Contents

■ SCHOLASTIC

DAILY Word Ladders

Grades 1–2

by **Timothy V. Rasinski**
Kent State University

New York • Toronto • London • Auckland • Sydney
Mexico City • New Delhi • Hong Kong • Buenos Aires

Teaching *Resources*

INTERACTIVE WHITEBOARD ACTIVITIES

To my own children—Mike, Emily, Mary, and Jenny—
Word Wizards in their own right.

A father couldn't ask for better kids.

Edited and produced by Immacula A. Rhodes

Cover design by Brian LaRossa

Cover and interior illustrations by Teresa Anderko

Interior design by Sydney Wright

ISBN: 978-0-545-37486-6

Text copyright © 2012, 2008 by Timothy V. Rasinski

Illustrations copyright © 2012, 2008 by Scholastic Inc.

Published by Scholastic Inc.

Printed in the U.S.A.

1 2 3 4 5 6 7 8 9 10   40   19 18 17 16 15 14 13 12

Welcome to Word Ladders!

In this book you'll find more than 150 mini word-study lessons that are also kid-pleasing games! To complete each Word Ladder takes just ten minutes but actively involves each learner in analyzing the structure and meaning of words. To play, students begin with one word and then make a series of other words by changing or rearranging the letters in the word before. With regular use, Word Ladders can go a long way toward developing your students' decoding and vocabulary skills.

How do Word Ladders work?

Let's say our first Word Ladder begins with the word *walk*. The directions will tell students to change one letter in *walk* to make a word that means "to speak." The word students will make, of course, is *talk*. The directions for the next word will then ask students to make a change in *talk* to form another word—perhaps *tale* or *tall*. Students will form new words as they work up the ladder until they reach the top rung. The final word is in some way related to the first word—for example, *run*. If students get stuck on a rung along the way, they can come back to it, because the words before and after will give them the clues they need to go on.

How do Word Ladders benefit students?

Word Ladders are great for building students' decoding, phonics, spelling, and vocabulary skills. When students add, take away, or rearrange letters to make a new word from one they have just made, they must examine sound-symbol relationships closely. This is just the kind of analysis that all children need to do in order to learn how to decode and spell accurately. And when the puzzle

adds a bit of meaning in the form of a definition (for example, "make a word that means *to say something*"), it helps extend students' understanding of words and concepts. All of these skills are key to students' success in learning to read and write. So even though Word Ladders will feel like a game, your students will be practicing essential literacy skills at the same time!

How do I teach a Word Ladder lesson?

Word Ladders are incredibly easy and quick to implement. Here are four simple steps:

1. Choose a Word Ladder to try. (The first five pages feature easier ladders, so you may want to start with those.)

2. Make a copy of the Word Ladder for each student.

3. Choose whether you want to do the Word Ladder with the class as a whole, or have students work alone, in pairs, or in groups. When working with the whole class, use the CD to display the ladder on your interactive whiteboard (see "Using the CD" sidebar for more). If students are emergent readers, you might read the clues to them and use a think-aloud method to model how to complete the activity. In addition, you might use the display to demonstrate how to fill in the word on each rung. As their skills develop, students can begin doing the Word Ladders independently.

4. At each new word, students will see two clues: the kinds of changes they need to make to the previous word ("change the first letter," "change the vowel," and so on), and a definition of or clue to the meaning of the new word. Sometimes this

clue will be a cloze sentence in which the word fits the context but is left out for children to fill in. Move from word to word in this way, up the whole Word Ladder.

Look for the **Bonus Boxes** with stars. These are particularly difficult words that you may want to preteach.

That's the lesson in a nutshell! It should take no longer than ten minutes to do. Once you're done, you might extend the lessons by having students sort the words into various categories. This can help them deepen their understanding of word relationships. For instance, they could sort them into:

- Grammatical categories. (Which words are nouns? Verbs?)

- Word structure. (Which words have a long vowel and which don't? Which contain a consonant blend?)

- Word meaning. (Which words express what a person can do or feel? Which do not?)

Additionally, you can create your own Word Ladders using copies of the blank puzzles on pages 166–168. Or you might invite students to make their own puzzles to exchange with classmates.

Tips for Working With Word Ladders

Try these tips to give students extra help in doing the Word Ladders:

- List all the "answers" for the ladder (that is, the words for each rung) in random order on the board for students to choose from as they go through the puzzle.

- Add your own clues to give students extra help as they work through each rung.

- If students are stuck on a particular rung, you might say the word aloud and see if students can spell it correctly by making appropriate changes in the previous word.

- Challenge students to come up with alternative definitions for the same words. Many words, like *bat, pet, bill,* and *lot,* have multiple meanings.

Using the CD

The CD features the same Word Ladders that are in the book, ready to display on your interactive whiteboard. The Word Ladders on the CD were created using Promethean's ActivInspire software. To use, simply download the free Personal Edition of the software at http://www.prometheanplanet.com/en-us/support/software/activinspire/ and install into your computer. (You may need to register first before downloading the software. Registration is free.)

Here are some tips for using the Word Ladders on the interactive whiteboard:

- Use the Page Browser to scan through the Word Ladders in the file. The ladders appear in the same order as they do in the book. To go to a desired page, simply tap on it on the browser.

- Invite students to use the Pen tool to write the answers on the write-on lines. To check if an answer is correct, drag down the Answer tab below the clue.

- To clear the page and hide the Answer tabs again, simply tap the reset button (two arrows forming a circle).

- Tap on the left or right arrows to move from page to page.

Name _____

Read the clues, then write the words.
Start at the bottom and climb to the top.

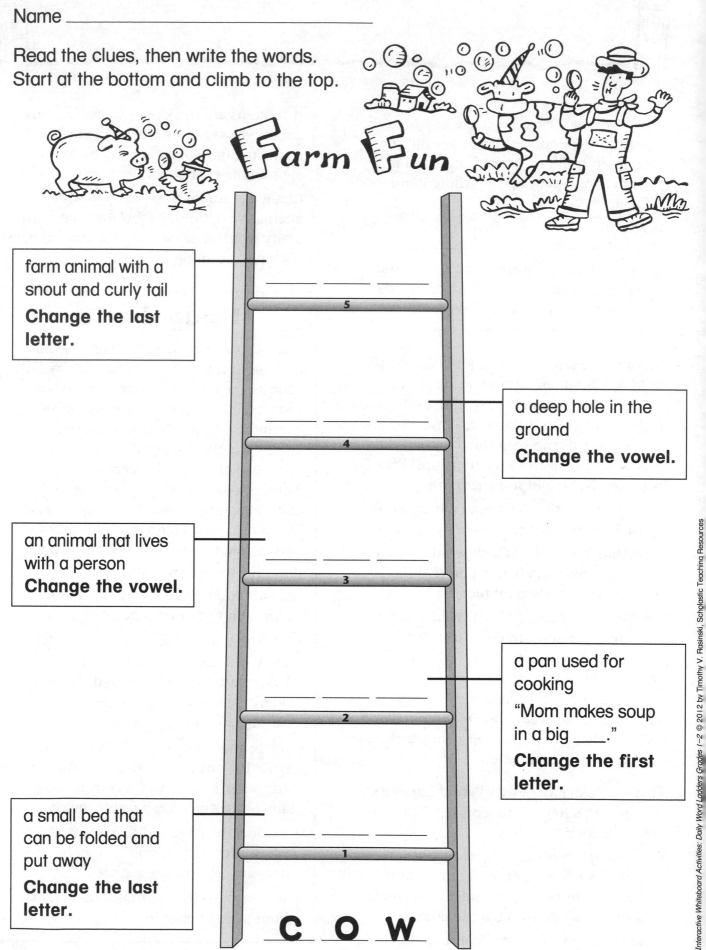

Farm Fun

farm animal with a snout and curly tail
Change the last letter.

5

a deep hole in the ground
Change the vowel.

4

an animal that lives with a person
Change the vowel.

3

a pan used for cooking
"Mom makes soup in a big ____."
Change the first letter.

2

a small bed that can be folded and put away
Change the last letter.

1

C   O   W

Interactive Whiteboard Activities: Daily Word Ladders Grades 1–2 © 2012 by Timothy V. Rasinski, Scholastic Teaching Resources

Name _____

Read the clues, then write the words.
Start at the bottom and climb to the top.

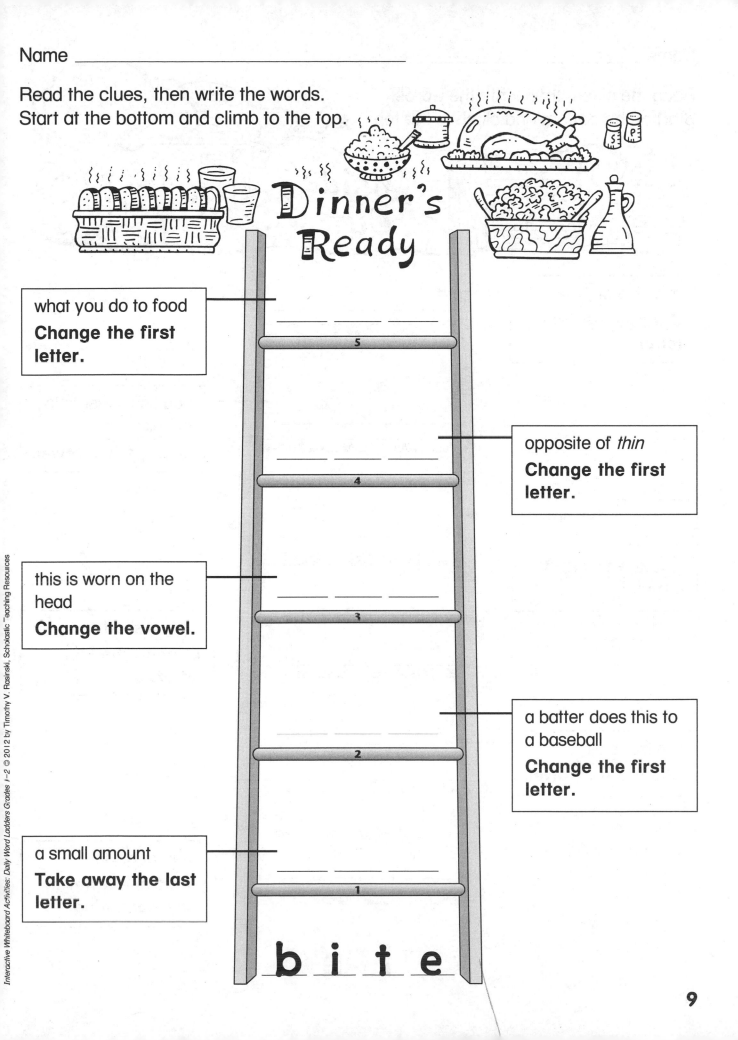

what you do to food
Change the first letter.

opposite of *thin*
Change the first letter.

this is worn on the head
Change the vowel.

a batter does this to a baseball
Change the first letter.

a small amount
Take away the last letter.

b i t e

Interactive Whiteboard Activities: Daily Word Ladders Grades 1–2 © 2012 by Timothy V. Rasinski, Scholastic Teaching Resources

Name _____

Read the clues, then write the words.
Start at the bottom and climb to the top.

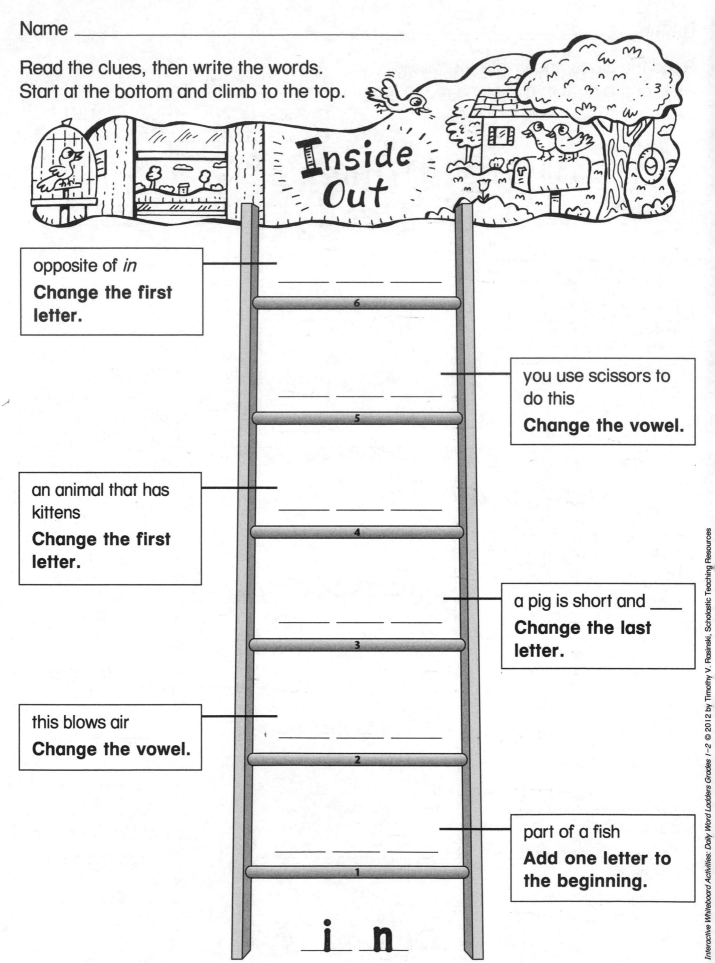

Inside Out

opposite of *in*
Change the first letter.

you use scissors to do this
Change the vowel.

an animal that has kittens
Change the first letter.

a pig is short and ___
Change the last letter.

this blows air
Change the vowel.

part of a fish
Add one letter to the beginning.

6

5

4

3

2

1

i n

10

Interactive Whiteboard Activities: Daily Word Ladders Grades 1–2 © 2012 by Timothy V. Rasinski, Scholastic Teaching Resources

Name _____

Read the clues, then write the words.
Start at the bottom and climb to the top.

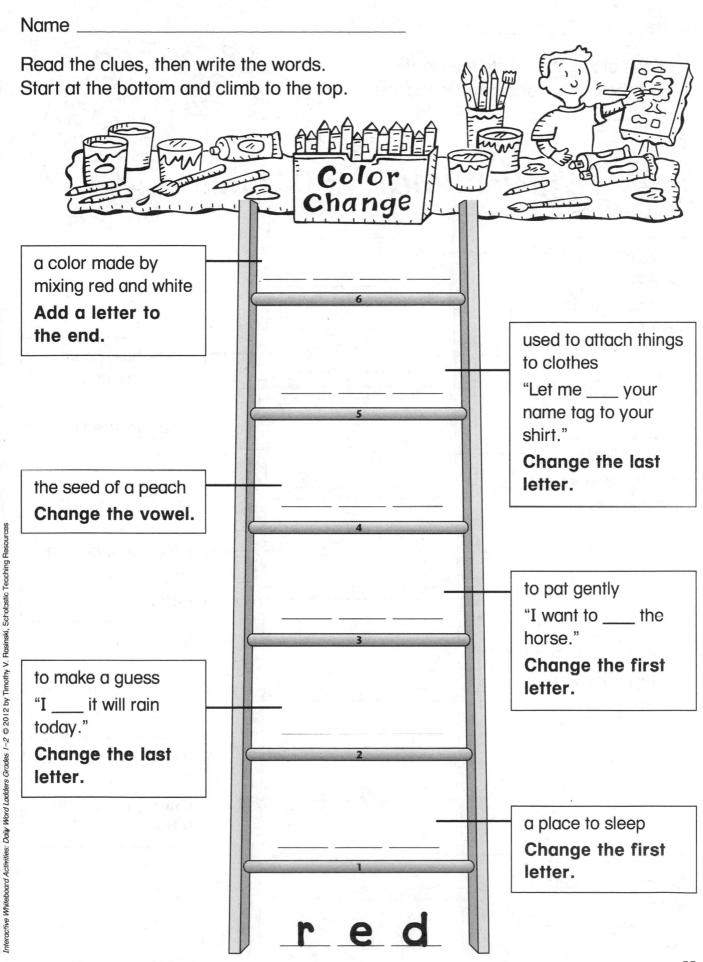

Color Change

a color made by
mixing red and white
**Add a letter to
the end.**

used to attach things
to clothes
"Let me ___ your
name tag to your
shirt."
**Change the last
letter.**

the seed of a peach
Change the vowel.

to pat gently
"I want to ___ the
horse."
**Change the first
letter.**

to make a guess
"I ___ it will rain
today."
**Change the last
letter.**

a place to sleep
**Change the first
letter.**

6

5

4

3

2

1

r e d

Interactive Whiteboard Activities: Daily Word Ladders Grades 1–2 © 2012 by Timothy V. Rasinski, Scholastic Teaching Resources

Name _____

Read the clues, then write the words.
Start at the bottom and climb to the top.

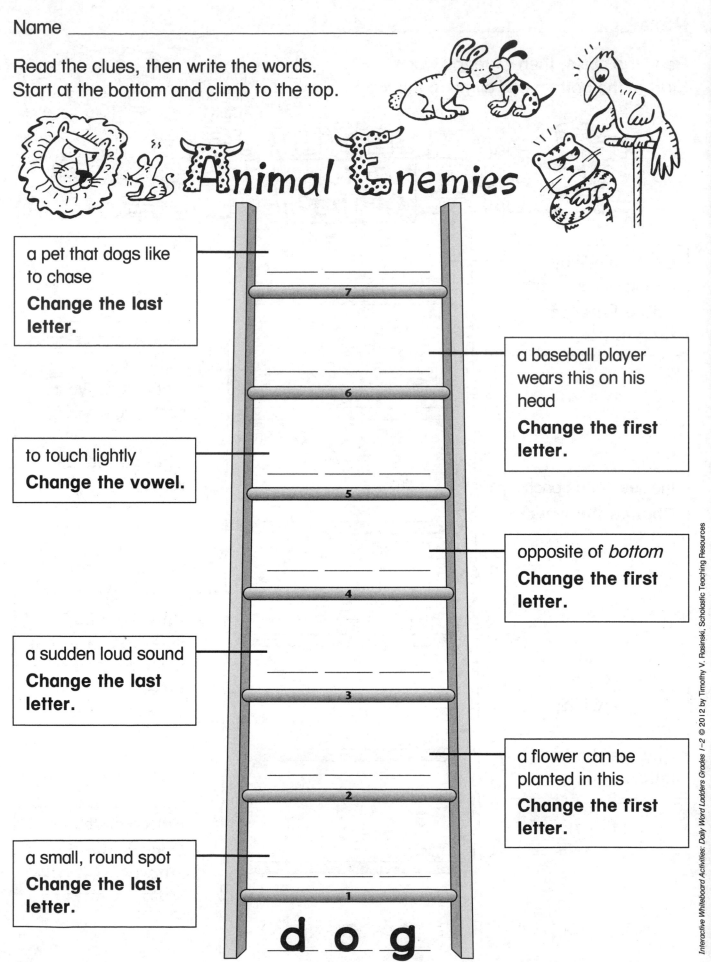

Animal Enemies

a pet that dogs like to chase
Change the last letter.

a baseball player wears this on his head
Change the first letter.

to touch lightly
Change the vowel.

opposite of *bottom*
Change the first letter.

a sudden loud sound
Change the last letter.

a flower can be planted in this
Change the first letter.

a small, round spot
Change the last letter.

7

6

5

4

3

2

1

d o g

Interactive Whiteboard Activities: Daily Word Ladders Grades 1–2 © 2012 by Timothy V. Rasinski, Scholastic Teaching Resources

Name _____

Read the clues, then write the words.
Start at the bottom and climb to the top.

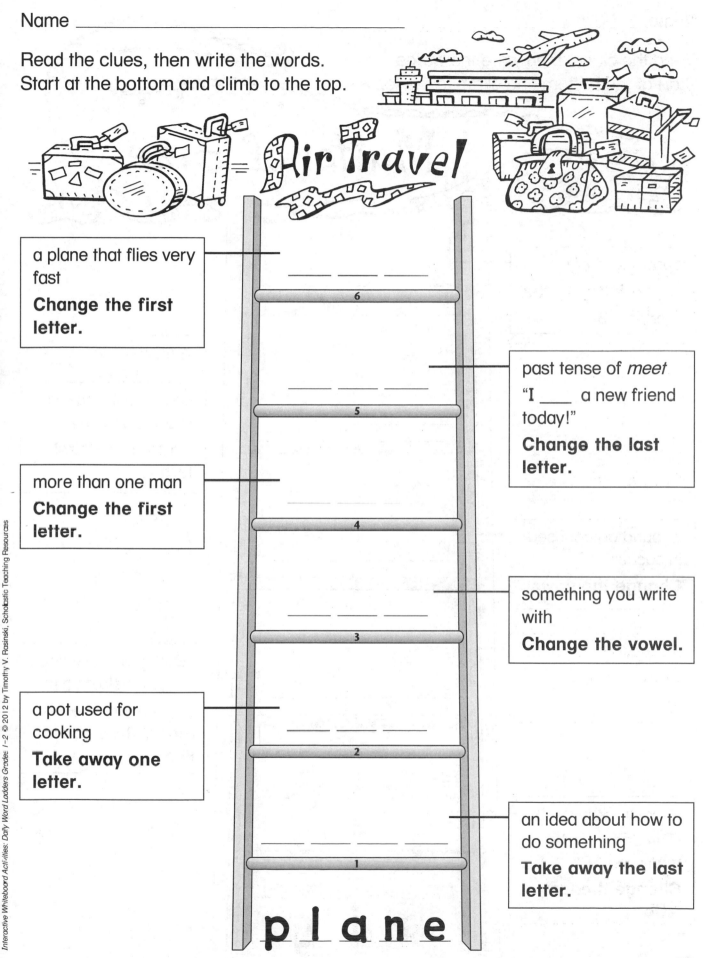

Air Travel

a plane that flies very fast
Change the first letter.

past tense of *meet*
"I ____ a new friend today!"
Change the last letter.

more than one man
Change the first letter.

something you write with
Change the vowel.

a pot used for cooking
Take away one letter.

an idea about how to do something
Take away the last letter.

6

5

4

3

2

1

p l a n e

Interactive Whiteboard Activities: Daily Word Ladders Grades 1–2 © 2012 by Timothy V. Rasinski, Scholastic Teaching Resources

Name _____

Read the clues, then write the words.
Start at the bottom and climb to the top.

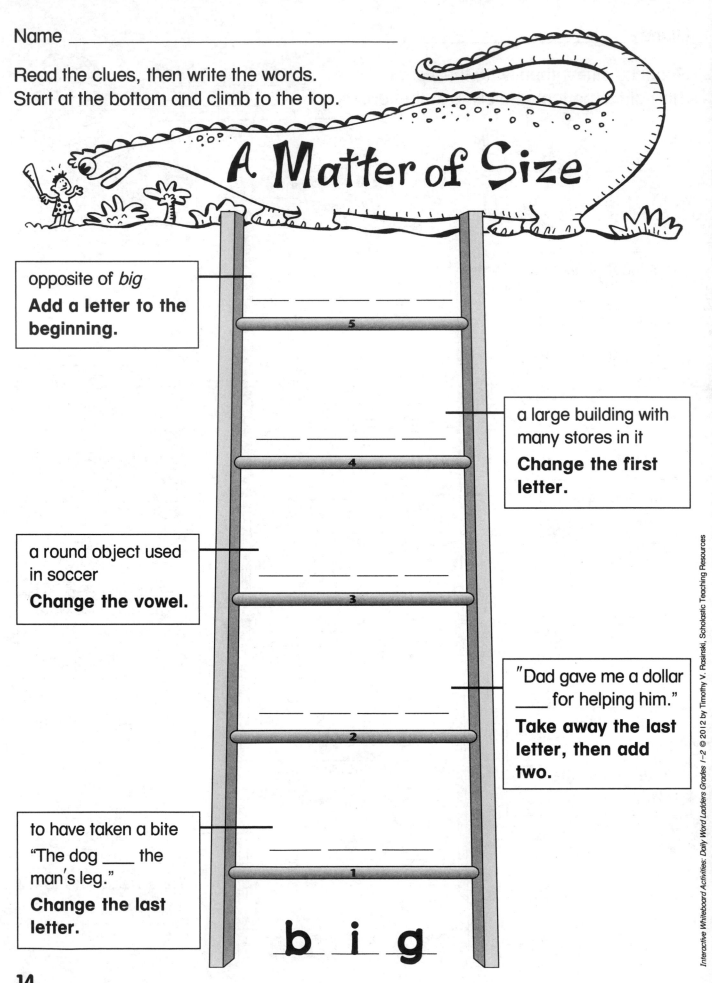

A Matter of Size

opposite of *big*
Add a letter to the beginning.

5

_ _ _ _ _

a large building with
many stores in it
Change the first letter.

4

_ _ _ _

a round object used
in soccer
Change the vowel.

3

_ _ _ _

"Dad gave me a dollar
___ for helping him."
Take away the last letter, then add two.

2

_ _ _

to have taken a bite
"The dog ___ the man's leg."
Change the last letter.

1

b i g

Interactive Whiteboard Activities: *Daily Word Ladders Grades 1–2* © 2012 by Timothy V. Rasinski, Scholastic Teaching Resources

Name _____

Read the clues, then write the words.
Start at the bottom and climb to the top.

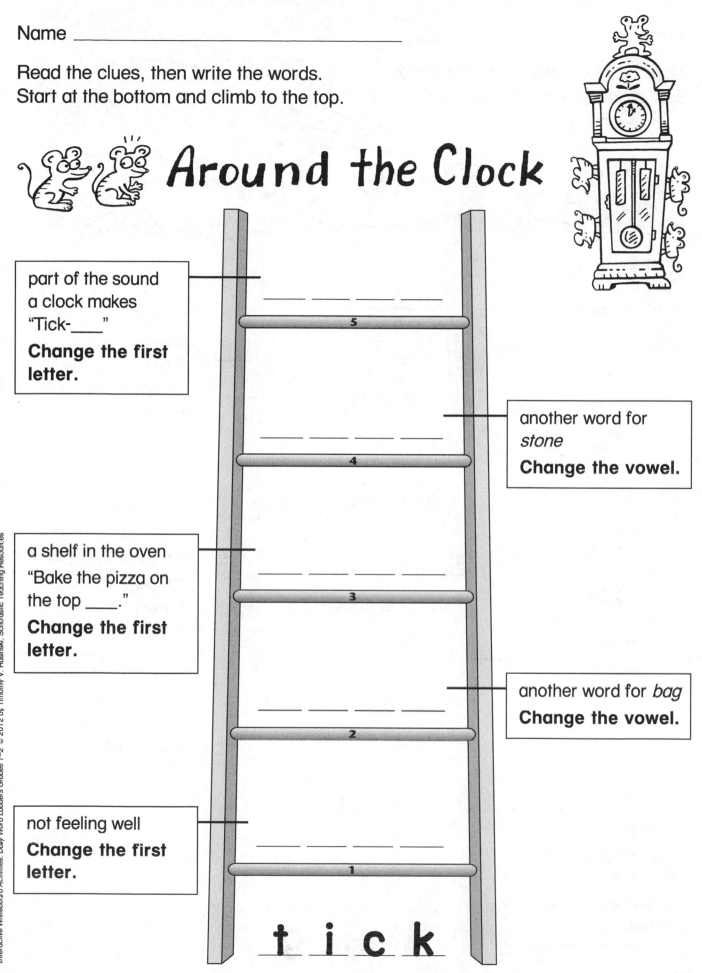

Around the Clock

part of the sound
a clock makes
"Tick-___"
**Change the first
letter.**

another word for
stone
Change the vowel.

a shelf in the oven
"Bake the pizza on
the top ___."
**Change the first
letter.**

another word for *bag*
Change the vowel.

not feeling well
**Change the first
letter.**

5

4

3

2

1

t i c k

Interactive Whiteboard Activities: Daily Word Ladders Grades 1–2 © 2012 by Timothy V. Rasinski, Scholastic Teaching Resources

Name _____

Read the clues, then write the words.
Start at the bottom and climb to the top.

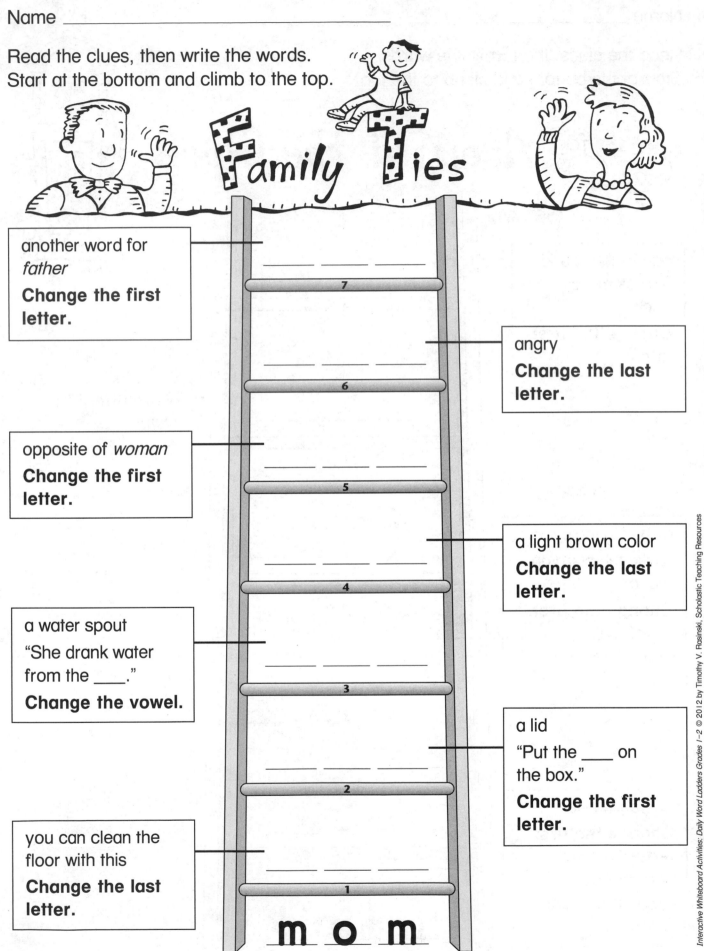

Family Ties

another word for *father*
Change the first letter.

7

angry
Change the last letter.

6

opposite of *woman*
Change the first letter.

5

a light brown color
Change the last letter.

4

a water spout
"She drank water from the ____."
Change the vowel.

3

a lid
"Put the ____ on the box."
Change the first letter.

2

you can clean the floor with this
Change the last letter.

1

m o m

Interactive Whiteboard Activities: Daily Word Ladders Grades 1–2 © 2012 by Timothy V. Rasinski, Scholastic Teaching Resources

Name _____

Read the clues, then write the words.
Start at the bottom and climb to the top.

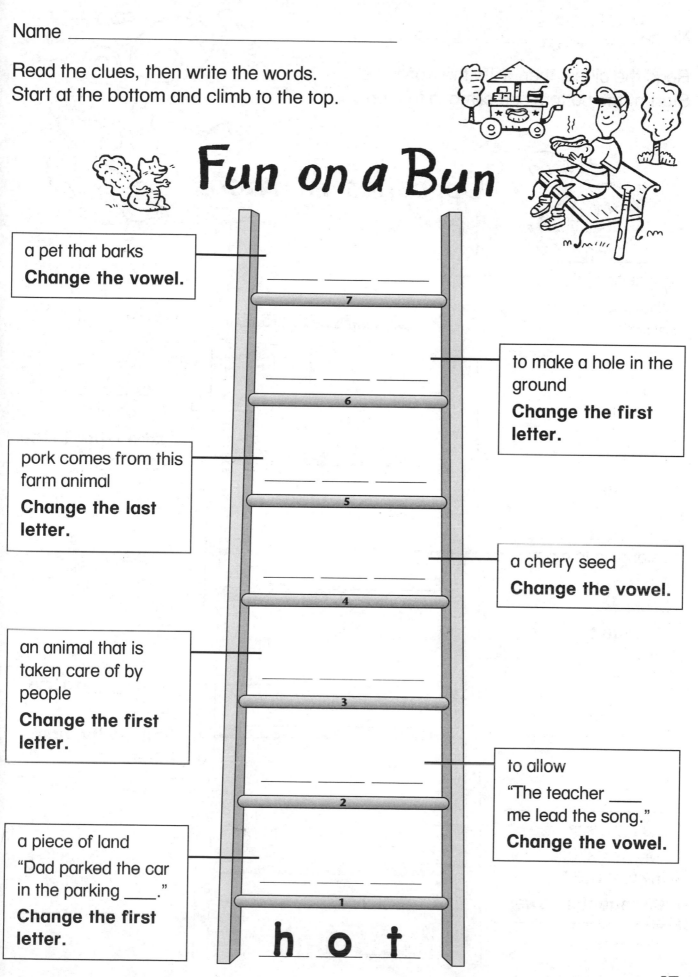

Fun on a Bun

a pet that barks
Change the vowel.

to make a hole in the ground
Change the first letter.

pork comes from this farm animal
Change the last letter.

a cherry seed
Change the vowel.

an animal that is taken care of by people
Change the first letter.

to allow
"The teacher ____ me lead the song."
Change the vowel.

a piece of land
"Dad parked the car in the parking ____."
Change the first letter.

7
6
5
4
3
2
1

h o t

Name _____

Read the clues, then write the words.
Start at the bottom and climb to the top.

Opposites Attract

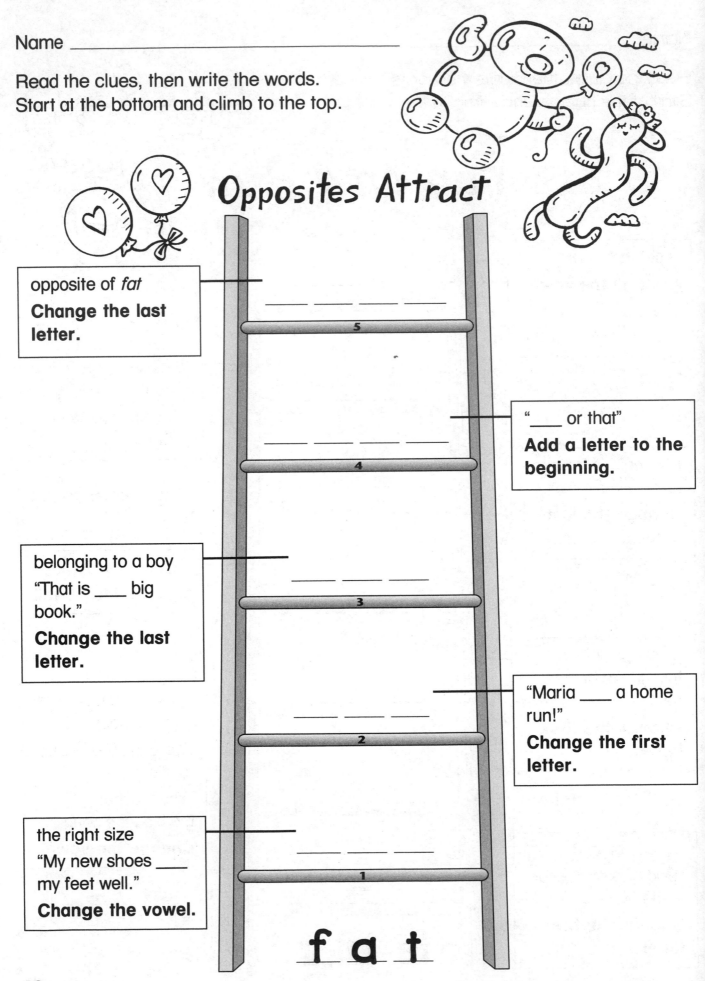

opposite of *fat*
Change the last letter.

5

"____ or that"
Add a letter to the beginning.

4

belonging to a boy
"That is ____ big book."
Change the last letter.

3

"Maria ____ a home run!"
Change the first letter.

2

the right size
"My new shoes ____ my feet well."
Change the vowel.

1

f a t

Name _____

Read the clues, then write the words.
Start at the bottom and climb to the top.

Sweet Sounds

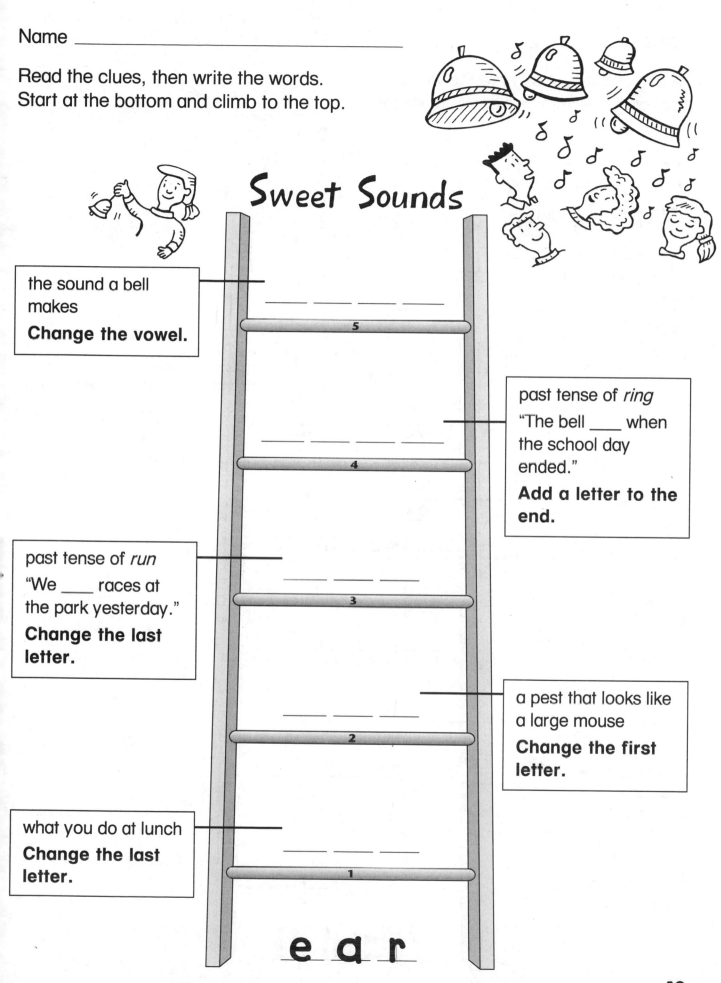

the sound a bell makes
Change the vowel.

past tense of *ring*
"The bell ___ when the school day ended."
Add a letter to the end.

past tense of *run*
"We ___ races at the park yesterday."
Change the last letter.

a pest that looks like a large mouse
Change the first letter.

what you do at lunch
Change the last letter.

e a r

Name _____

Read the clues, then write the words.
Start at the bottom and climb to the top.

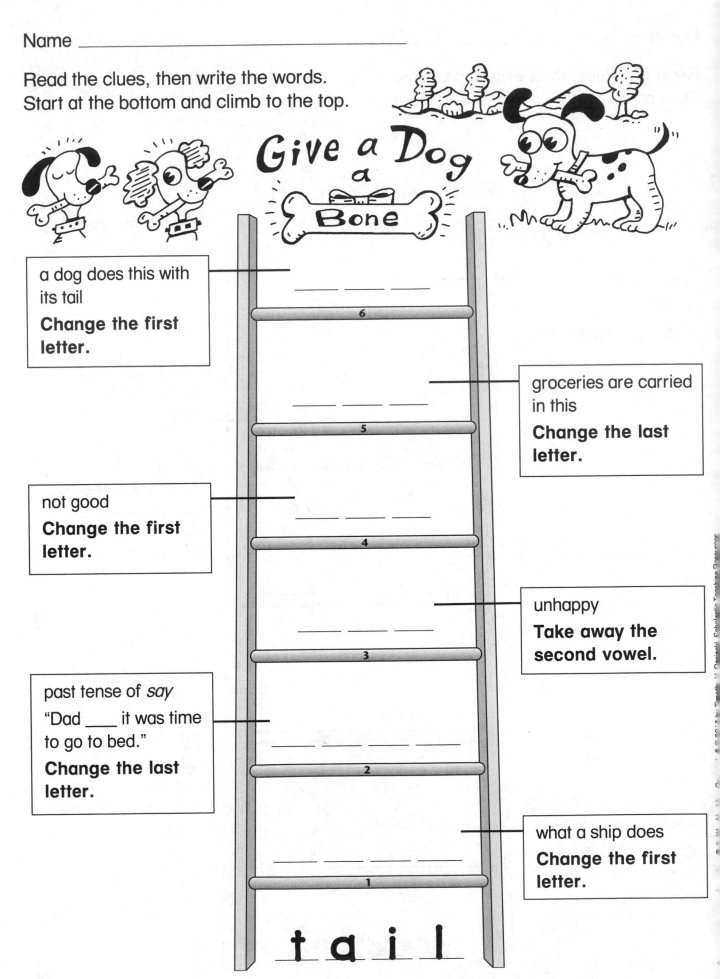

Give a Dog a Bone

a dog does this with its tail
Change the first letter.

groceries are carried in this
Change the last letter.

not good
Change the first letter.

unhappy
Take away the second vowel.

past tense of *say*
"Dad ____ it was time to go to bed."
Change the last letter.

what a ship does
Change the first letter.

t a i l

Name _____

Read the clues, then write the words.
Start at the bottom and climb to the top.

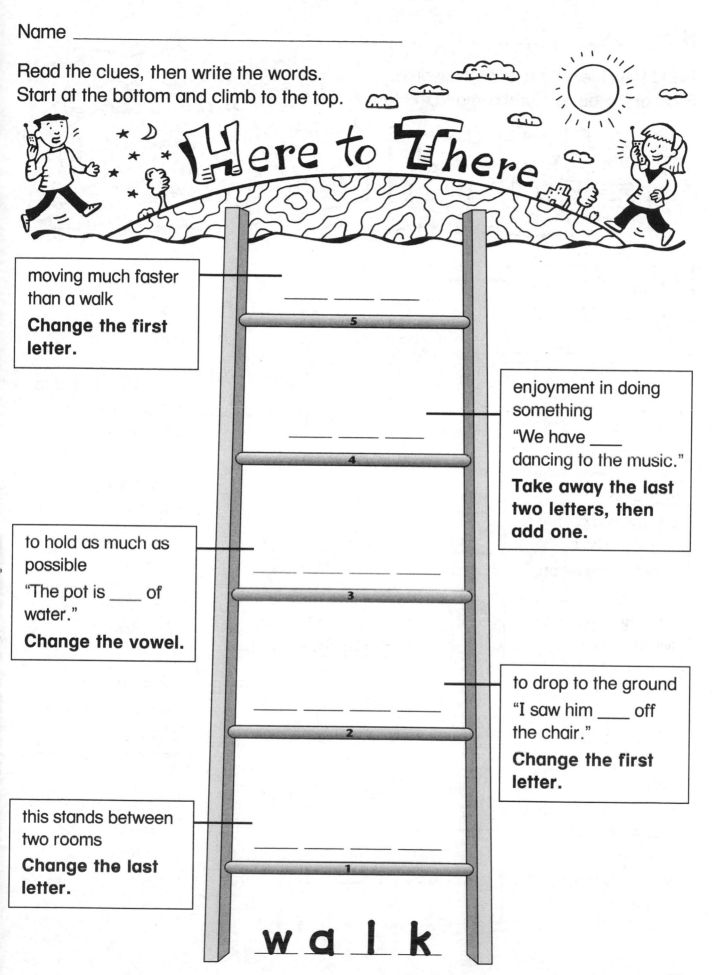

Here to There

moving much faster than a walk
Change the first letter.

_ _ _ _

5

enjoyment in doing something
"We have ___ dancing to the music."
Take away the last two letters, then add one.

_ _ _ _

4

to hold as much as possible
"The pot is ___ of water."
Change the vowel.

_ _ _ _

3

to drop to the ground
"I saw him ___ off the chair."
Change the first letter.

_ _ _ _

2

this stands between two rooms
Change the last letter.

_ _ _ _

1

w a l k

Name _____

Read the clues, then write the words.
Start at the bottom and climb to the top.

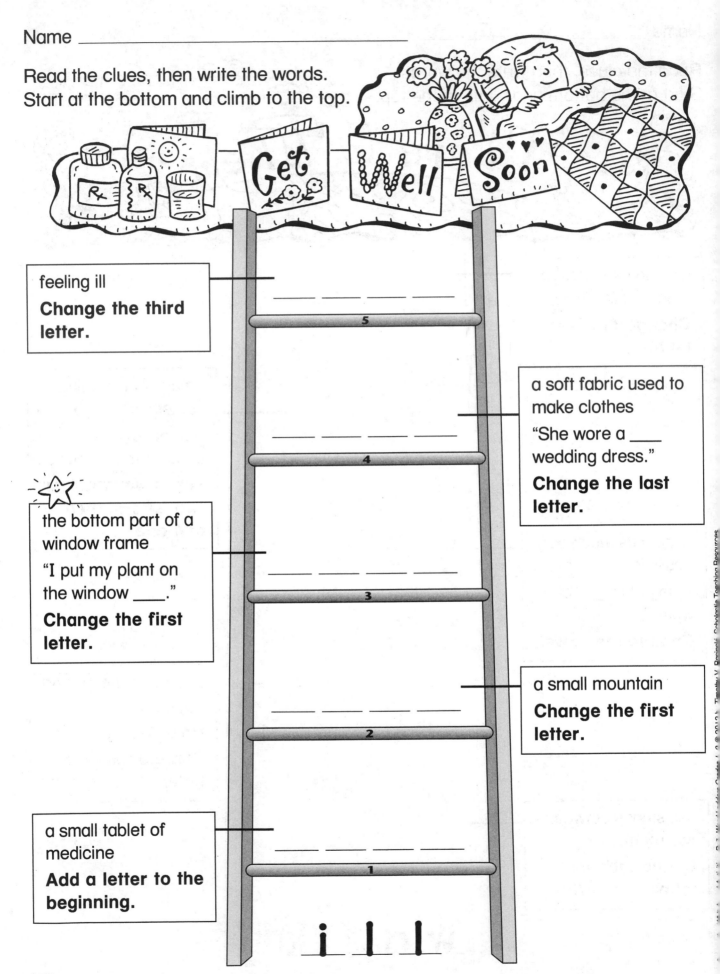

feeling ill
Change the third letter.

_ _ _ _ (5)

a soft fabric used to make clothes
"She wore a ___ wedding dress."
Change the last letter.

_ _ _ _ (4)

the bottom part of a window frame
"I put my plant on the window ___."
Change the first letter.

_ _ _ _ (3)

a small mountain
Change the first letter.

_ _ _ _ (2)

a small tablet of medicine
Add a letter to the beginning.

_ _ _ _ (1)

i l l

Name _____

Read the clues, then write the words.
Start at the bottom and climb to the top.

In the Can

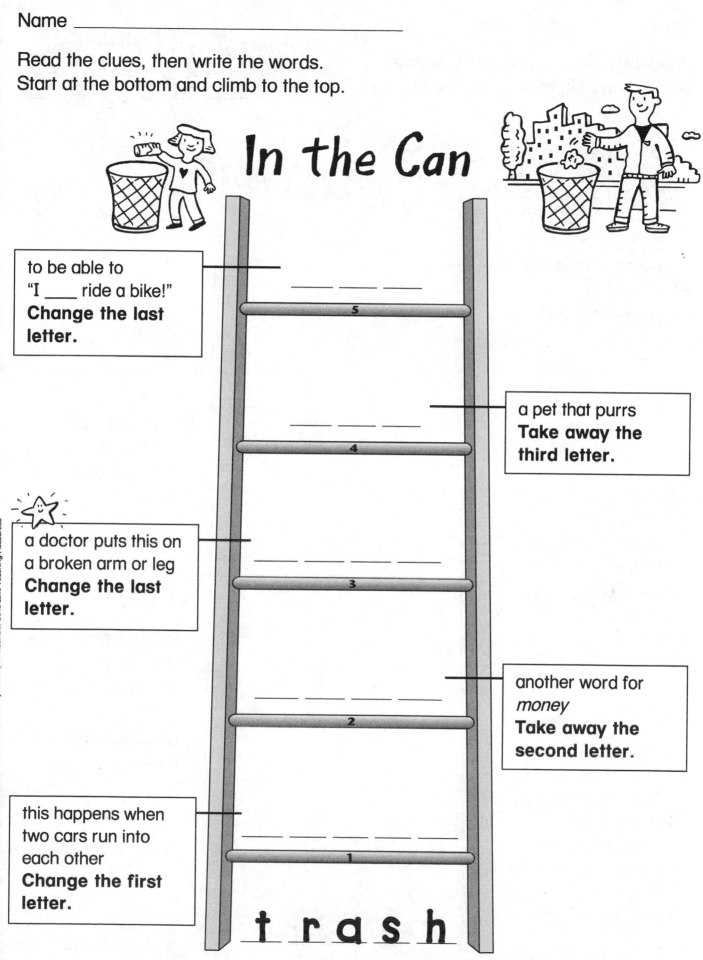

to be able to
"I ____ ride a bike!"
Change the last letter.

_____ _____ _____   5

a pet that purrs
Take away the third letter.

_____ _____ _____   4

a doctor puts this on a broken arm or leg
Change the last letter.

_____ _____ _____ _____   3

another word for *money*
Take away the second letter.

_____ _____ _____ _____   2

this happens when two cars run into each other
Change the first letter.

_____ _____ _____ _____ _____   1

t r a s h

Name _____

Read the clues, then write the words.
Start at the bottom and climb to the top.

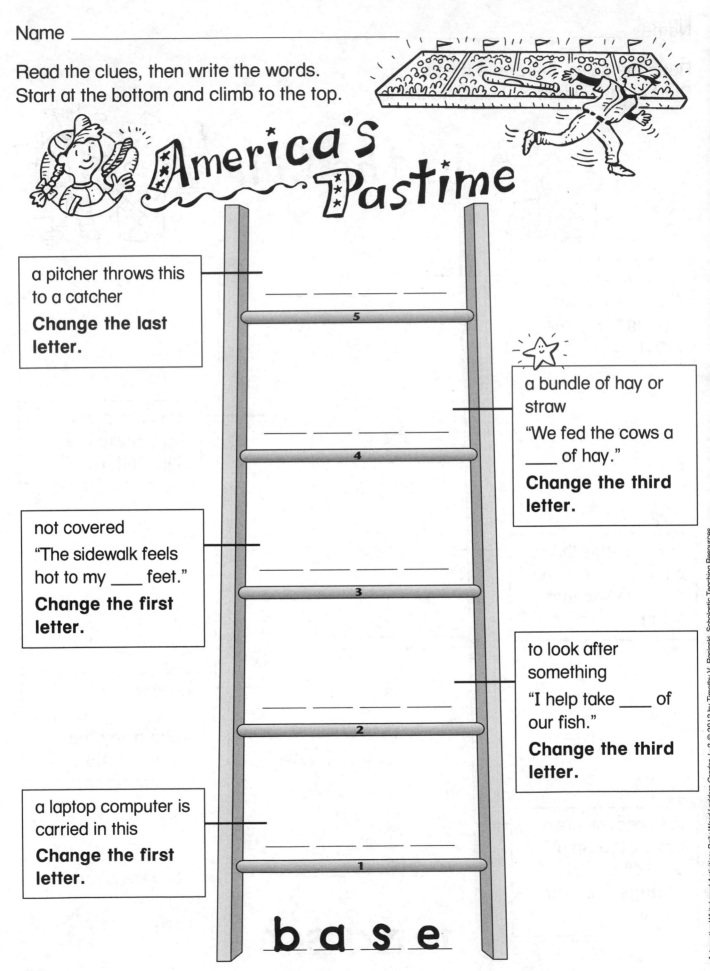

America's Pastime

a pitcher throws this to a catcher
Change the last letter.

_ _ _ _ _   5

a bundle of hay or straw
"We fed the cows a ___ of hay."
Change the third letter.

_ _ _ _ _   4

not covered
"The sidewalk feels hot to my ___ feet."
Change the first letter.

_ _ _ _ _   3

to look after something
"I help take ___ of our fish."
Change the third letter.

_ _ _ _ _   2

a laptop computer is carried in this
Change the first letter.

_ _ _ _ _   1

b a s e

Interactive Whiteboard Activities: Daily Word Ladders Grades 1–2 © 2012 by Timothy V. Rasinski, Scholastic Teaching Resources

Name _____

Read the clues, then write the words.
Start at the bottom and climb to the top.

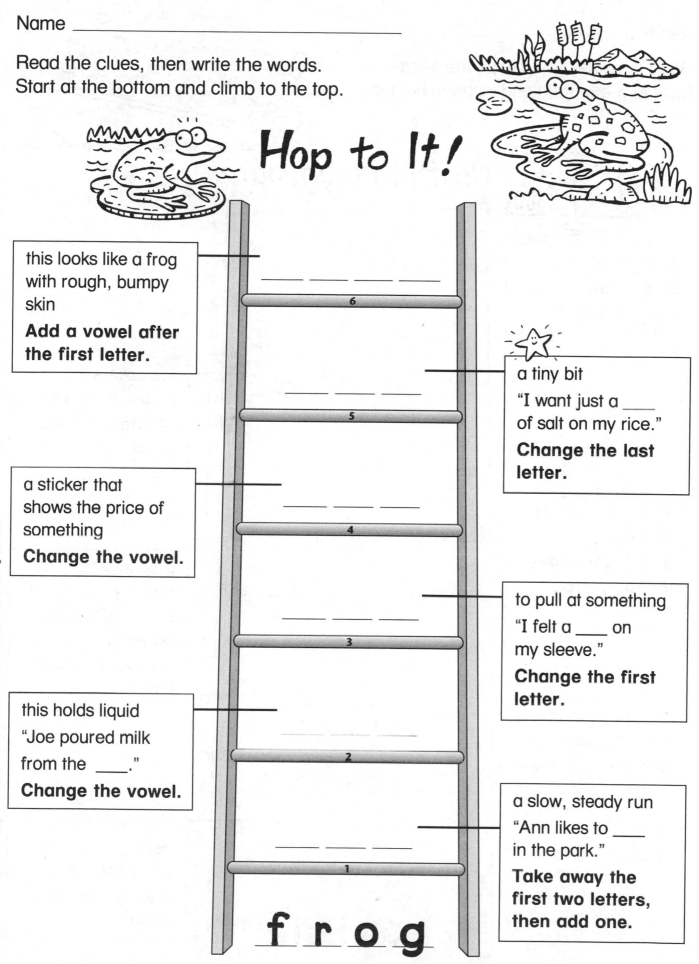

Hop to It!

this looks like a frog
with rough, bumpy
skin
**Add a vowel after
the first letter.**

a sticker that
shows the price of
something
Change the vowel.

this holds liquid
"Joe poured milk
from the ___."
Change the vowel.

a tiny bit
"I want just a ____
of salt on my rice."
**Change the last
letter.**

to pull at something
"I felt a ___ on
my sleeve."
**Change the first
letter.**

a slow, steady run
"Ann likes to ___
in the park."
**Take away the
first two letters,
then add one.**

6

5

4

3

2

1

f r o g

25

Name _____

Read the clues, then write the words.
Start at the bottom and climb to the top.

On the Playground

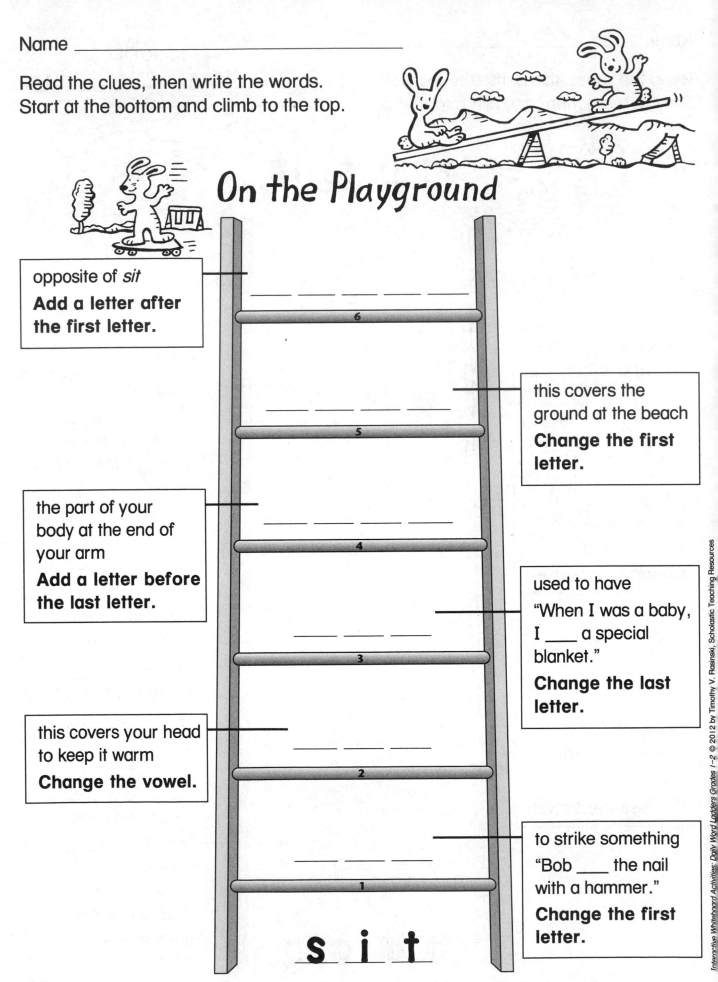

opposite of *sit*
Add a letter after the first letter.

this covers the ground at the beach
Change the first letter.

the part of your body at the end of your arm
Add a letter before the last letter.

used to have
"When I was a baby, I ___ a special blanket."
Change the last letter.

this covers your head to keep it warm
Change the vowel.

to strike something
"Bob ___ the nail with a hammer."
Change the first letter.

s i t

6
5
4
3
2
1

Interactive Whiteboard Activities: Daily Word Ladders Grades 1–2 © 2012 by Timothy V. Rasinski, Scholastic Teaching Resources

Name _____

Read the clues, then write the words.
Start at the bottom and climb to the top.

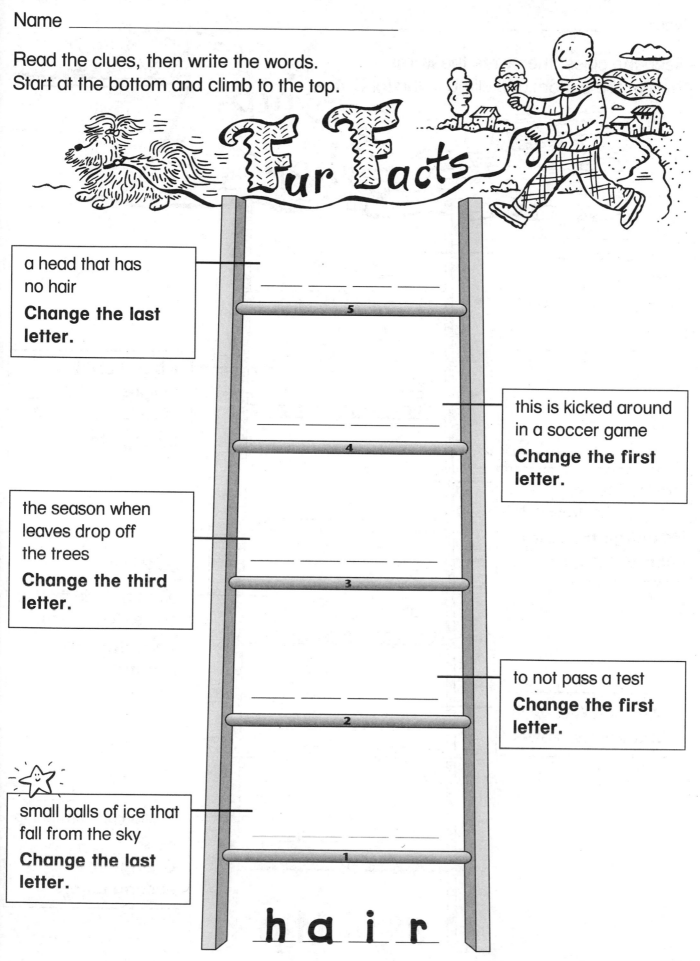

a head that has
no hair
**Change the last
letter.**

this is kicked around
in a soccer game
**Change the first
letter.**

the season when
leaves drop off
the trees
**Change the third
letter.**

to not pass a test
**Change the first
letter.**

small balls of ice that
fall from the sky
**Change the last
letter.**

h a i r

Name _____

Read the clues, then write the words.
Start at the bottom and climb to the top.

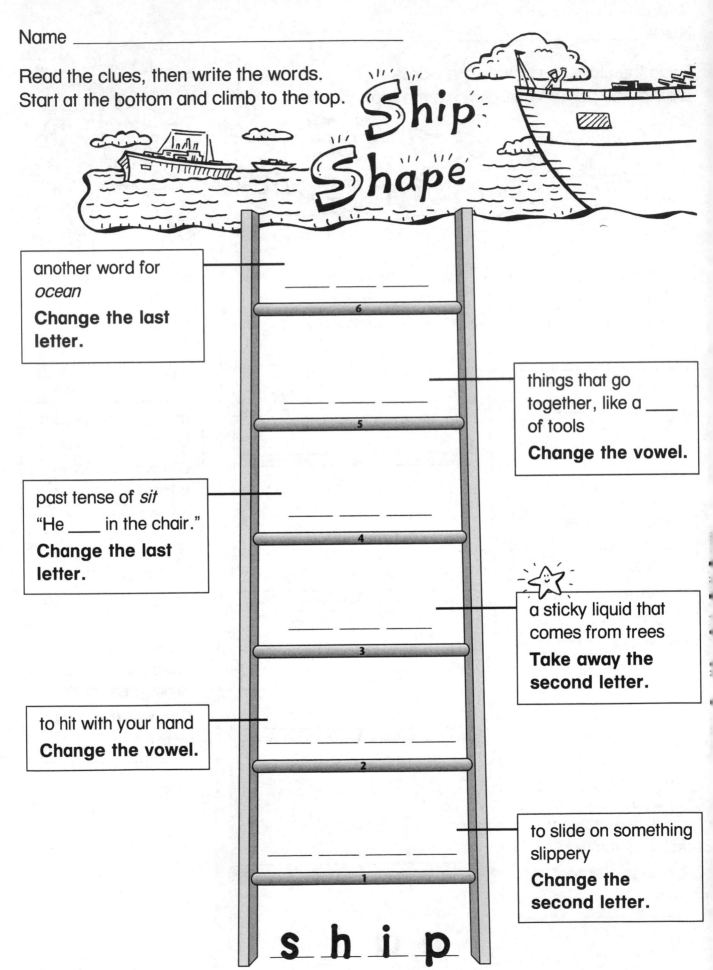

Ship
Shape

another word for *ocean*
Change the last letter.

things that go together, like a ____ of tools
Change the vowel.

past tense of *sit*
"He ____ in the chair."
Change the last letter.

a sticky liquid that comes from trees
Take away the second letter.

to hit with your hand
Change the vowel.

to slide on something slippery
Change the second letter.

s h i p

Name _____

Read the clues, then write the words.
Start at the bottom and climb to the top.

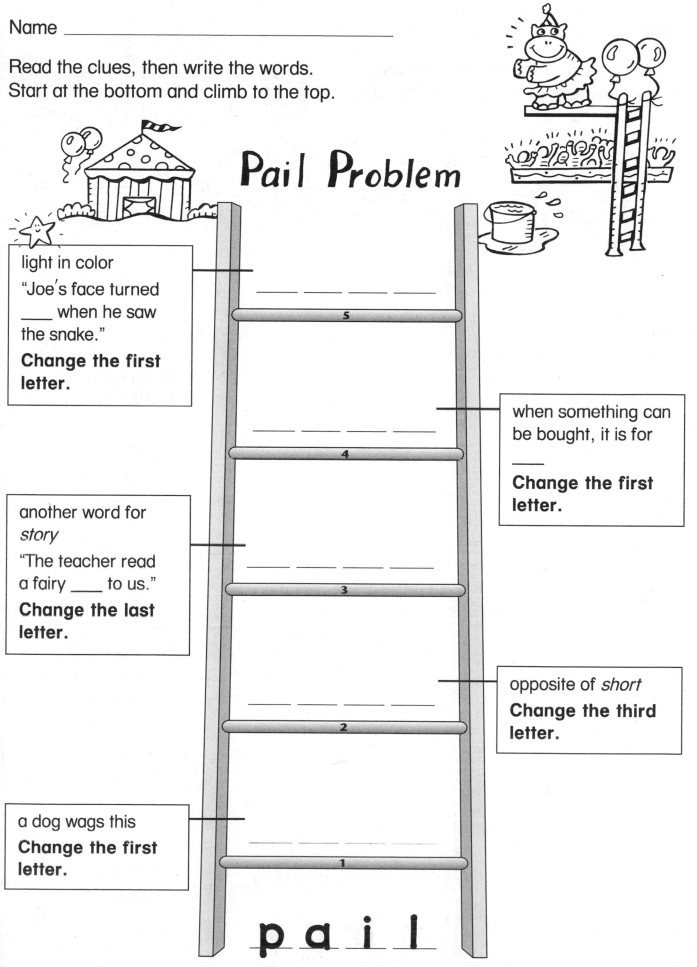

Pail Problem

light in color

"Joe's face turned ____ when he saw the snake."

Change the first letter.

when something can be bought, it is for

____

Change the first letter.

another word for *story*

"The teacher read a fairy ____ to us."

Change the last letter.

opposite of *short*
Change the third letter.

a dog wags this
Change the first letter.

p a i l

Name _____

Read the clues, then write the words.
Start at the bottom and climb to the top.

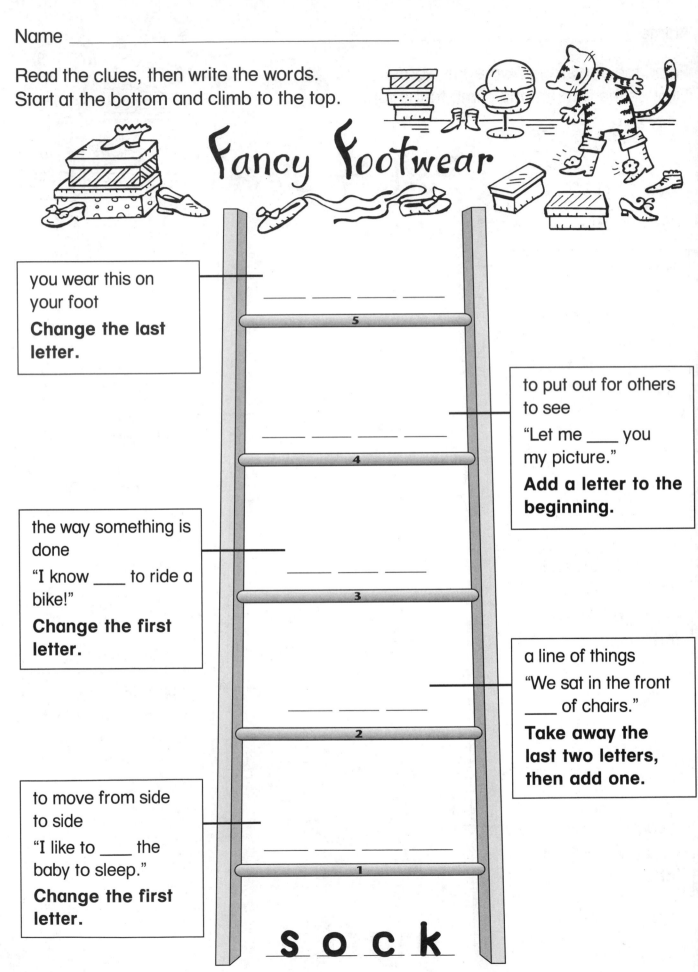

Fancy Footwear

you wear this on your foot
Change the last letter.

to put out for others to see
"Let me ___ you my picture."
Add a letter to the beginning.

the way something is done
"I know ___ to ride a bike!"
Change the first letter.

a line of things
"We sat in the front ___ of chairs."
Take away the last two letters, then add one.

to move from side to side
"I like to ___ the baby to sleep."
Change the first letter.

s o c k

Name _____

Read the clues, then write the words.
Start at the bottom and climb to the top.

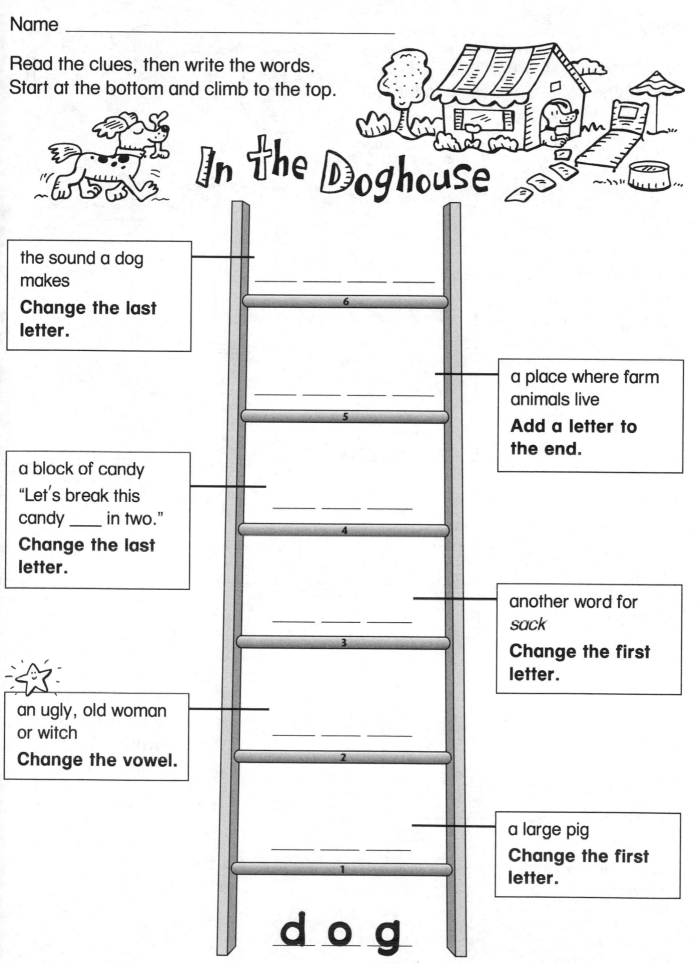

In the Doghouse

the sound a dog makes
Change the last letter.

a place where farm animals live
Add a letter to the end.

a block of candy
"Let's break this candy ____ in two."
Change the last letter.

another word for *sack*
Change the first letter.

an ugly, old woman or witch
Change the vowel.

a large pig
Change the first letter.

6

5

4

3

2

1

d o g

Name _____

Read the clues, then write the words.
Start at the bottom and climb to the top.

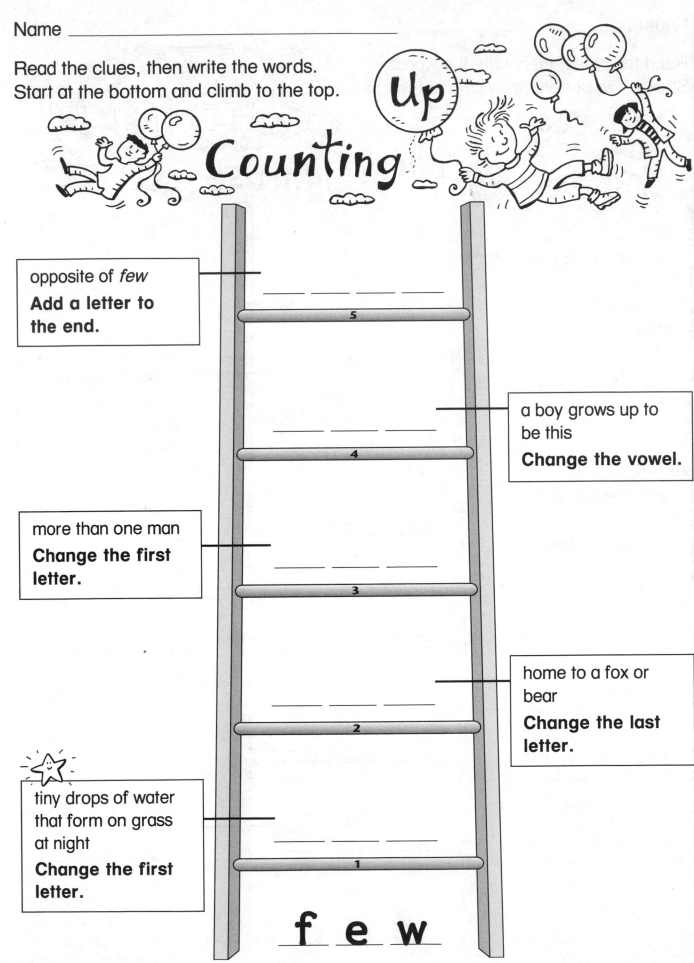

Counting **Up**

opposite of *few*
Add a letter to the end.

_ _ _ _ _

a boy grows up to be this
Change the vowel.

more than one man
Change the first letter.

home to a fox or bear
Change the last letter.

tiny drops of water that form on grass at night
Change the first letter.

f e w

Name _____

Read the clues, then write the words.
Start at the bottom and climb to the top.

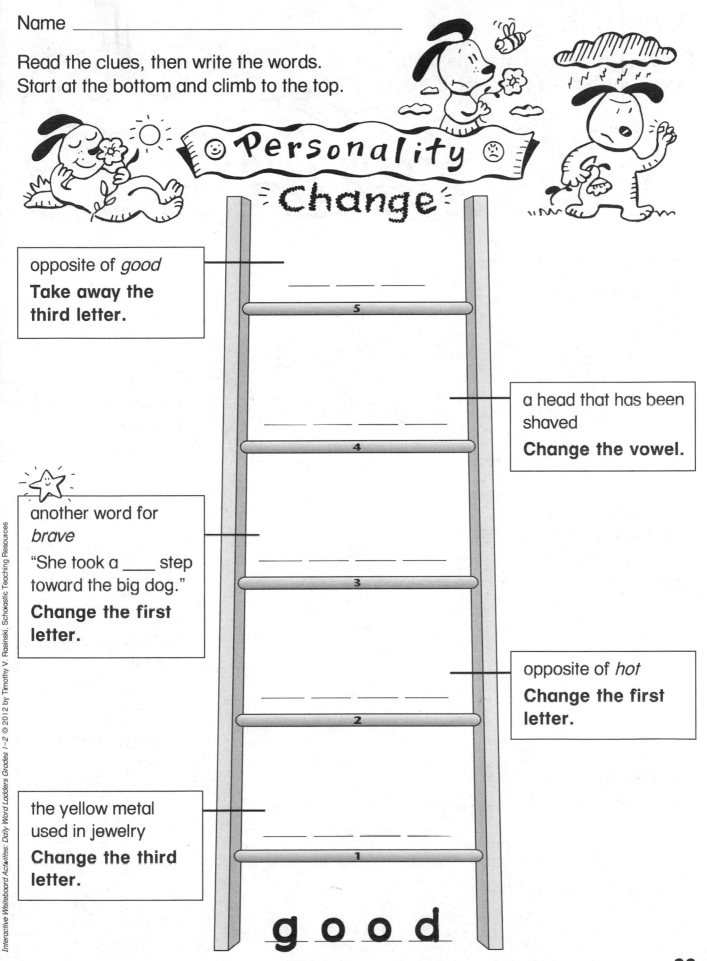

Personality Change

opposite of *good*
Take away the third letter.

_____ _____ _____ _____
5

a head that has been shaved
Change the vowel.

_____ _____ _____ _____
4

another word for *brave*
"She took a _____ step toward the big dog."
Change the first letter.

_____ _____ _____ _____
3

opposite of *hot*
Change the first letter.

_____ _____ _____
2

the yellow metal used in jewelry
Change the third letter.

_____ _____ _____ _____
1

g o o d

Name _____

Read the clues, then write the words.
Start at the bottom and climb to the top.

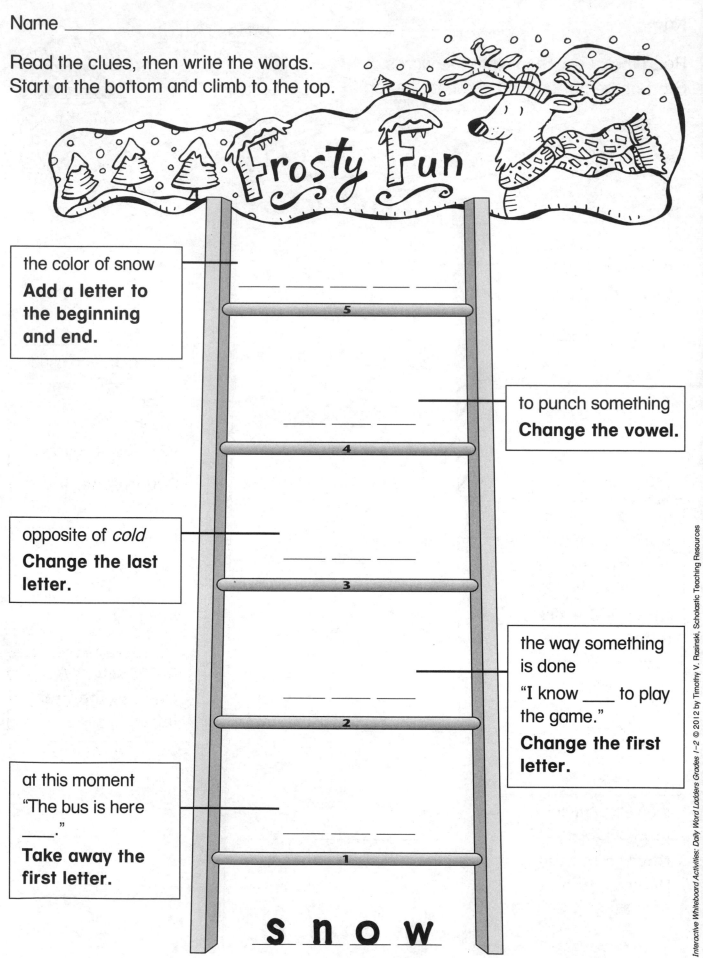

Frosty Fun

the color of snow
Add a letter to the beginning and end.

5 ___ ___ ___ ___ ___

to punch something
Change the vowel.

4 ___ ___ ___ ___

opposite of *cold*
Change the last letter.

3 ___ ___ ___ ___

the way something is done
"I know ___ to play the game."
Change the first letter.

2 ___ ___ ___

at this moment
"The bus is here ___."
Take away the first letter.

1 ___ ___ ___ ___

s   n   o   w

Interactive Whiteboard Activities: Daily Word Ladders Grades 1–2 © 2012 by Timothy V. Rasinski, Scholastic Teaching Resources

Name _____

Read the clues, then write the words.
Start at the bottom and climb to the top.

Warm and Cozy

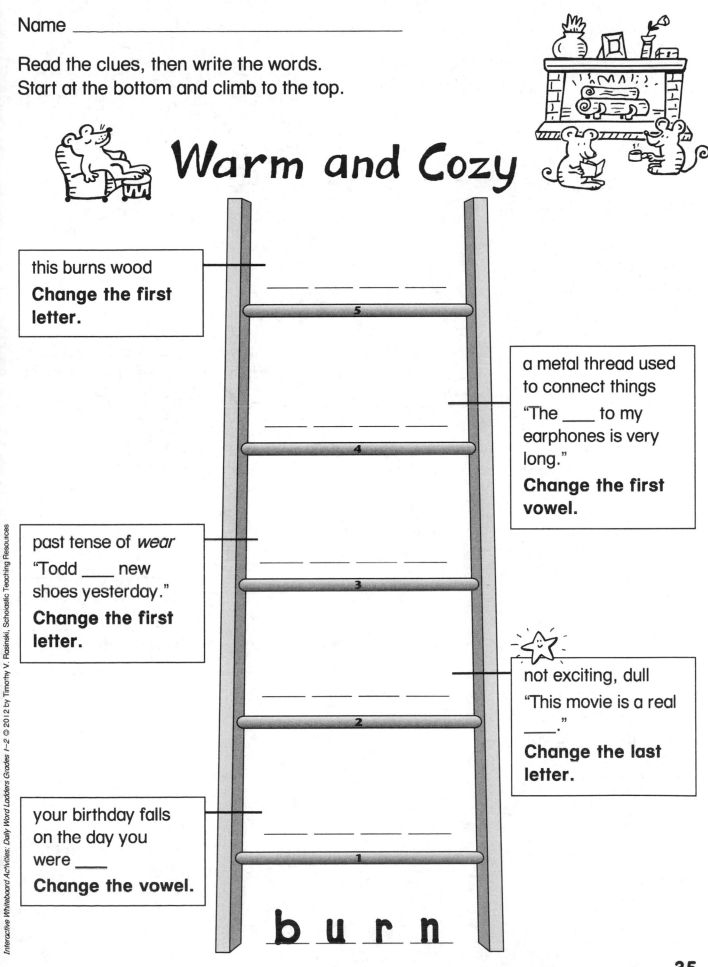

this burns wood
Change the first letter.

_____ 5 _____

a metal thread used to connect things
"The ____ to my earphones is very long."
Change the first vowel.

_____ 4 _____

past tense of *wear*
"Todd ____ new shoes yesterday."
Change the first letter.

_____ 3 _____

not exciting, dull
"This movie is a real ____."
Change the last letter.

_____ 2 _____

your birthday falls on the day you were ____
Change the vowel.

_____ 1 _____

b u r n

Interactive Whiteboard Activities: Daily Word Ladders Grades 1–2 © 2012 by Timothy V. Rasinski, Scholastic Teaching Resources

Name _____

Read the clues, then write the words.
Start at the bottom and climb to the top.

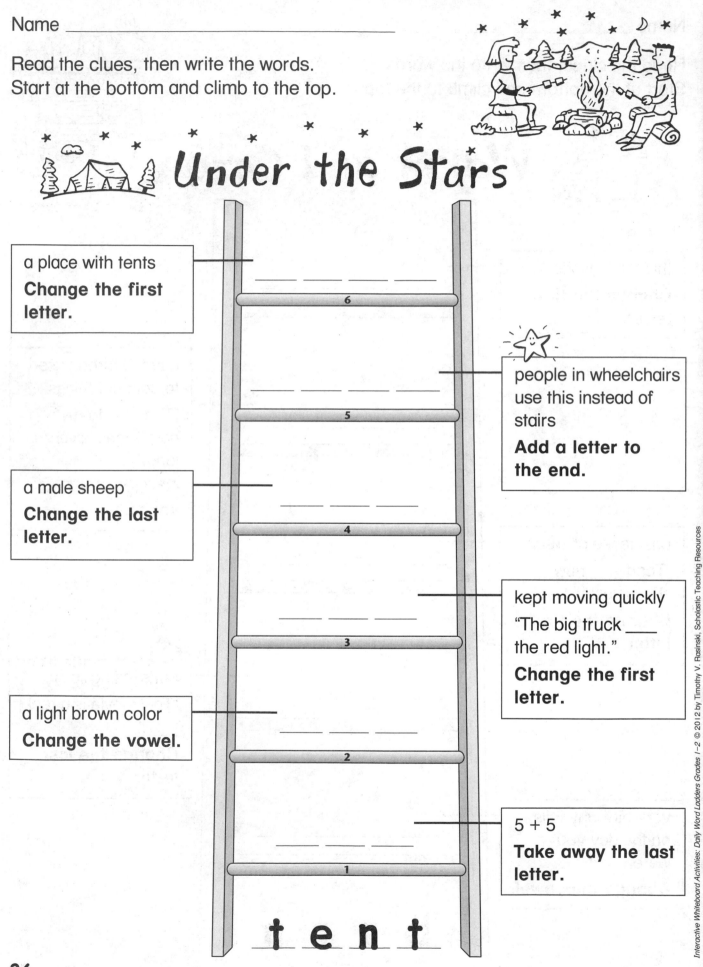

Under the Stars

a place with tents
Change the first letter.

6 ___ ___ ___ ___

people in wheelchairs use this instead of stairs
Add a letter to the end.

5 ___ ___ ___ ___

a male sheep
Change the last letter.

4 ___ ___ ___

kept moving quickly
"The big truck ____ the red light."
Change the first letter.

3 ___ ___ ___

a light brown color
Change the vowel.

2 ___ ___ ___

5 + 5
Take away the last letter.

1 ___ ___ ___

t e n t

Interactive Whiteboard Activities: Daily Word Ladders Grades 1–2 © 2012 by Timothy V. Rasinski; Scholastic Teaching Resources

Name _____

Read the clues, then write the words.
Start at the bottom and climb to the top.

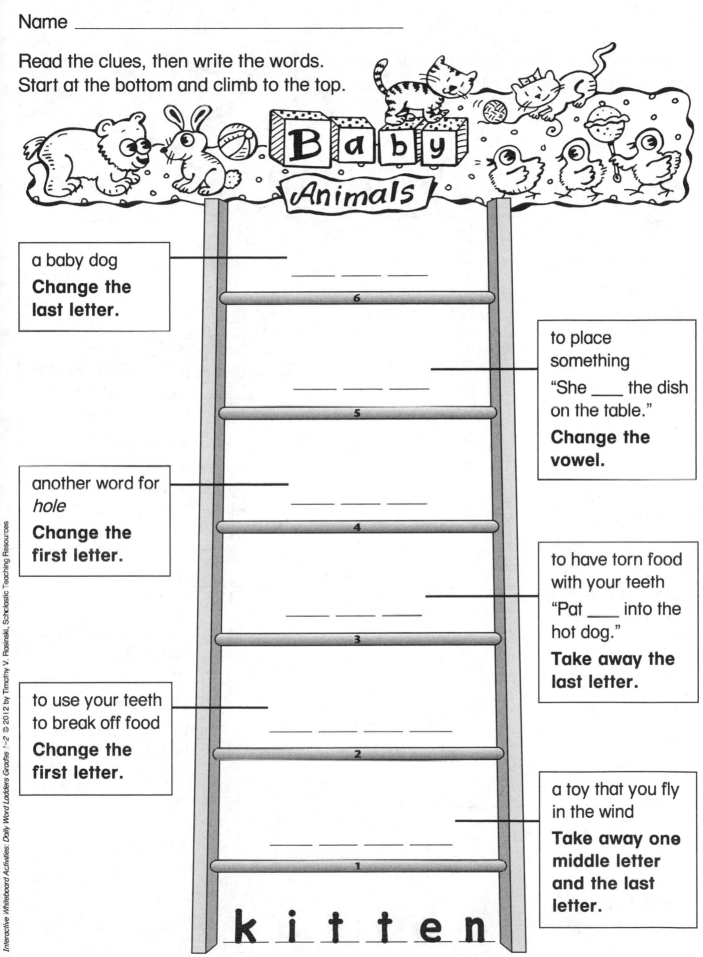

a baby dog
Change the last letter.

to place something
"She ____ the dish on the table."
Change the vowel.

another word for *hole*
Change the first letter.

to have torn food with your teeth
"Pat ____ into the hot dog."
Take away the last letter.

to use your teeth to break off food
Change the first letter.

a toy that you fly in the wind
Take away one middle letter and the last letter.

6

5

4

3

2

1

k i t t e n

Interactive Whiteboard Activities: Daily Word Ladders Grades 1–2 © 2012 by Timothy V. Rasinski, Scholastic Teaching Resources

Name _____

Read the clues, then write the words.
Start at the bottom and climb to the top.

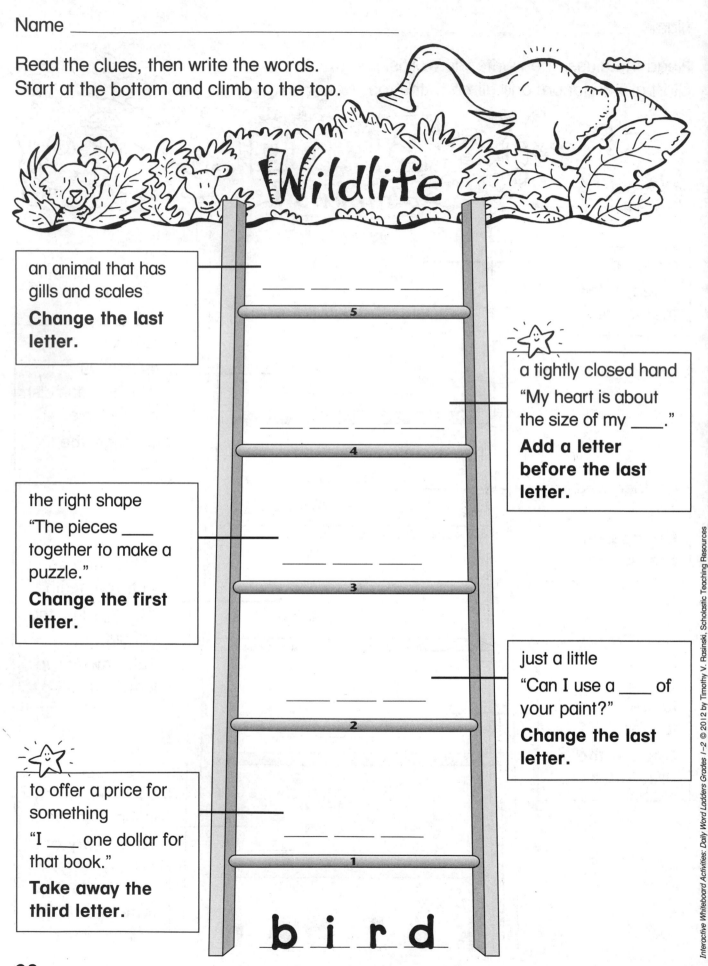

an animal that has
gills and scales
**Change the last
letter.**

a tightly closed hand
"My heart is about
the size of my ___."
**Add a letter
before the last
letter.**

the right shape
"The pieces ___
together to make a
puzzle."
**Change the first
letter.**

just a little
"Can I use a ___ of
your paint?"
**Change the last
letter.**

to offer a price for
something
"I ___ one dollar for
that book."
**Take away the
third letter.**

b i r d

Interactive Whiteboard Activities: Daily Word Ladders Grades 1–2 © 2012 by Timothy V. Rasinski, Scholastic Teaching Resources

Name _____

Read the clues, then write the words.
Start at the bottom and climb to the top.

Raise Your Voice

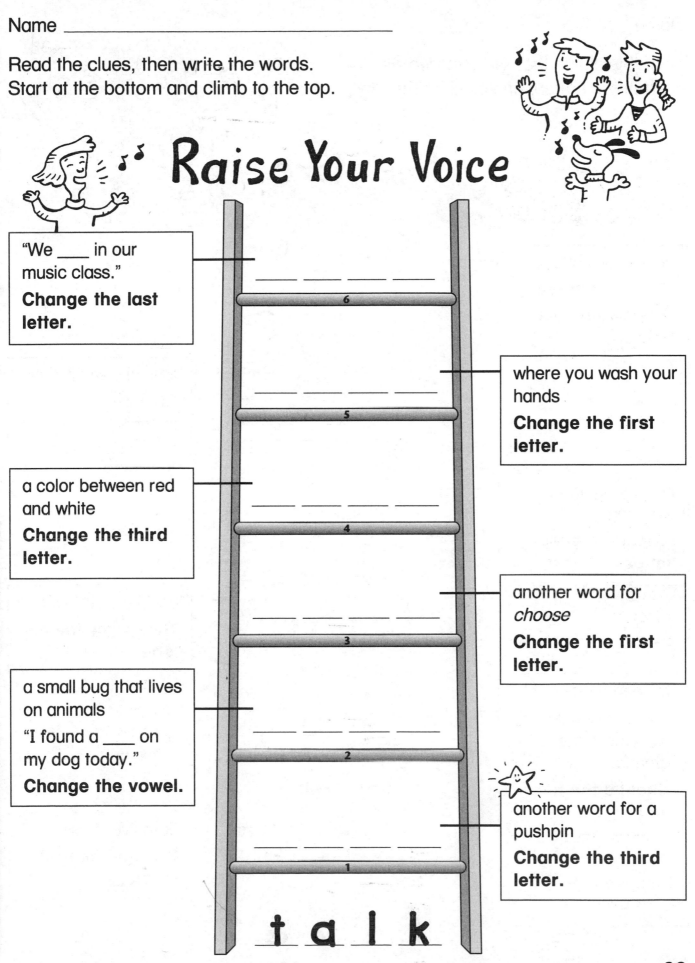

"We ___ in our music class."
Change the last letter.

where you wash your hands
Change the first letter.

a color between red and white
Change the third letter.

another word for *choose*
Change the first letter.

a small bug that lives on animals
"I found a ___ on my dog today."
Change the vowel.

another word for a pushpin
Change the third letter.

6

5

4

3

2

1

t a l k

Interactive Whiteboard Activities: Daily Word Ladders Grades 1–2 © 2012 by Timothy V. Rasinski, Scholastic Teaching Resources

Name _____

Read the clues, then write the words.
Start at the bottom and climb to the top.

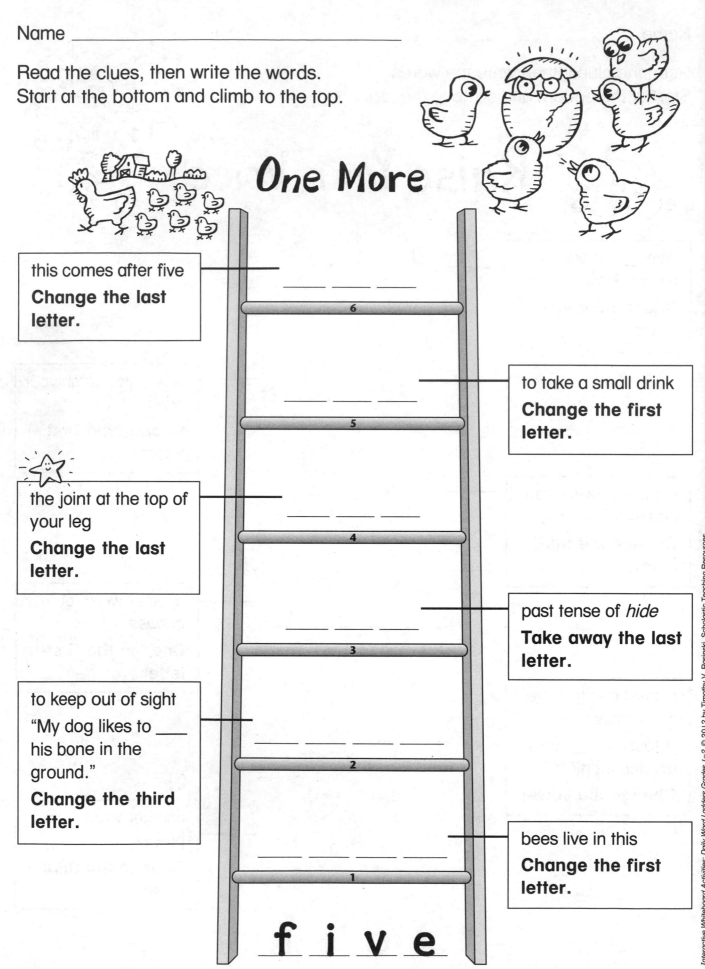

One More

this comes after five
Change the last letter.

6 _ _ _ _ _

to take a small drink
Change the first letter.

5 _ _ _ _

the joint at the top of your leg
Change the last letter.

4 _ _ _ _

past tense of *hide*
Take away the last letter.

3 _ _ _ _

to keep out of sight
"My dog likes to ___ his bone in the ground."
Change the third letter.

2 _ _ _ _

bees live in this
Change the first letter.

1 _ _ _ _

f i v e

Interactive Whiteboard Activities: Daily Word Ladders Grades 1–2 © 2012 by Timothy V. Rasinski, Scholastic Teaching Resources

Name _____

Read the clues, then write the words.
Start at the bottom and climb to the top.

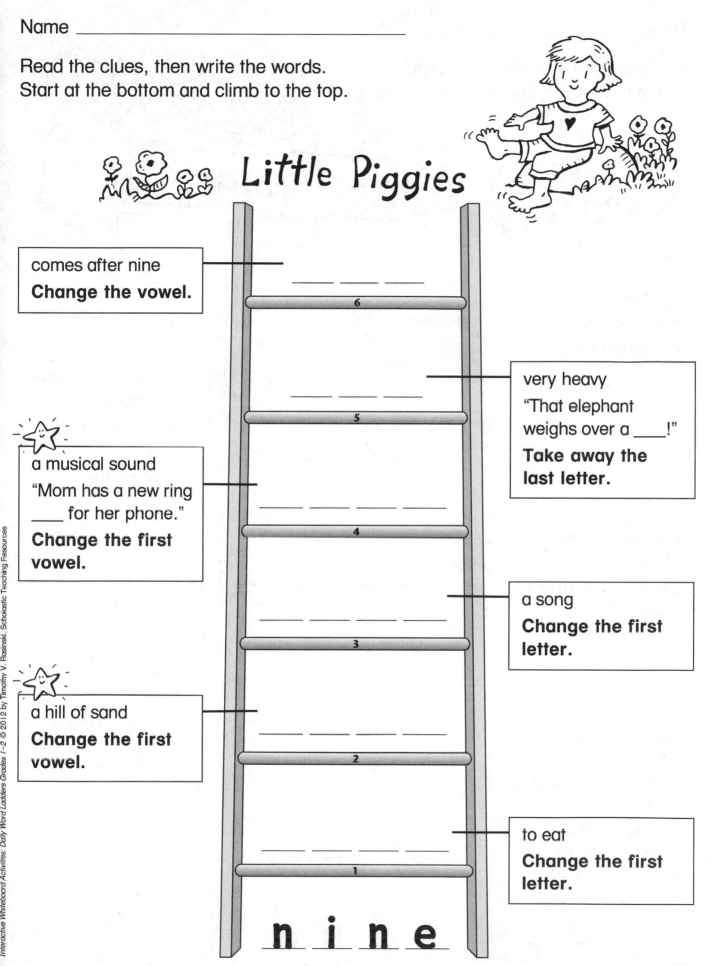

Little Piggies

comes after nine
Change the vowel.

_ _ _ _ 6

very heavy
"That elephant weighs over a ___!"
Take away the last letter.

_ _ _ _ 5

a musical sound
"Mom has a new ring ___ for her phone."
Change the first vowel.

_ _ _ _ 4

a song
Change the first letter.

_ _ _ _ 3

a hill of sand
Change the first vowel.

_ _ _ _ 2

to eat
Change the first letter.

_ _ _ _ 1

n i n e

Interactive Whiteboard Activities: Daily Word Ladders Grades 1–2 © 2012 by Timothy V. Rasinski. Scholastic Teaching Resources

Name _____

Read the clues, then write the words.
Start at the bottom and climb to the top.

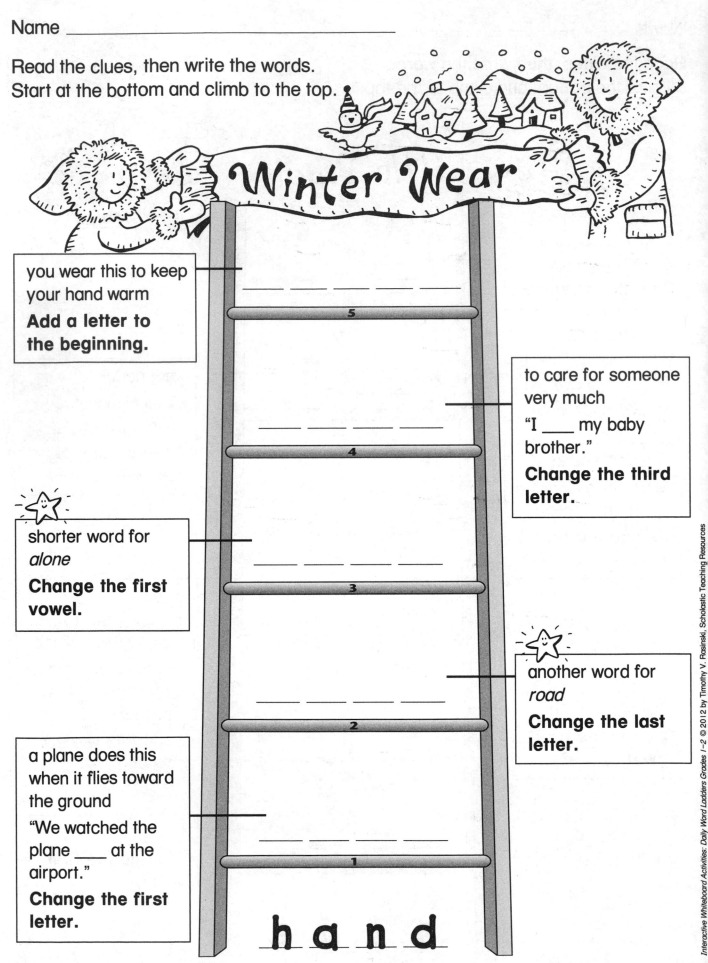

Winter Wear

you wear this to keep your hand warm
Add a letter to the beginning.

to care for someone very much
"I ___ my baby brother."
Change the third letter.

shorter word for *alone*
Change the first vowel.

another word for *road*
Change the last letter.

a plane does this when it flies toward the ground
"We watched the plane ___ at the airport."
Change the first letter.

5

4

3

2

1

h a n d

42

Interactive Whiteboard Activities: Daily Word Ladders Grades 1–2 © 2012 by Timothy V. Rasinski, Scholastic Teaching Resources

Name _____

Read the clues, then write the words.
Start at the bottom and climb to the top.

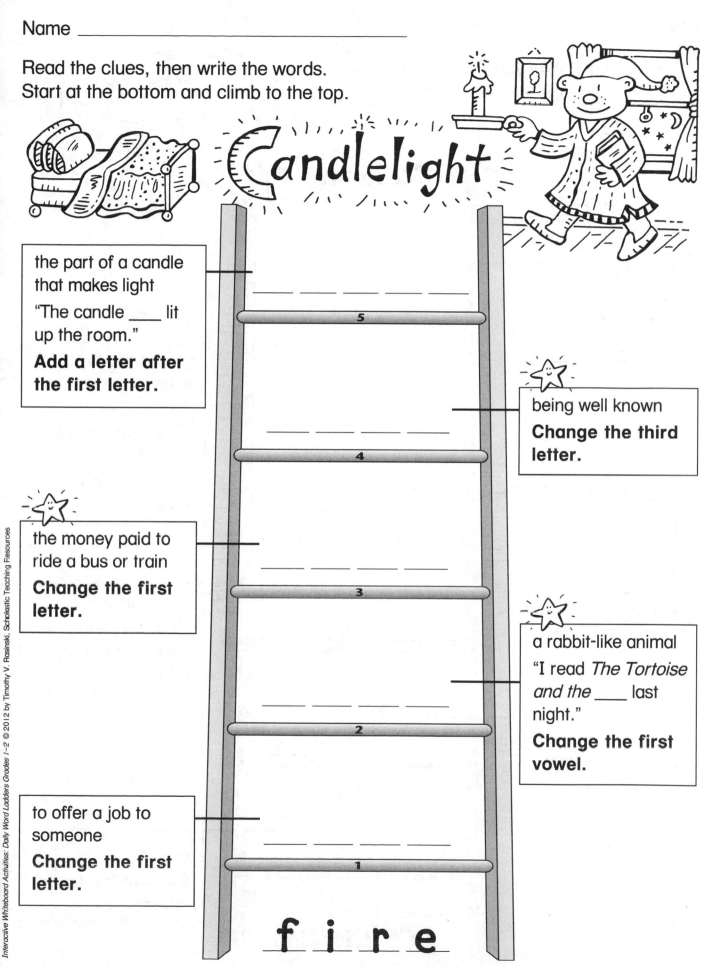

Candlelight

the part of a candle that makes light

"The candle ____ lit up the room."

Add a letter after the first letter.

being well known
Change the third letter.

the money paid to ride a bus or train
Change the first letter.

a rabbit-like animal

"I read *The Tortoise and the* ____ *last night.*"

Change the first vowel.

to offer a job to someone
Change the first letter.

5

4

3

2

1

f i r e

Interactive Whiteboard Activities: Daily Word Ladders Grades 1–2 © 2012 by Timothy V. Rasinski, Scholastic Teaching Resources

Name _____

Read the clues, then write the words.
Start at the bottom and climb to the top.

Eyeglass Holders

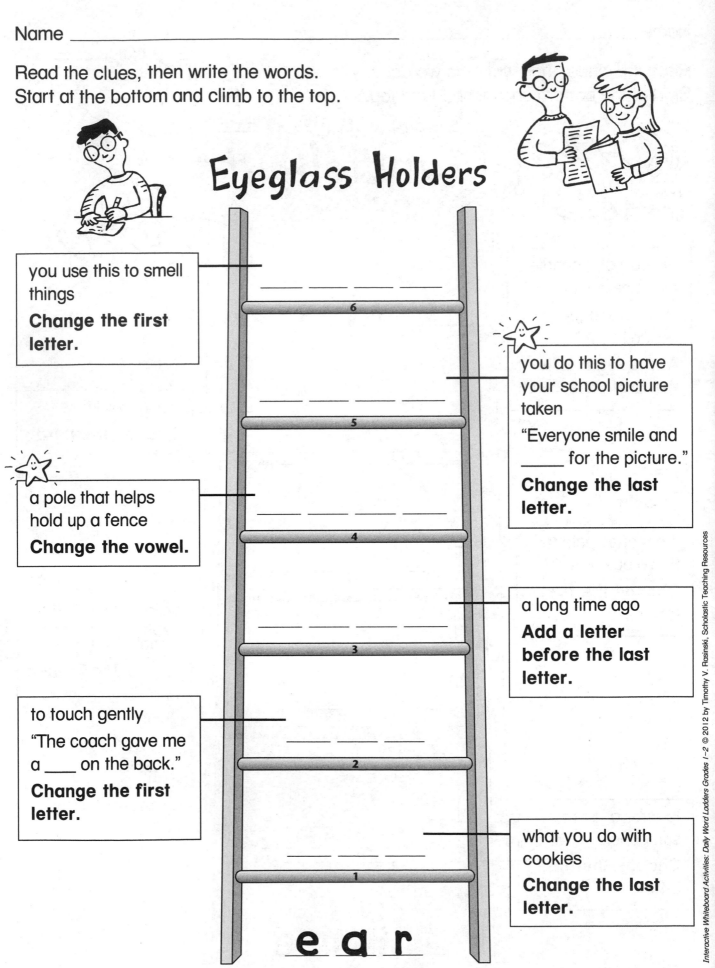

you use this to smell things
Change the first letter.

you do this to have your school picture taken
"Everyone smile and _____ for the picture."
Change the last letter.

a pole that helps hold up a fence
Change the vowel.

a long time ago
Add a letter before the last letter.

to touch gently
"The coach gave me a ____ on the back."
Change the first letter.

what you do with cookies
Change the last letter.

e a r

Interactive Whiteboard Activities: Daily Word Ladders Grades 1–2 © 2012 by Timothy V. Rasinski, Scholastic Teaching Resources

Name _____

Read the clues, then write the words.
Start at the bottom and climb to the top.

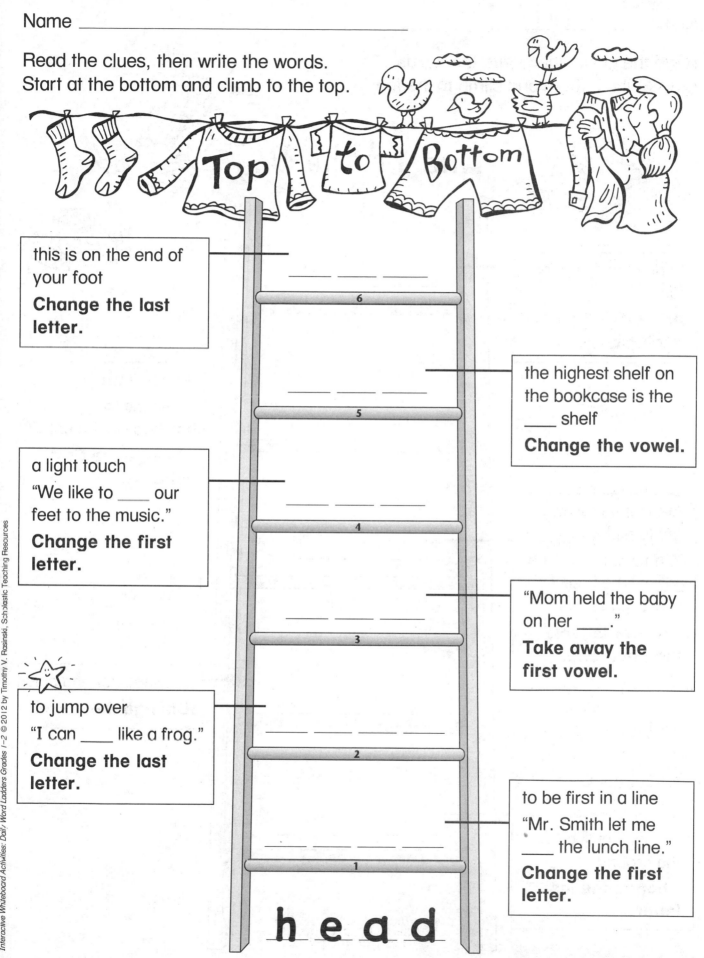

this is on the end of your foot
Change the last letter.

the highest shelf on the bookcase is the ___ shelf
Change the vowel.

a light touch
"We like to ___ our feet to the music."
Change the first letter.

"Mom held the baby on her ___."
Take away the first vowel.

to jump over
"I can ___ like a frog."
Change the last letter.

to be first in a line
"Mr. Smith let me ___ the lunch line."
Change the first letter.

6

5

4

3

2

1

h e a d

Interactive Whiteboard Activities: Daily Word Ladders Grades 1–2 © 2012 by Timothy V. Rasinski, Scholastic Teaching Resources

Name _____

Read the clues, then write the words.
Start at the bottom and climb to the top.

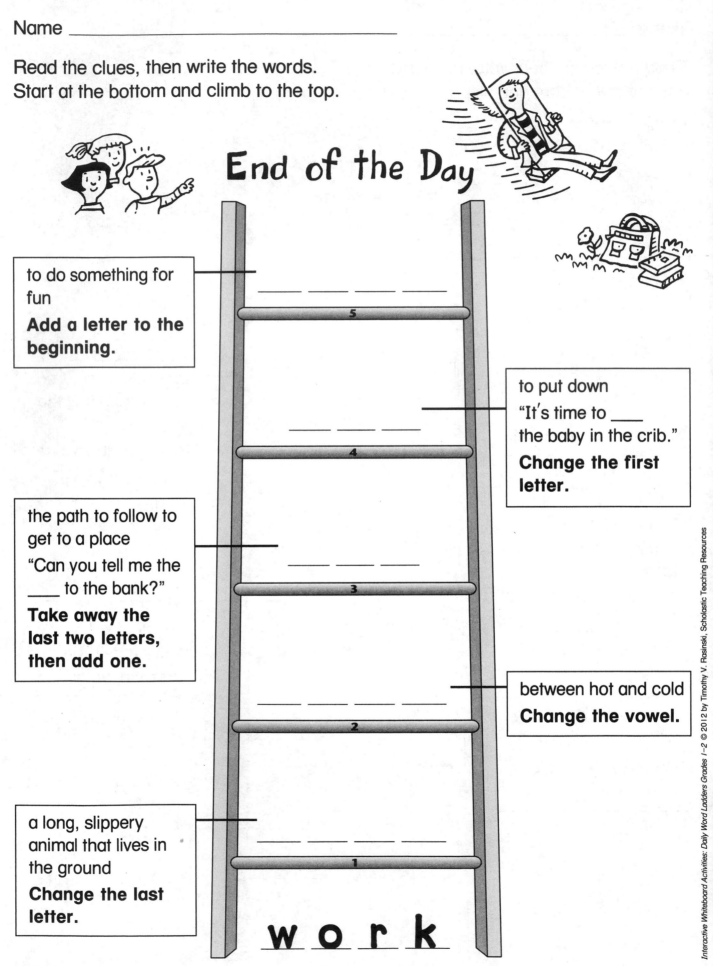

End of the Day

to do something for fun
Add a letter to the beginning.

_ _ _ _ _   (5)

to put down
"It's time to ___ the baby in the crib."
Change the first letter.

_ _ _ _   (4)

the path to follow to get to a place
"Can you tell me the ___ to the bank?"
Take away the last two letters, then add one.

_ _ _ _   (3)

between hot and cold
Change the vowel.

_ _ _ _   (2)

a long, slippery animal that lives in the ground
Change the last letter.

_ _ _ _   (1)

w o r k

Interactive Whiteboard Activities: Daily Word Ladders Grades 1–2 © 2012 by Timothy V. Rasinski, Scholastic Teaching Resources

Name _____

Read the clues, then write the words.
Start at the bottom and climb to the top.

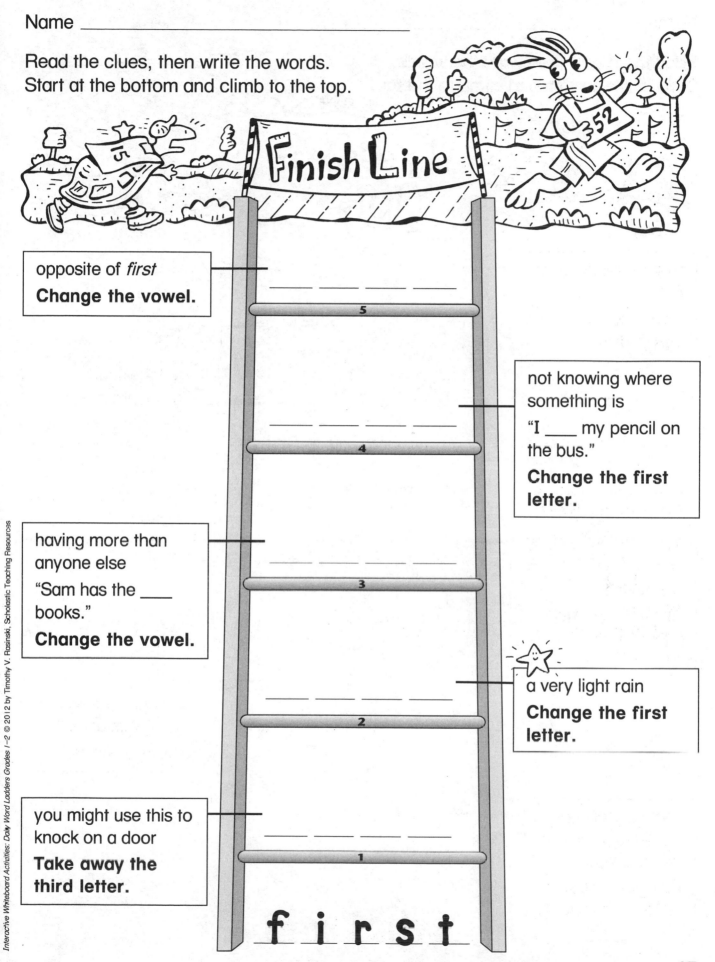

Finish Line

opposite of *first*
Change the vowel.

_ _ _ _

5

not knowing where
something is
"I ____ my pencil on
the bus."
**Change the first
letter.**

_ _ _ _

4

having more than
anyone else
"Sam has the ____
books."
Change the vowel.

_ _ _ _

3

a very light rain
**Change the first
letter.**

_ _ _ _

2

you might use this to
knock on a door
**Take away the
third letter.**

_ _ _ _

1

f i r s t

Name _____

Read the clues, then write the words.
Start at the bottom and climb to the top.

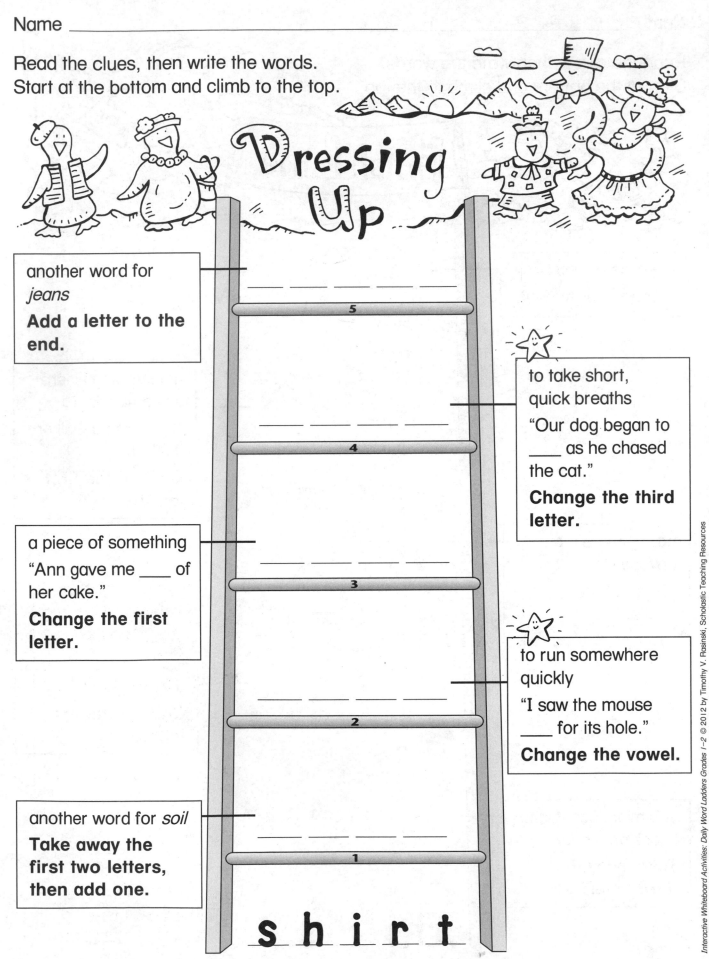

Dressing Up

another word for *jeans*
Add a letter to the end.

to take short, quick breaths
"Our dog began to ___ as he chased the cat."
Change the third letter.

a piece of something
"Ann gave me ___ of her cake."
Change the first letter.

to run somewhere quickly
"I saw the mouse ___ for its hole."
Change the vowel.

another word for *soil*
Take away the first two letters, then add one.

5

4

3

2

1

s h i r t

Interactive Whiteboard Activities: Daily Word Ladders Grades 1–2 © 2012 by Timothy V. Rasinski, Scholastic Teaching Resources

Name _____

Read the clues, then write the words.
Start at the bottom and climb to the top.

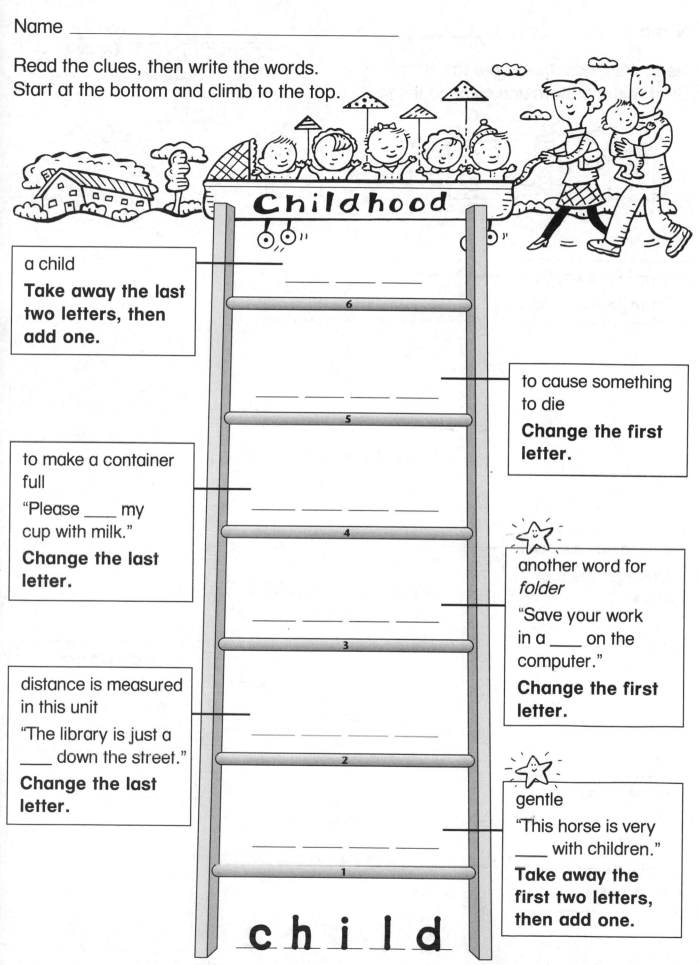

Childhood

a child
Take away the last two letters, then add one.

to make a container full
"Please ____ my cup with milk."
Change the last letter.

distance is measured in this unit
"The library is just a ____ down the street."
Change the last letter.

to cause something to die
Change the first letter.

another word for *folder*
"Save your work in a ____ on the computer."
Change the first letter.

gentle
"This horse is very ____ with children."
Take away the first two letters, then add one.

6

5

4

3

2

1

c h i l d

Name _____

Read the clues, then write the words.
Start at the bottom and climb to the top.

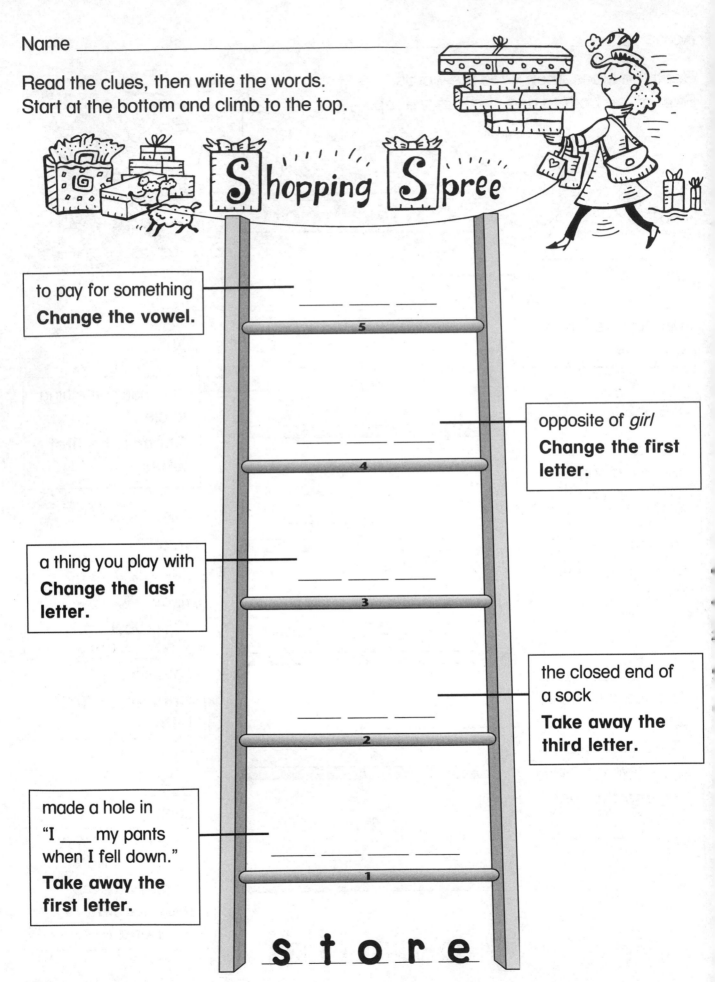

Shopping Spree

to pay for something
Change the vowel.

_____ _____ _____ _____

5

opposite of *girl*
Change the first letter.

_____ _____ _____

4

a thing you play with
Change the last letter.

_____ _____ _____

3

the closed end of a sock
Take away the third letter.

_____ _____ _____

2

made a hole in
"I ___ my pants when I fell down."
Take away the first letter.

_____ _____ _____ _____

1

s t o r e

Name _____

Read the clues, then write the words.
Start at the bottom and climb to the top.

a part of your skeleton
Change the first letter.

_ _ _ _
6

the shade of a color
"I used a dark ____ of blue to color the sky in my picture."
Add a vowel to the end.

_ _ _ _
5

"Our school bus weighs more than a ____."
Add a letter to the beginning.

_ _ _ _
4

_ _ _
3

opposite of *off*
Change the vowel.

opposite of *out*
Take away the first letter.

_ _ _
2

_ _ _ _
1

another word for *family*
Take away the first letter.

s   k   i   n

Name _____

Read the clues, then write the words.
Start at the bottom and climb to the top.

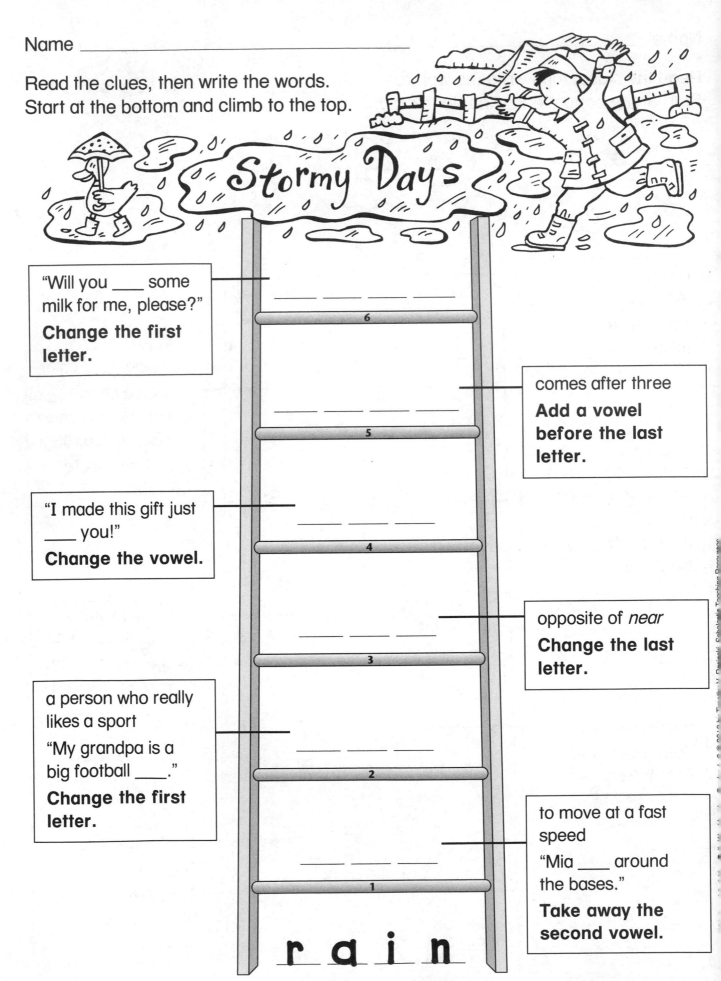

Stormy Days

"Will you ____ some milk for me, please?"
Change the first letter.

comes after three
Add a vowel before the last letter.

"I made this gift just ____ you!"
Change the vowel.

opposite of *near*
Change the last letter.

a person who really likes a sport
"My grandpa is a big football ____."
Change the first letter.

to move at a fast speed
"Mia ____ around the bases."
Take away the second vowel.

6 _ _ _ _
5 _ _ _ _
4 _ _ _ _
3 _ _ _ _ _
2 _ _ _ _
1 _ _ _ _ _

r a i n

Name _____

Read the clues, then write the words.
Start at the bottom and climb to the top.

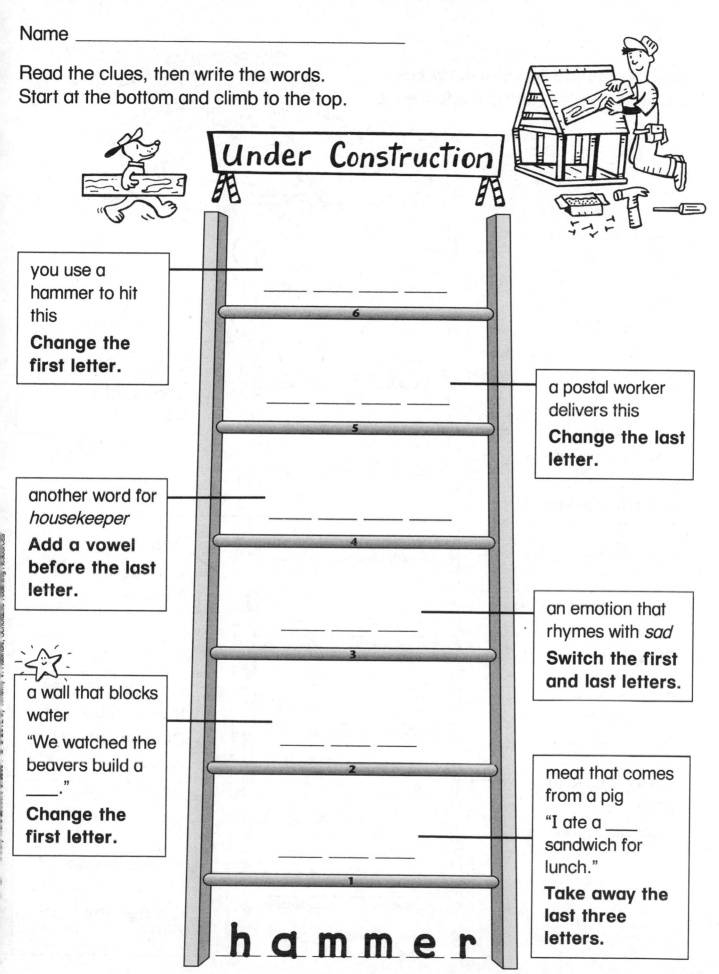

Under Construction

you use a hammer to hit this
Change the first letter.

6 _ _ _ _ _ _

a postal worker delivers this
Change the last letter.

5 _ _ _ _ _

another word for *housekeeper*
Add a vowel before the last letter.

4 _ _ _ _ _

an emotion that rhymes with *sad*
Switch the first and last letters.

3 _ _ _ _

a wall that blocks water
"We watched the beavers build a ____."
Change the first letter.

2 _ _ _ _

meat that comes from a pig
"I ate a ____ sandwich for lunch."
Take away the last three letters.

1 _ _ _ _ _

h a m m e r

Name _____

Read the clues, then write the words.
Start at the bottom and climb to the top.

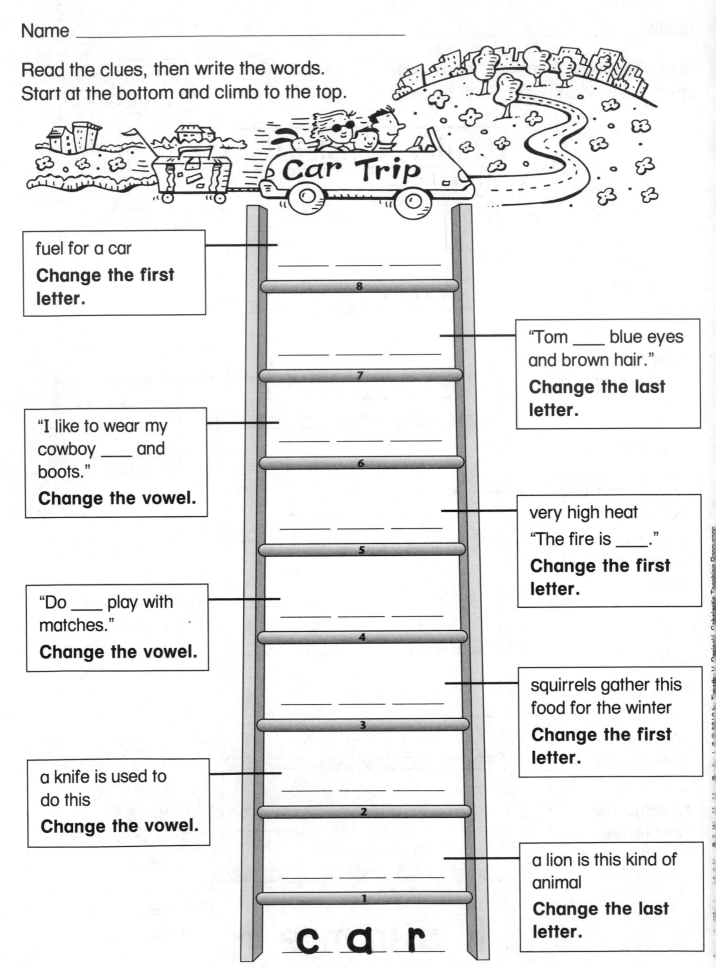

Car Trip

fuel for a car
Change the first letter.

_ _ _ _ _   8

"Tom ___ blue eyes and brown hair."
Change the last letter.

_ _ _ _ _   7

"I like to wear my cowboy ___ and boots."
Change the vowel.

_ _ _ _ _   6

very high heat
"The fire is ___."
Change the first letter.

_ _ _ _ _   5

"Do ___ play with matches."
Change the vowel.

_ _ _ _ _   4

squirrels gather this food for the winter
Change the first letter.

_ _ _ _ _   3

a knife is used to do this
Change the vowel.

_ _ _ _ _   2

a lion is this kind of animal
Change the last letter.

_ _ _ _ _   1

c a r

Name _____

Read the clues, then write the words.
Start at the bottom and climb to the top.

Climbing Limbs

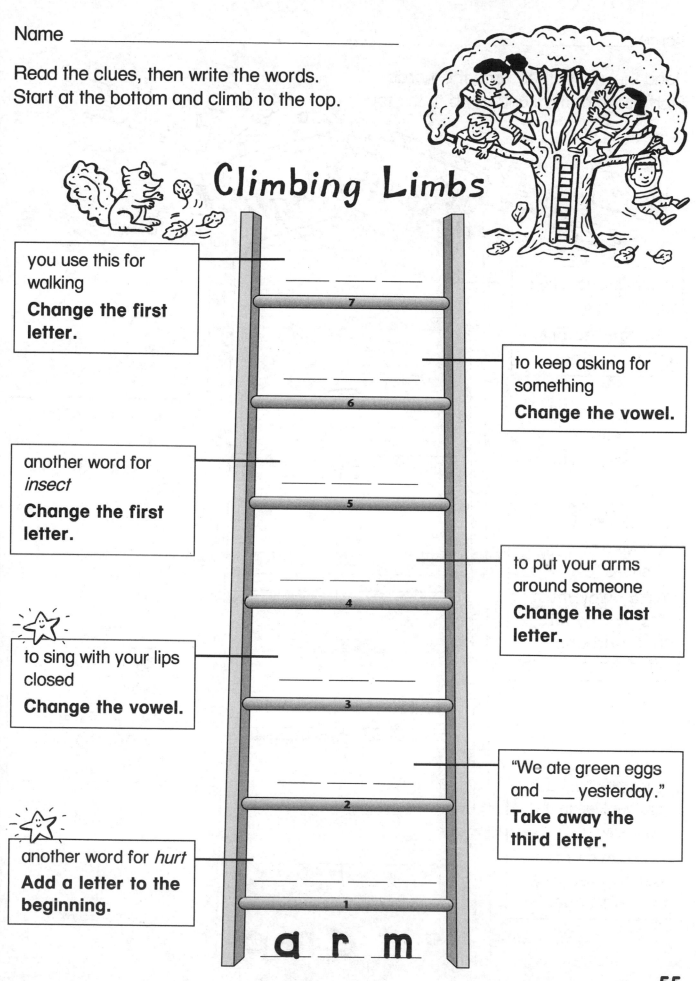

you use this for walking
Change the first letter.

to keep asking for something
Change the vowel.

another word for *insect*
Change the first letter.

to put your arms around someone
Change the last letter.

to sing with your lips closed
Change the vowel.

"We ate green eggs and ___ yesterday."
Take away the third letter.

another word for *hurt*
Add a letter to the beginning.

a r m

Name _____

Read the clues, then write the words.
Start at the bottom and climb to the top.

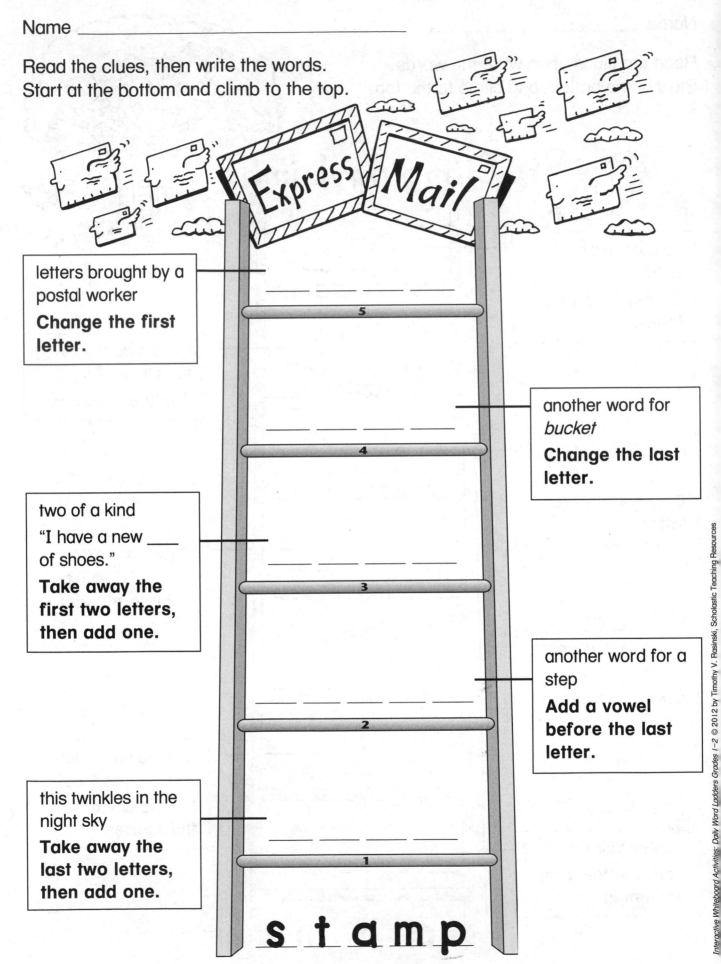

letters brought by a postal worker
Change the first letter.

another word for *bucket*
Change the last letter.

two of a kind
"I have a new ___ of shoes."
Take away the first two letters, then add one.

another word for a step
Add a vowel before the last letter.

this twinkles in the night sky
Take away the last two letters, then add one.

s t a m p

56

Interactive Whiteboard Activities: Daily Word Ladders Grades 1–2 © 2012 by Timothy V. Rasinski, Scholastic Teaching Resources

Name _____

Read the clues, then write the words.
Start at the bottom and climb to the top.

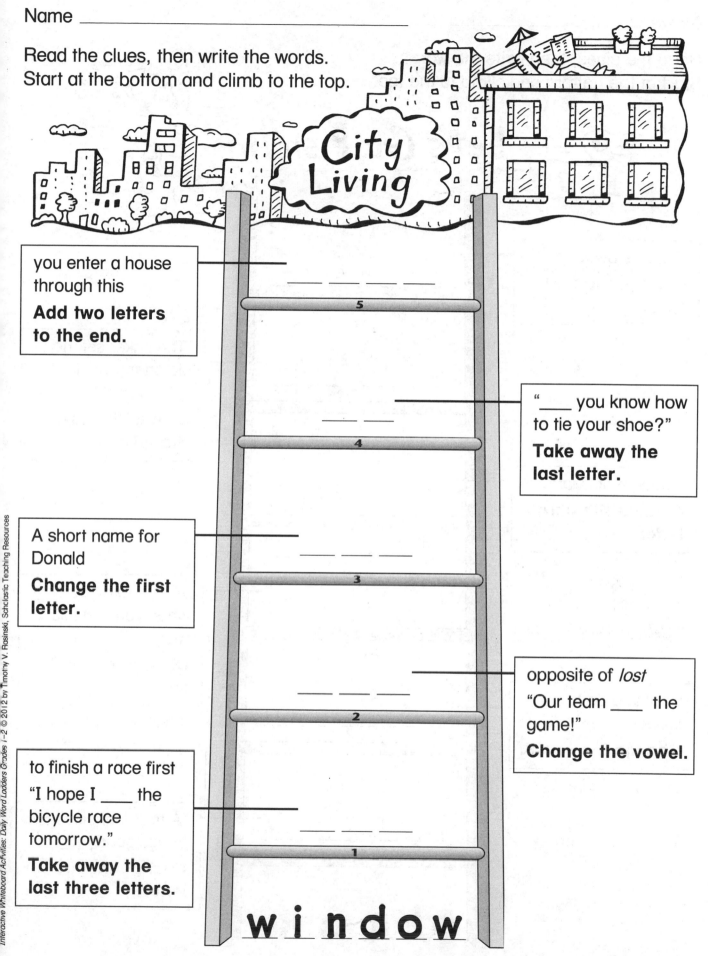

City Living

you enter a house through this
Add two letters to the end.

_____ _____ _____

5

" ____ you know how to tie your shoe?"
Take away the last letter.

_____ _____ _____

4

A short name for Donald
Change the first letter.

_____ _____ _____ _____

3

opposite of *lost*
"Our team ____ the game!"
Change the vowel.

_____ _____ _____ _____

2

to finish a race first
"I hope I ____ the bicycle race tomorrow."
Take away the last three letters.

_____ _____ _____

1

w i n d o w

Name _____

Read the clues, then write the words.
Start at the bottom and climb to the top.

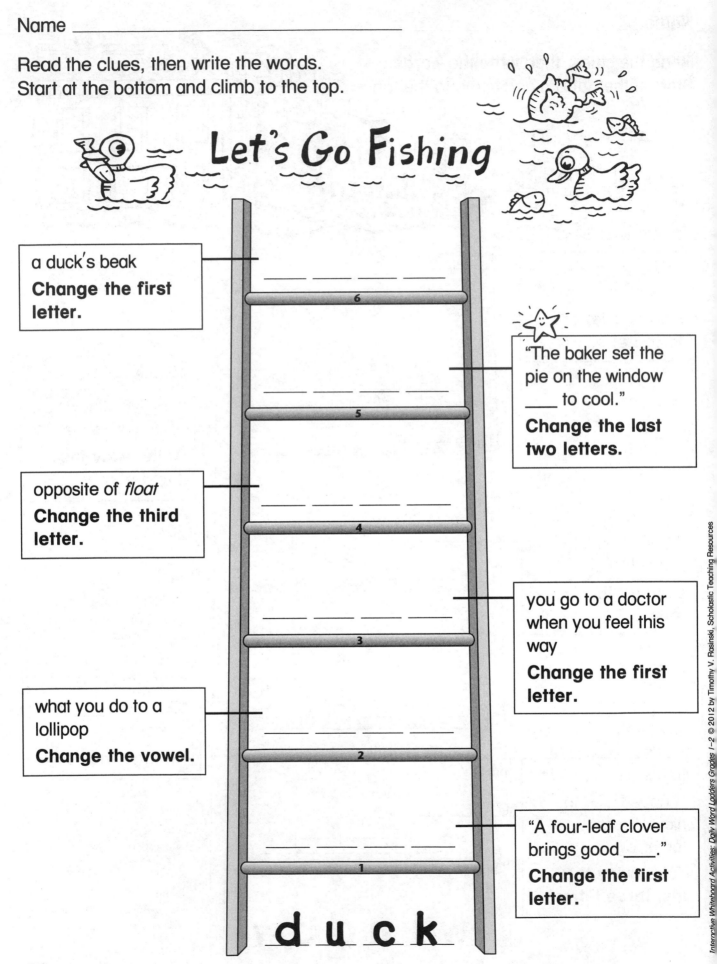

Let's Go Fishing

a duck's beak
Change the first letter.

6 _____ _____

"The baker set the pie on the window ___ to cool."
Change the last two letters.

5 _____ _____

opposite of *float*
Change the third letter.

4 _____ _____

you go to a doctor when you feel this way
Change the first letter.

3 _____ _____

what you do to a lollipop
Change the vowel.

2 _____ _____

"A four-leaf clover brings good ___."
Change the first letter.

1 _____ _____

d u c k

Interactive Whiteboard Activities: Daily Word Ladders Grades 1–2 © 2012 by Timothy V. Rasinski, Scholastic Teaching Resources

Name _____

Read the clues, then write the words.
Start at the bottom and climb to the top.

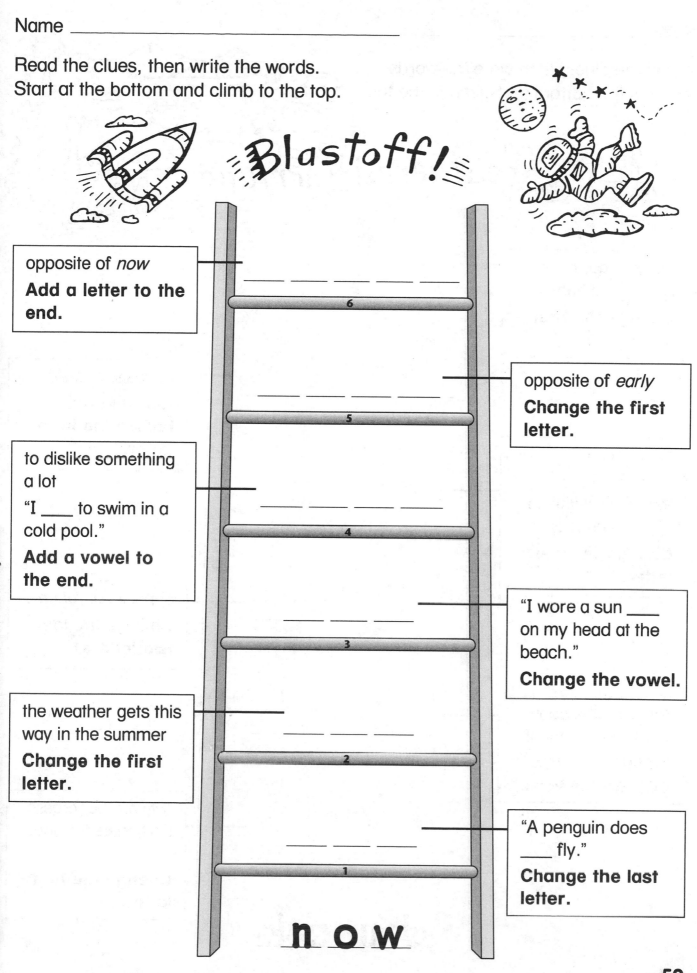

Blastoff!

opposite of *now*
Add a letter to the end.

_ _ _ _ _

6

opposite of *early*
Change the first letter.

_ _ _ _

5

to dislike something a lot
"I ___ to swim in a cold pool."
Add a vowel to the end.

_ _ _ _

4

"I wore a sun ___ on my head at the beach."
Change the vowel.

_ _ _

3

the weather gets this way in the summer
Change the first letter.

_ _ _

2

"A penguin does ___ fly."
Change the last letter.

_ _ _

1

n o w

Name _____

Read the clues, then write the words.
Start at the bottom and climb to the top.

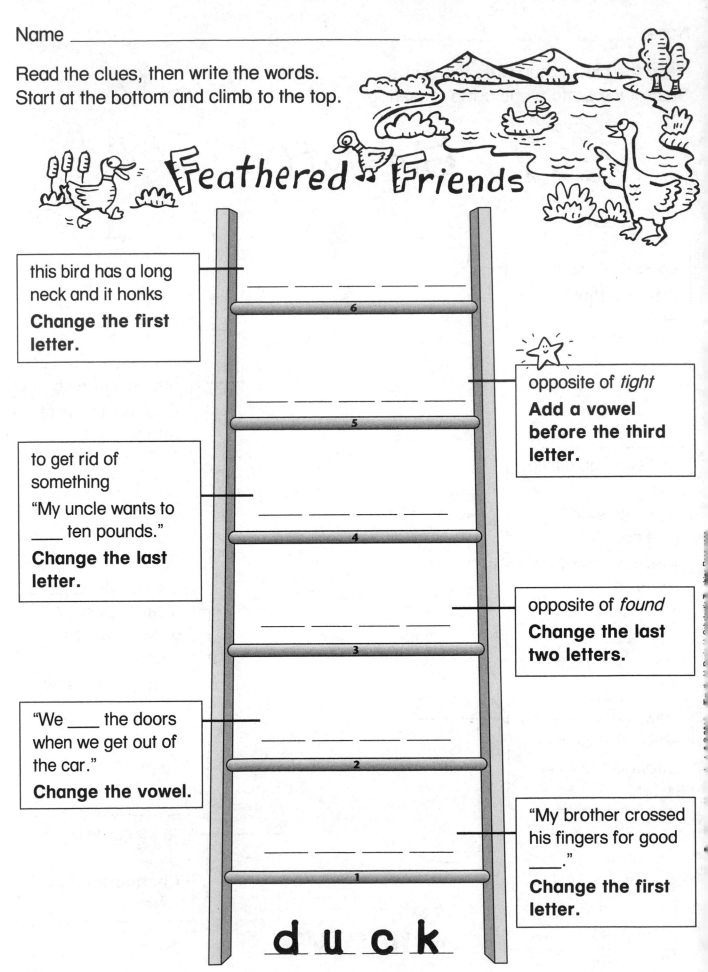

Feathered Friends

this bird has a long
neck and it honks
**Change the first
letter.**

opposite of *tight*
**Add a vowel
before the third
letter.**

to get rid of
something
"My uncle wants to
___ ten pounds."
**Change the last
letter.**

opposite of *found*
**Change the last
two letters.**

"We ___ the doors
when we get out of
the car."
Change the vowel.

"My brother crossed
his fingers for good
___."
**Change the first
letter.**

6

5

4

3

2

1

d u c k

Name _____

Read the clues, then write the words.
Start at the bottom and climb to the top.

In the Attic

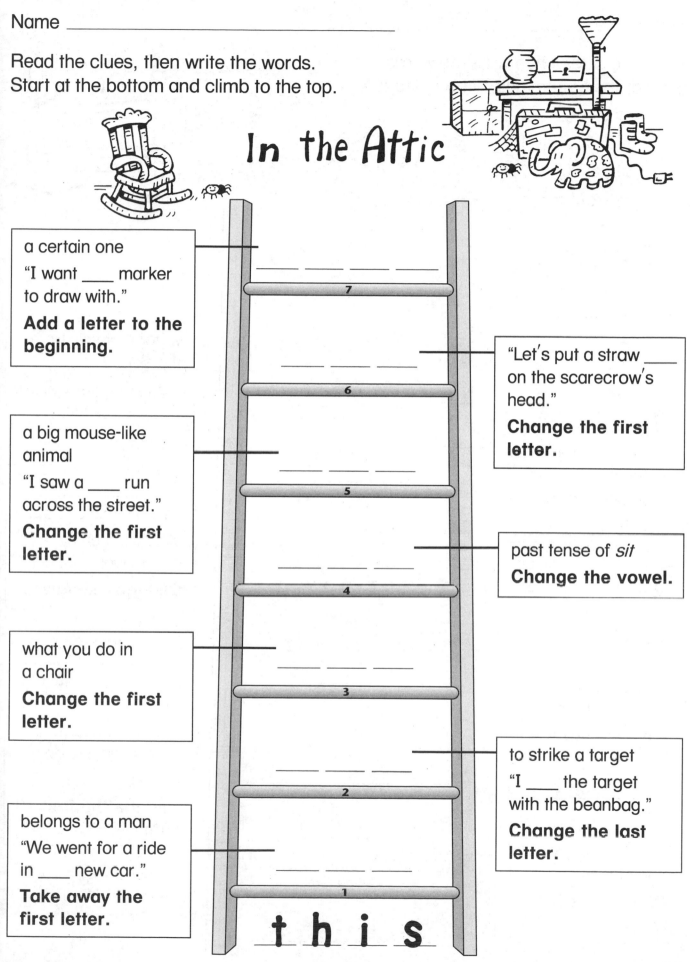

a certain one

"I want ____ marker to draw with."

Add a letter to the beginning.

a big mouse-like animal

"I saw a ____ run across the street."

Change the first letter.

what you do in a chair

Change the first letter.

belongs to a man

"We went for a ride in ____ new car."

Take away the first letter.

"Let's put a straw ____ on the scarecrow's head."

Change the first letter.

past tense of *sit*
Change the vowel.

to strike a target

"I ____ the target with the beanbag."

Change the last letter.

7

6

5

4

3

2

1

t h i s

Name _____

Read the clues, then write the words.
Start at the bottom and climb to the top.

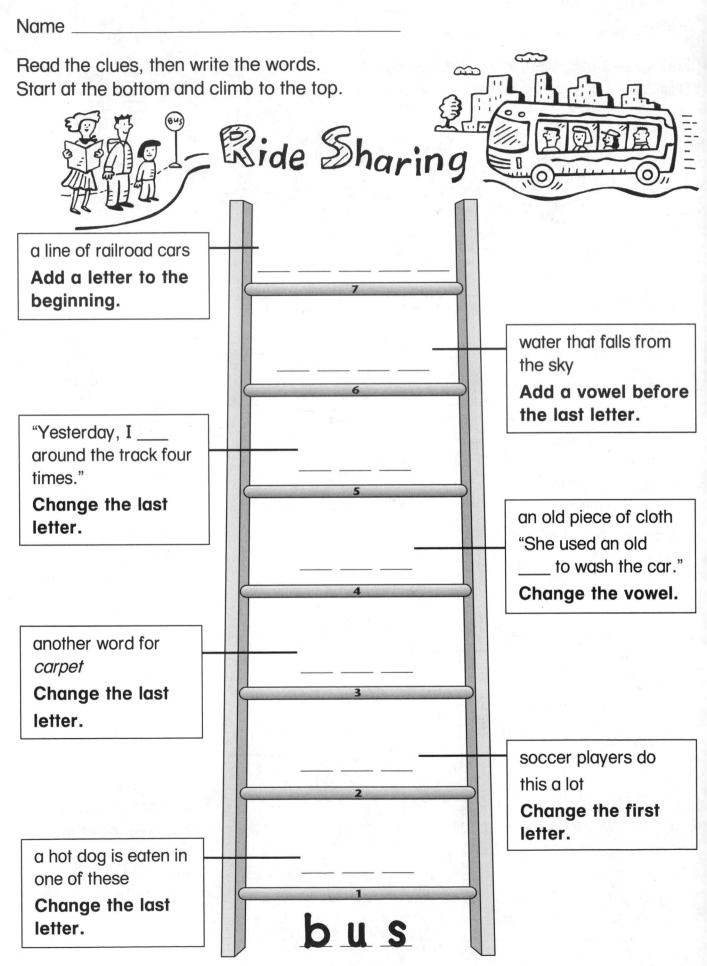

Ride Sharing

a line of railroad cars
Add a letter to the beginning.

7

water that falls from the sky
Add a vowel before the last letter.

6

"Yesterday, I ___ around the track four times."
Change the last letter.

5

an old piece of cloth
"She used an old ___ to wash the car."
Change the vowel.

4

another word for *carpet*
Change the last letter.

3

soccer players do this a lot
Change the first letter.

2

a hot dog is eaten in one of these
Change the last letter.

1

b u s

Name _____

Read the clues, then write the words.
Start at the bottom and climb to the top.

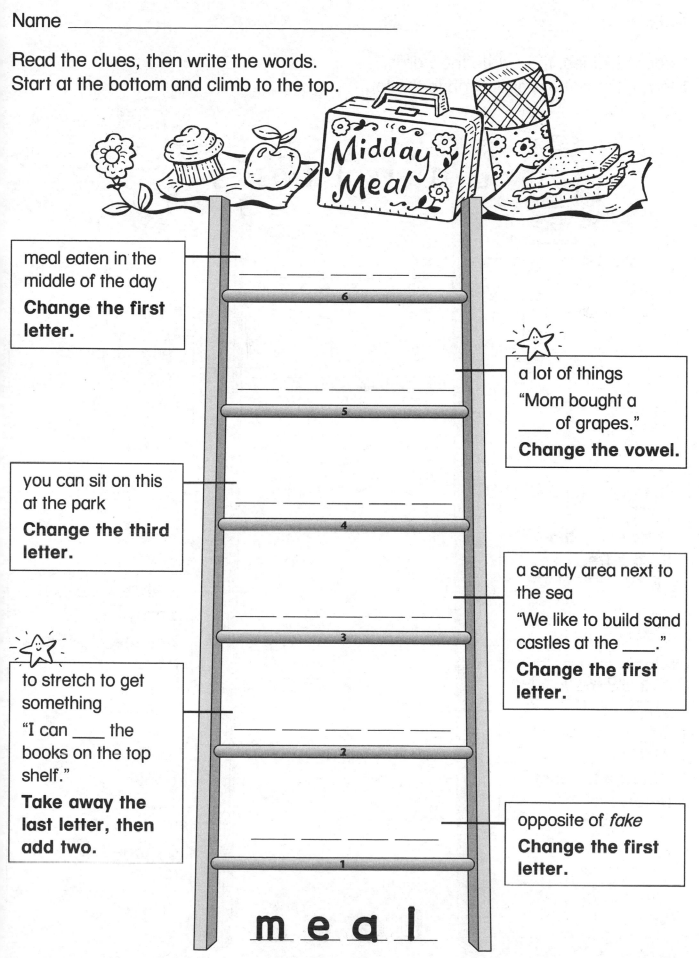

meal eaten in the middle of the day
Change the first letter.

a lot of things
"Mom bought a ___ of grapes."
Change the vowel.

you can sit on this at the park
Change the third letter.

a sandy area next to the sea
"We like to build sand castles at the ___."
Change the first letter.

to stretch to get something
"I can ___ the books on the top shelf."
Take away the last letter, then add two.

opposite of *fake*
Change the first letter.

6

5

4

3

2

1

m e a l

Name _____

Read the clues, then write the words.
Start at the bottom and climb to the top.

Super Dill!

Different Tastes

to really dislike
something
**Add a vowel to
the end.**

you wear this on
your head
Change the vowel.

"A pot of boiling water
is very ____."
**Take away the
third letter.**

a person who gives
a party
**Change the first
letter.**

when you don't know
where you are
"We got ____ in the
woods."
**Change the last
letter.**

opposite of *win*
**Change the third
letter.**

6

5

4

3

2

1

l o v e

Name _____

Read the clues, then write the words.
Start at the bottom and climb to the top.

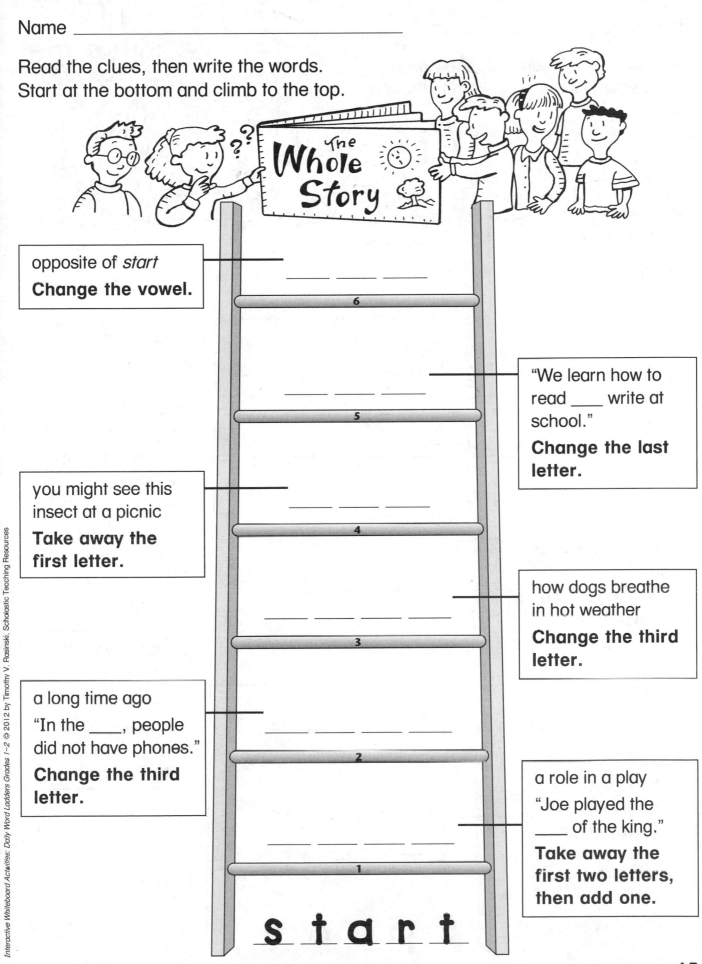

opposite of *start*
Change the vowel.

"We learn how to read ___ write at school."
Change the last letter.

you might see this insect at a picnic
Take away the first letter.

how dogs breathe in hot weather
Change the third letter.

a long time ago
"In the ___, people did not have phones."
Change the third letter.

a role in a play
"Joe played the ___ of the king."
Take away the first two letters, then add one.

6

5

4

3

2

1

s t a r t

Interactive Whiteboard Activities: Daily Word Ladders Grades 1–2 © 2012 by Timothy V. Rasinski, Scholastic Teaching Resources

Name _____

Read the clues, then write the words.
Start at the bottom and climb to the top.

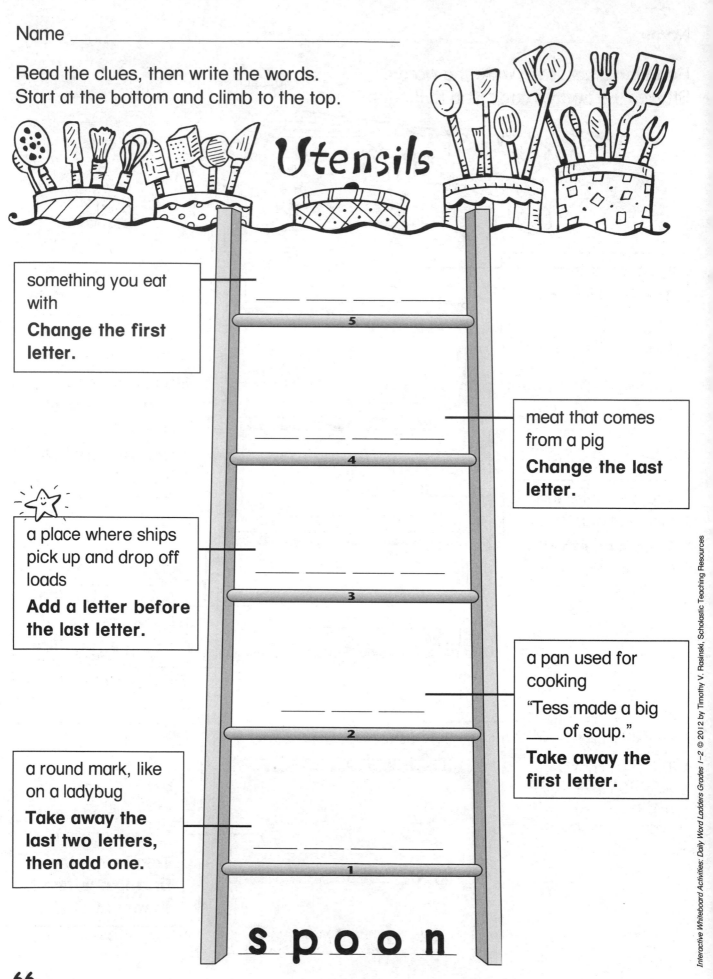

Utensils

something you eat with
Change the first letter.

— 5 —

meat that comes from a pig
Change the last letter.

— 4 —

a place where ships pick up and drop off loads
Add a letter before the last letter.

— 3 —

a pan used for cooking
"Tess made a big ___ of soup."
Take away the first letter.

— 2 —

a round mark, like on a ladybug
Take away the last two letters, then add one.

— 1 —

s p o o n

Interactive Whiteboard Activities: Daily Word Ladders Grades 1–2 © 2012 by Timothy V. Rasinski, Scholastic Teaching Resources

Name _____

Read the clues, then write the words.
Start at the bottom and climb to the top.

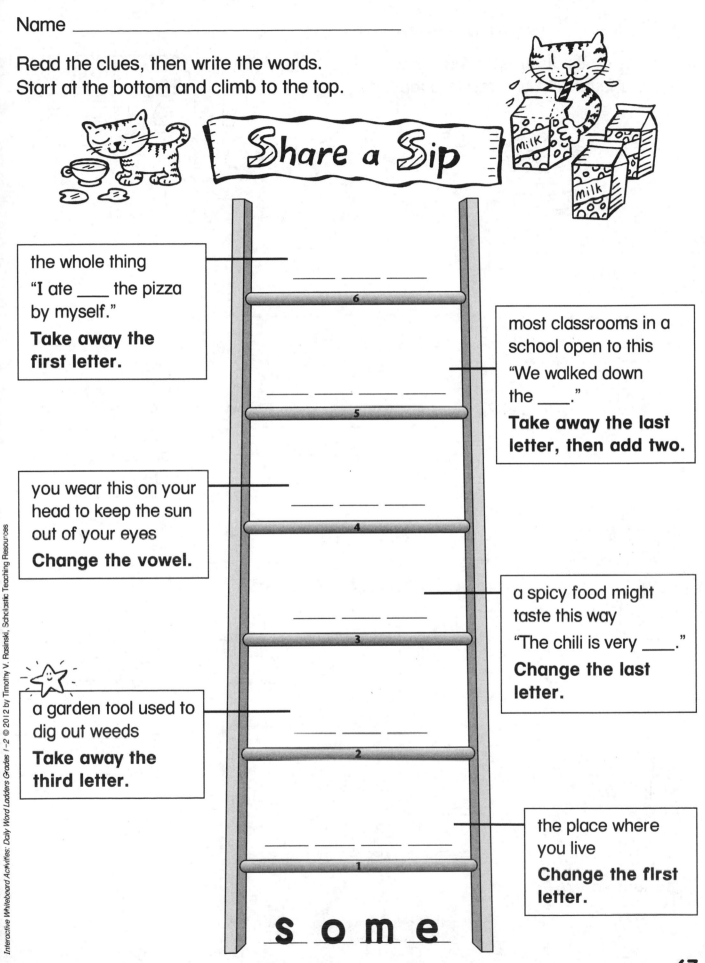

Share a Sip

the whole thing
"I ate ____ the pizza by myself."
Take away the first letter.

most classrooms in a school open to this
"We walked down the ____."
Take away the last letter, then add two.

you wear this on your head to keep the sun out of your eyes
Change the vowel.

a spicy food might taste this way
"The chili is very ____."
Change the last letter.

a garden tool used to dig out weeds
Take away the third letter.

the place where you live
Change the first letter.

6
5
4
3
2
1

s o m e

Interactive Whiteboard Activities: Daily Word Ladders Grades 1–2 © 2012 by Timothy V. Rasinski, Scholastic Teaching Resources

Name _____

Read the clues, then write the words.
Start at the bottom and climb to the top.

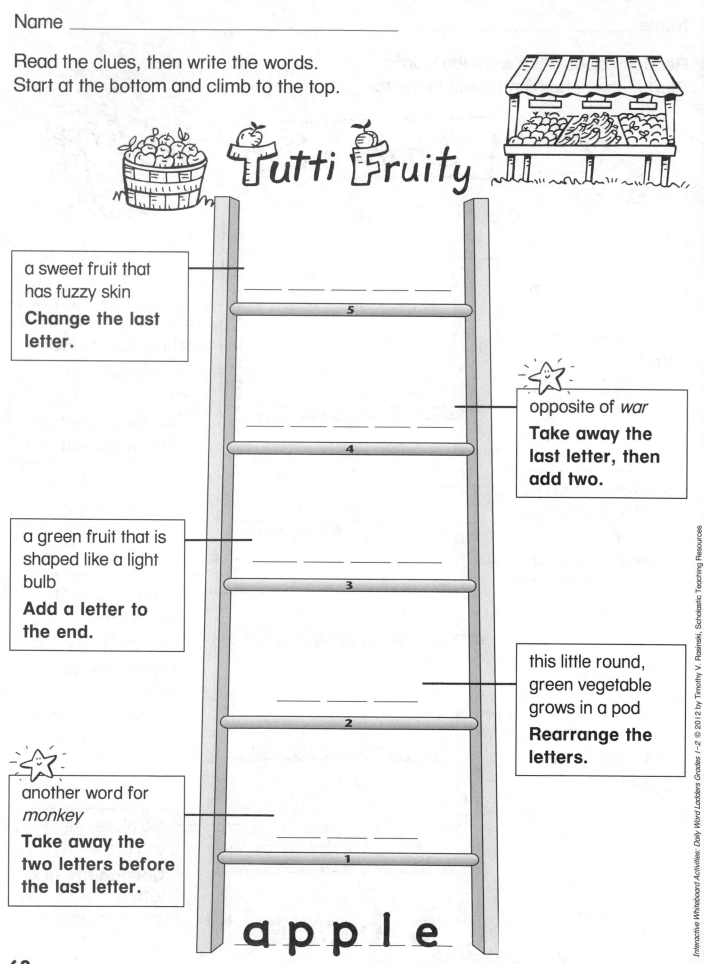

Tutti Fruity

a sweet fruit that has fuzzy skin
Change the last letter.

5 ___ ___ ___ ___ ___

opposite of *war*
Take away the last letter, then add two.

4 ___ ___ ___ ___

a green fruit that is shaped like a light bulb
Add a letter to the end.

3 ___ ___ ___ ___ ___

this little round, green vegetable grows in a pod
Rearrange the letters.

2 ___ ___ ___

another word for *monkey*
Take away the two letters before the last letter.

1 ___ ___ ___

a p p l e

68

Interactive Whiteboard Activities: Daily Word Ladders Grades 1–2 © 2012 by Timothy V. Rasinski, Scholastic Teaching Resources

Name _____

Read the clues, then write the words.
Start at the bottom and climb to the top.

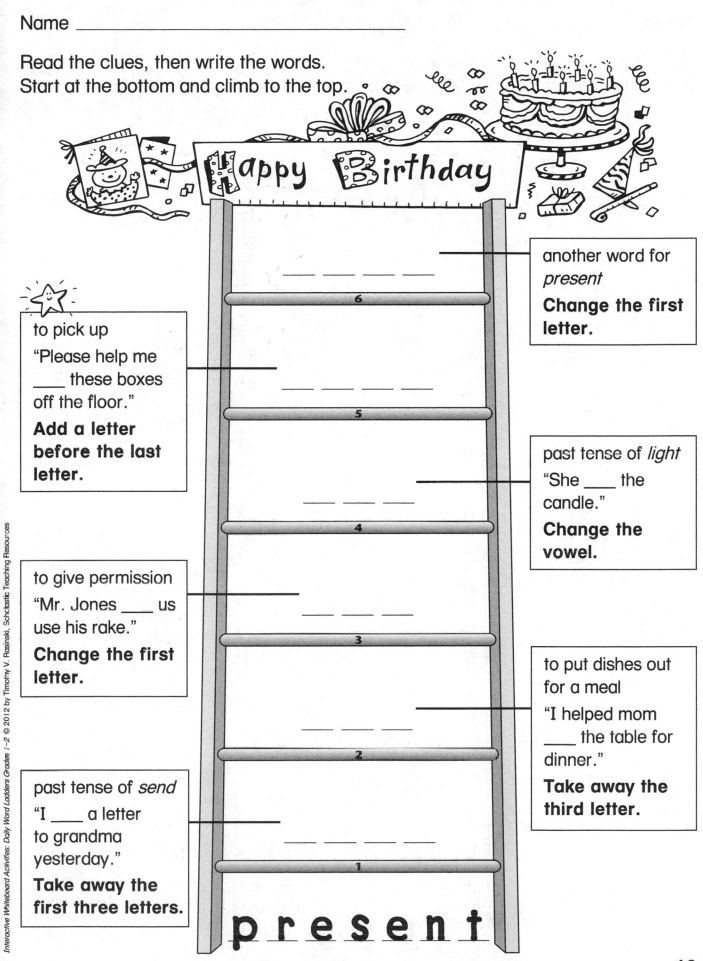

Happy Birthday

another word for
present
Change the first letter.

to pick up
"Please help me
___ these boxes
off the floor."
Add a letter before the last letter.

past tense of *light*
"She ___ the candle."
Change the vowel.

to give permission
"Mr. Jones ___ us use his rake."
Change the first letter.

to put dishes out for a meal
"I helped mom ___ the table for dinner."
Take away the third letter.

past tense of *send*
"I ___ a letter to grandma yesterday."
Take away the first three letters.

p r e s e n t

Name _____

Read the clues, then write the words.
Start at the bottom and climb to the top.

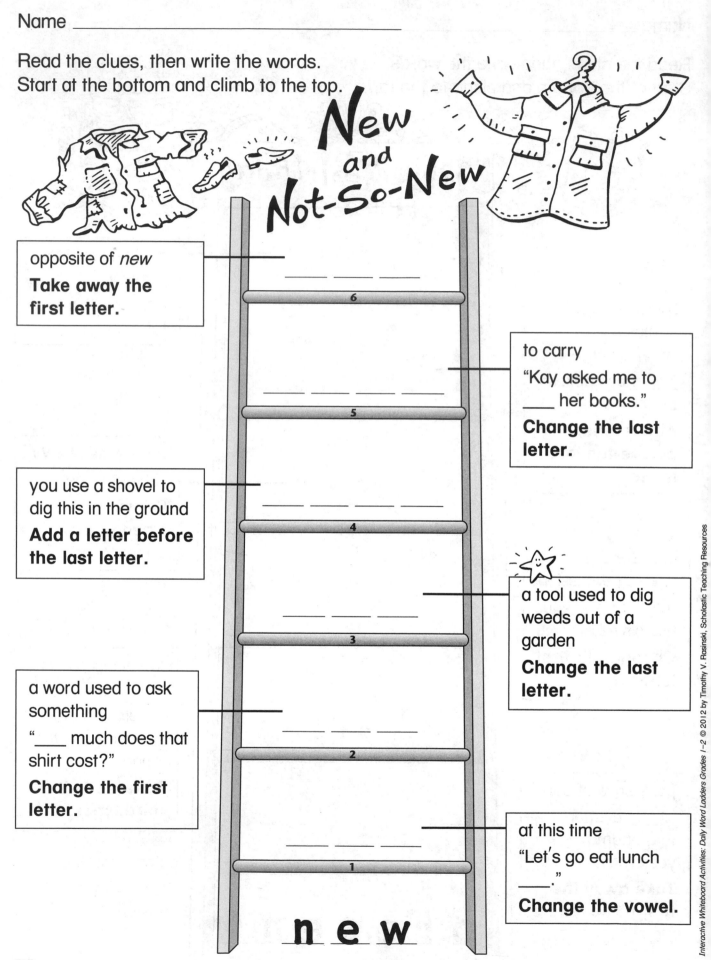

New
and
Not-So-New

opposite of *new*
Take away the first letter.

_ _ _

6

to carry
"Kay asked me to
___ her books."
Change the last letter.

_ _ _

5

you use a shovel to
dig this in the ground
Add a letter before the last letter.

_ _ _ _

4

a tool used to dig
weeds out of a
garden
Change the last letter.

_ _ _

3

a word used to ask
something
"___ much does that
shirt cost?"
Change the first letter.

_ _ _

2

at this time
"Let's go eat lunch
___."
Change the vowel.

_ _ _

1

n e w

Name _____

Read the clues, then write the words.
Start at the bottom and climb to the top.

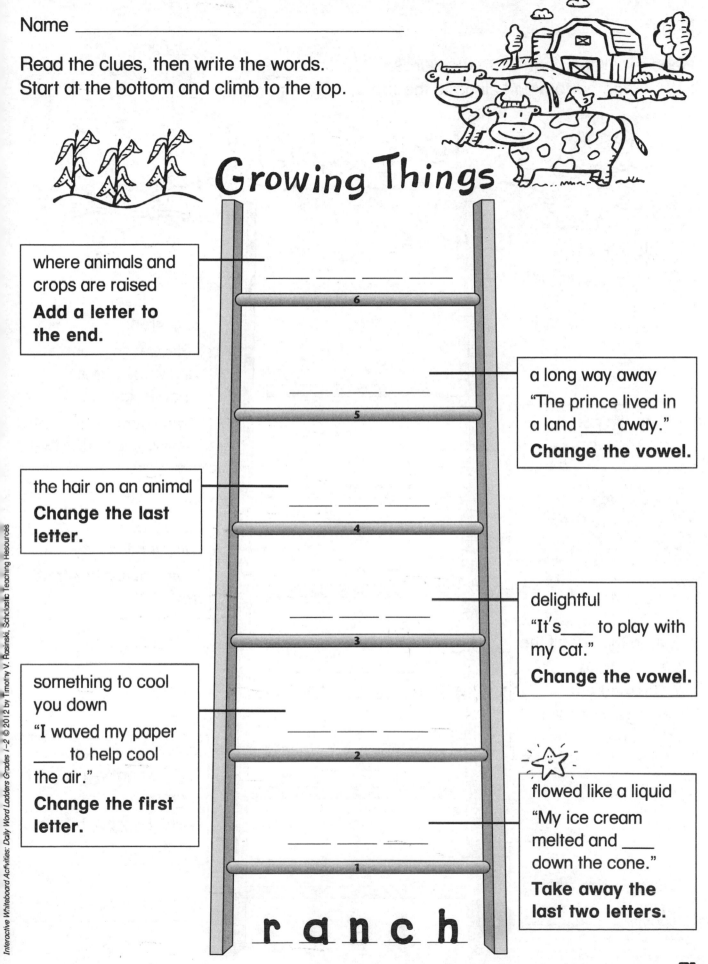

Growing Things

where animals and
crops are raised
**Add a letter to
the end.**

_ _ _ _ _ _   6

a long way away
"The prince lived in
a land ___ away."
Change the vowel.

_ _ _ _   5

the hair on an animal
**Change the last
letter.**

_ _ _ _   4

delightful
"It's___ to play with
my cat."
Change the vowel.

_ _ _ _   3

something to cool
you down
"I waved my paper
___ to help cool
the air."
**Change the first
letter.**

_ _ _ _   2

flowed like a liquid
"My ice cream
melted and ___
down the cone."
**Take away the
last two letters.**

_ _ _ _   1

r a n c h

Name _____

Read the clues, then write the words.
Start at the bottom and climb to the top.

Cluck, Cluck!

a baby chicken
Change the vowel.
(rung 7)

to see if something is correct
"Please ____ your answers on the answer key."
Take away the first letter, then add two.
(rung 6)

a wooden porch
"We sat outside on the ____."
Take away the last letter, then add two.
(rung 5)

where a fox lives
Take away the last letter.
(rung 4)

"When the car hit the post, it left a ____ in the door."
Change the first letter.
(rung 3)

"My family sleeps in a ____ when we go camping."
Add a letter to the end.
(rung 2)

7 + 3
Change the first letter.
(rung 1)

h e n

Interactive Whiteboard Activities: Daily Word Ladders Grades 1–2 © 2012 by Timothy V. Rasinski. Scholastic Teaching Resources

Name _____

Read the clues, then write the words.
Start at the bottom and climb to the top.

Simon Says

opposite of *sit*
Add a letter to the beginning and end.

"Her skin turned ___ after she sat in the sun."
Change the first letter.

a kind of food container
"Mom bought a ___ of beans at the store."
Change the last letter.

the lid of a toothpaste tube
"Please put the ___ back on the toothpaste."
Change the vowel.

many people drink coffee in this
Change the first letter.

a dog is called this after it's born
Take away the third letter.

this is used to put air in a bike tire
Change the first letter.

j u m p

7
6
5
4
3
2
1

Name _____

Read the clues, then write the words.
Start at the bottom and climb to the top.

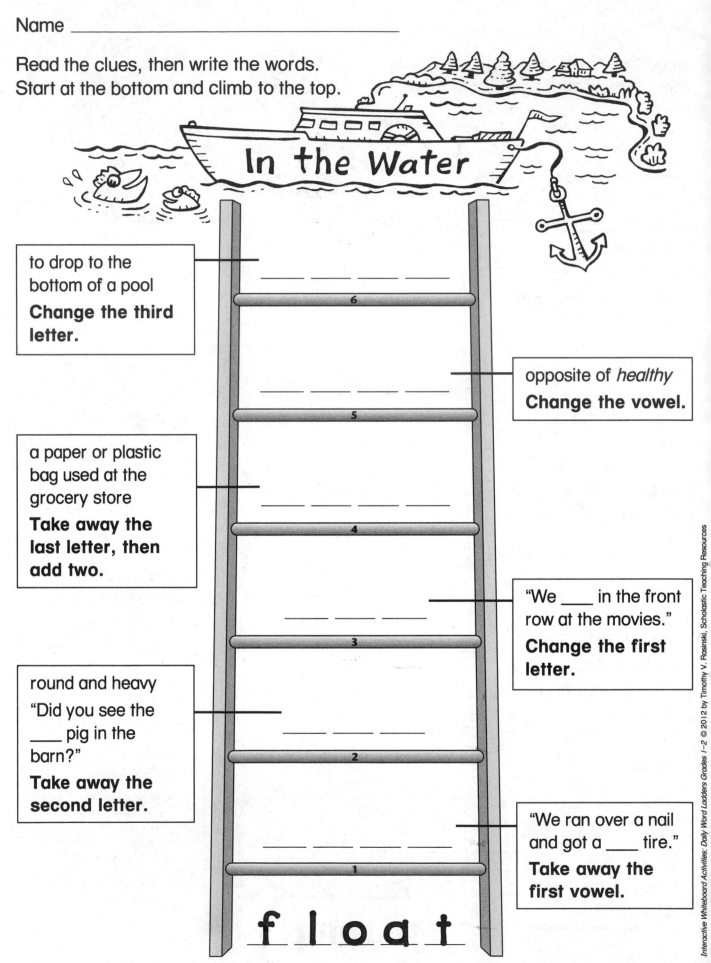

In the Water

to drop to the bottom of a pool
Change the third letter.

6 _ _ _ _

opposite of *healthy*
Change the vowel.

5 _ _ _ _ _

a paper or plastic bag used at the grocery store
Take away the last letter, then add two.

4 _ _ _ _ _

"We ___ in the front row at the movies."
Change the first letter.

3 _ _ _ _

round and heavy
"Did you see the ___ pig in the barn?"
Take away the second letter.

2 _ _ _ _

"We ran over a nail and got a ___ tire."
Take away the first vowel.

1 _ _ _ _ _

f l o a t

Interactive Whiteboard Activities: Daily Word Ladders Grades 1–2 © 2012 by Timothy V. Rasinski, Scholastic Teaching Resources

Name _____

Read the clues, then write the words.
Start at the bottom and climb to the top.

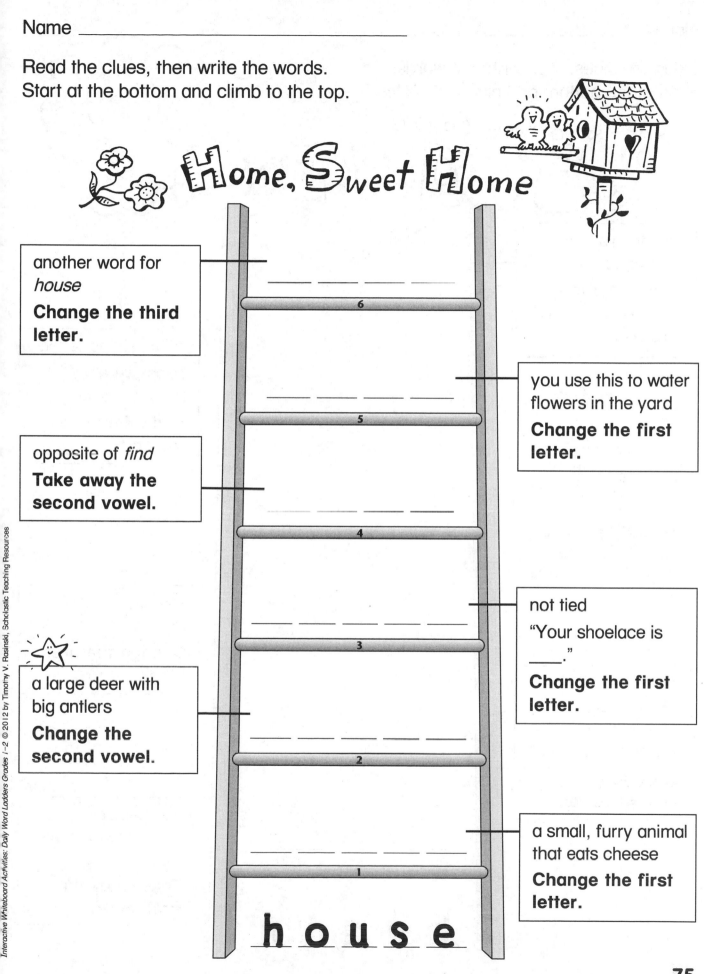

Home, Sweet Home

another word for *house*
Change the third letter.

you use this to water flowers in the yard
Change the first letter.

opposite of *find*
Take away the second vowel.

not tied
"Your shoelace is ____."
Change the first letter.

a large deer with big antlers
Change the second vowel.

a small, furry animal that eats cheese
Change the first letter.

6

5

4

3

2

1

h o u s e

Name _____

Read the clues, then write the words.
Start at the bottom and climb to the top.

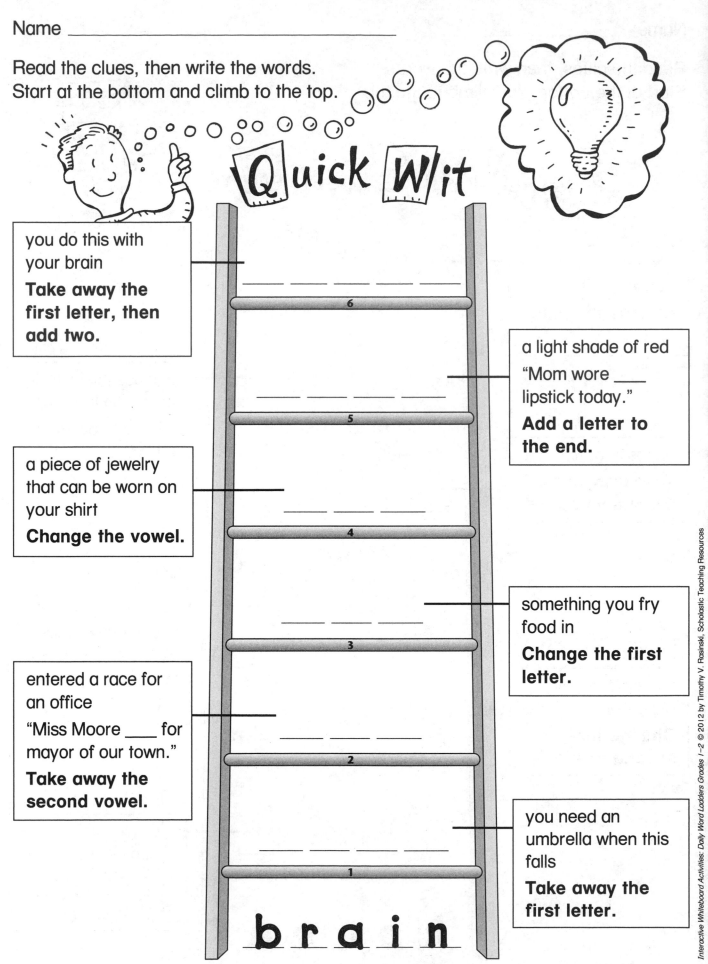

Quick Wit

you do this with your brain
Take away the first letter, then add two.

a light shade of red
"Mom wore ___ lipstick today."
Add a letter to the end.

a piece of jewelry that can be worn on your shirt
Change the vowel.

something you fry food in
Change the first letter.

entered a race for an office
"Miss Moore ___ for mayor of our town."
Take away the second vowel.

you need an umbrella when this falls
Take away the first letter.

6

5

4

3

2

1

b r a i n

Name _____

Read the clues, then write the words.
Start at the bottom and climb to the top.

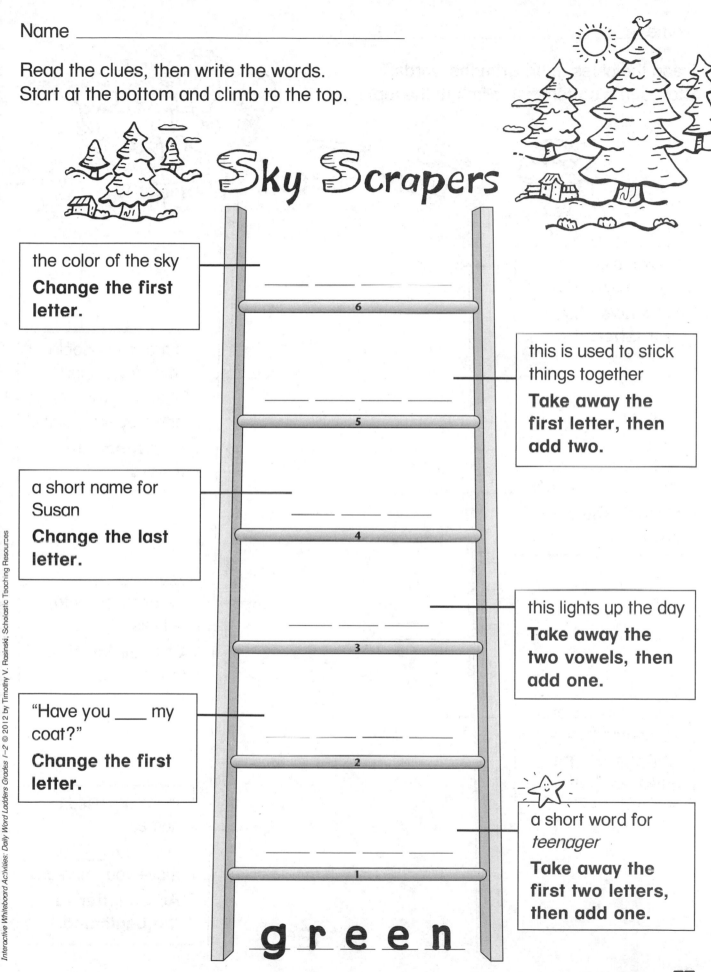

Sky Scrapers

the color of the sky
Change the first letter.

this is used to stick things together
Take away the first letter, then add two.

a short name for Susan
Change the last letter.

this lights up the day
Take away the two vowels, then add one.

"Have you ___ my coat?"
Change the first letter.

a short word for *teenager*
Take away the first two letters, then add one.

6

5

4

3

2

1

g r e e n

Name _____

Read the clues, then write the words.
Start at the bottom and climb to the top.

Cool Treat

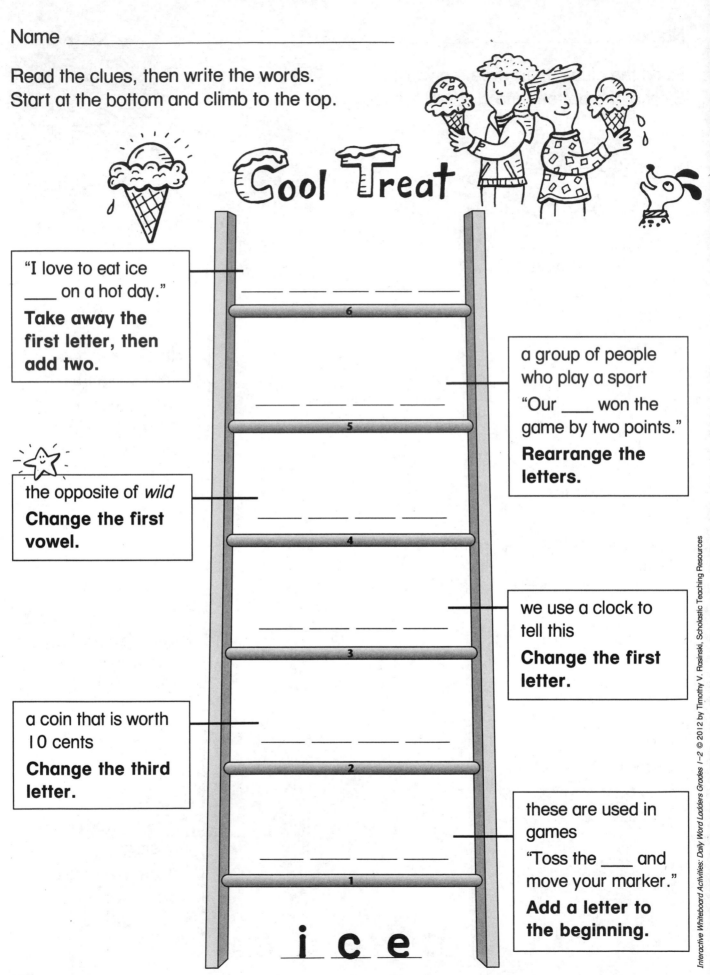

"I love to eat ice ____ on a hot day."
Take away the first letter, then add two.

6 ____ ____ ____ ____ ____

a group of people who play a sport
"Our ____ won the game by two points."
Rearrange the letters.

5 ____ ____ ____ ____

the opposite of *wild*
Change the first vowel.

4 ____ ____ ____ ____

we use a clock to tell this
Change the first letter.

a coin that is worth 10 cents
Change the third letter.

3 ____ ____ ____ ____

these are used in games
"Toss the ____ and move your marker."
Add a letter to the beginning.

2 ____ ____ ____

1 ____ ____ ____

i c e

Interactive Whiteboard Activities: Daily Word Ladders Grades 1–2 © 2012 by Timothy V. Rasinski, Scholastic Teaching Resources

Name _____

Read the clues, then write the words.
Start at the bottom and climb to the top.

All Wet

this falls during a thunder storm
Add a vowel before the last letter.

_____ _____ _____ _____
6

"Sue ____ faster than everyone else in the race."
Change the last letter.

_____ _____ _____ _____
5

a large pest that rhymes with *cat*
Change the vowel.

_____ _____ _____ _____
4

food does this when it goes bad
"The bananas turned brown and began to ____."
Change the last letter.

_____ _____ _____ _____
3

"I caught a fish with my new ____ and reel."
Take away the first two letters, then add one.

_____ _____ _____ _____
2

a clump of dirt
Take away the second vowel.

_____ _____ _____ _____
1

c l o u d

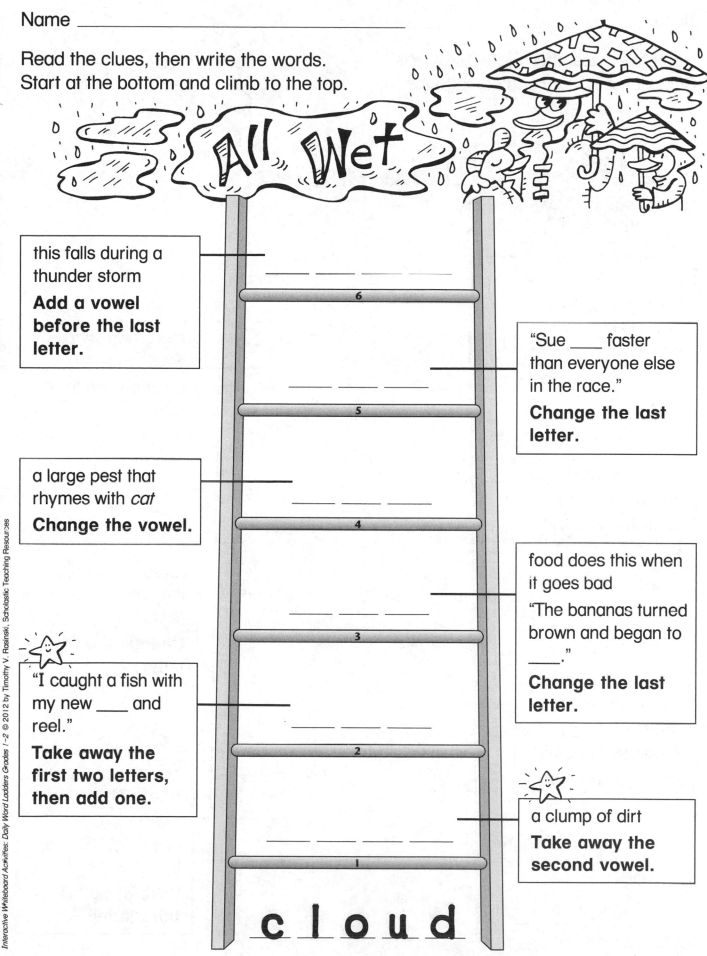

Name _____

Read the clues, then write the words.
Start at the bottom and climb to the top.

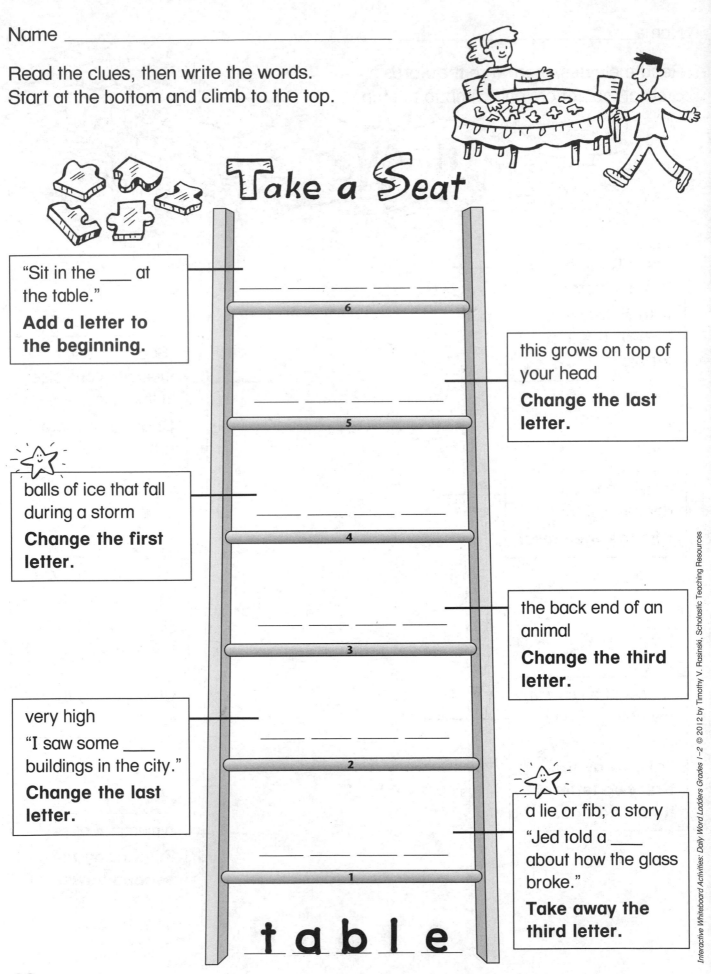

Take a Seat

"Sit in the ___ at the table."
Add a letter to the beginning.

this grows on top of your head
Change the last letter.

balls of ice that fall during a storm
Change the first letter.

the back end of an animal
Change the third letter.

very high
"I saw some ___ buildings in the city."
Change the last letter.

a lie or fib; a story
"Jed told a ___ about how the glass broke."
Take away the third letter.

6

5

4

3

2

1

t a b l e

Interactive Whiteboard Activities: Daily Word Ladders Grades 1–2 © 2012 by Timothy V. Rasinski, Scholastic Teaching Resources

Name _____

Read the clues, then write the words.
Start at the bottom and climb to the top.

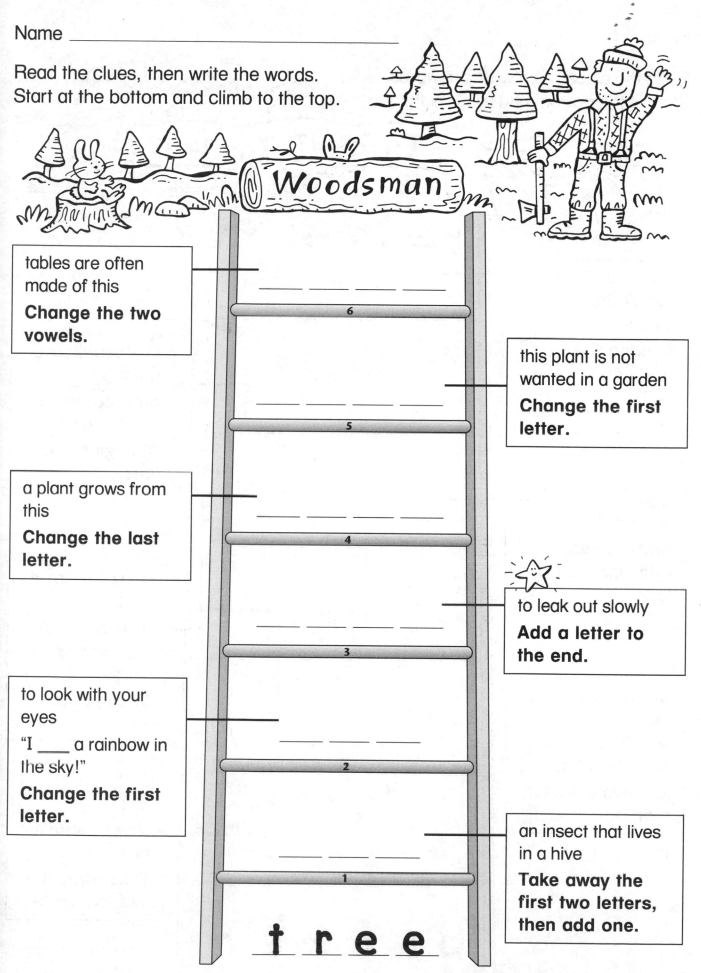

Woodsman

tables are often made of this
Change the two vowels.

this plant is not wanted in a garden
Change the first letter.

a plant grows from this
Change the last letter.

to leak out slowly
Add a letter to the end.

to look with your eyes
"I ____ a rainbow in the sky!"
Change the first letter.

an insect that lives in a hive
Take away the first two letters, then add one.

6

5

4

3

2

1

t r e e

81

Name _____

Read the clues, then write the words.
Start at the bottom and climb to the top.

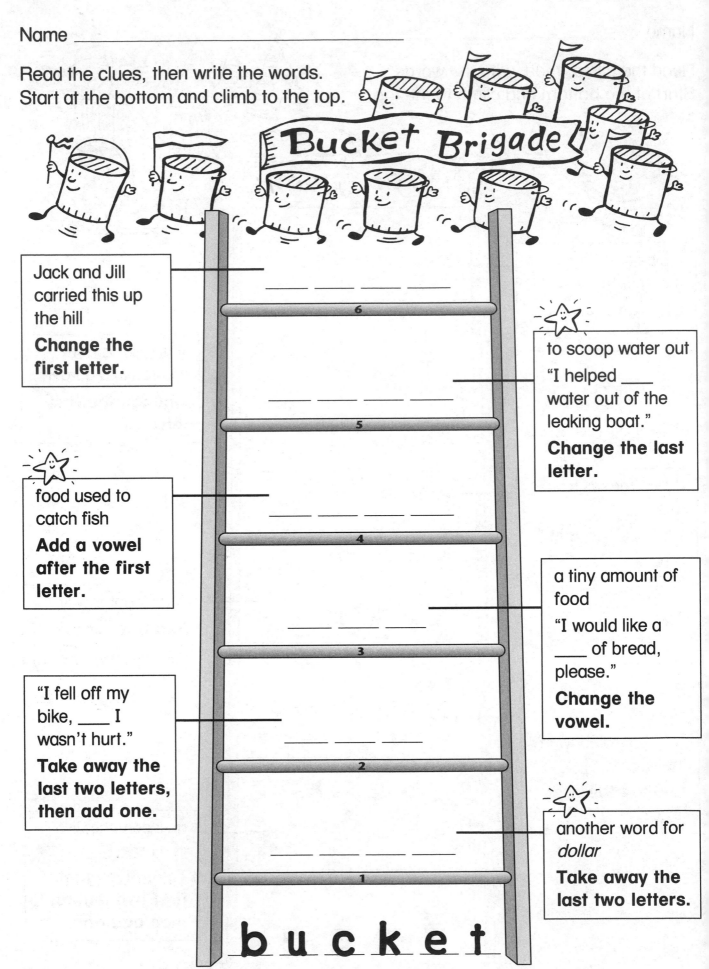

Bucket Brigade

Jack and Jill carried this up the hill
Change the first letter.

to scoop water out
"I helped ___ water out of the leaking boat."
Change the last letter.

food used to catch fish
Add a vowel after the first letter.

a tiny amount of food
"I would like a ___ of bread, please."
Change the vowel.

"I fell off my bike, ___ I wasn't hurt."
Take away the last two letters, then add one.

another word for *dollar*
Take away the last two letters.

6
5
4
3
2
1

b u c k e t

Name _____

Read the clues, then write the words.
Start at the bottom and climb to the top.

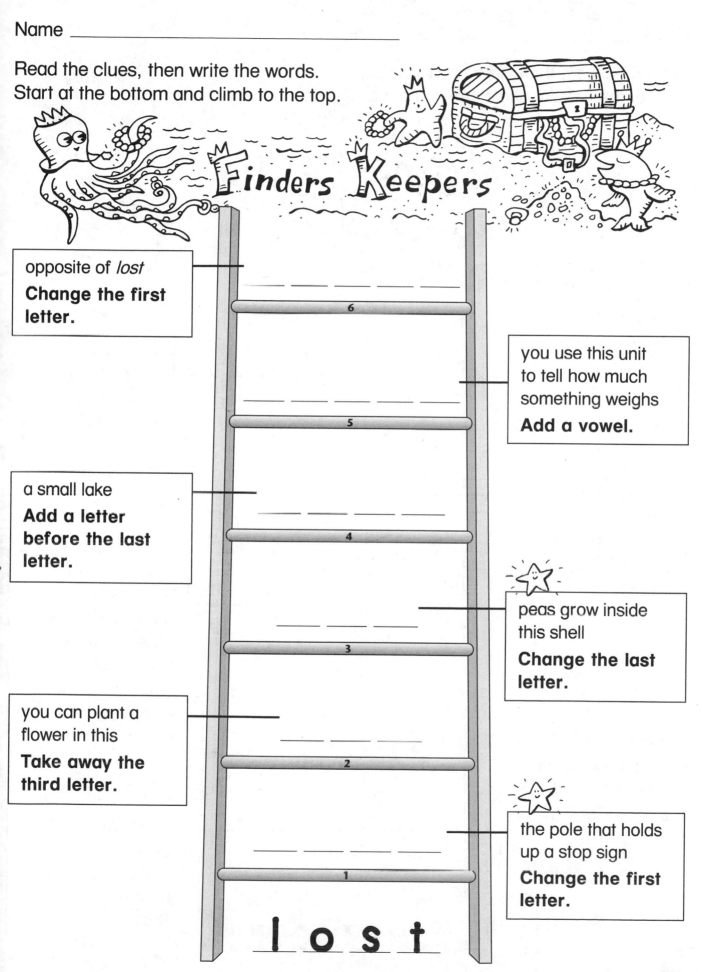

Finders Keepers

opposite of *lost*
Change the first letter.

you use this unit to tell how much something weighs
Add a vowel.

a small lake
Add a letter before the last letter.

peas grow inside this shell
Change the last letter.

you can plant a flower in this
Take away the third letter.

the pole that holds up a stop sign
Change the first letter.

6

5

4

3

2

1

l o s t

Name _____

Read the clues, then write the words.
Start at the bottom and climb to the top.

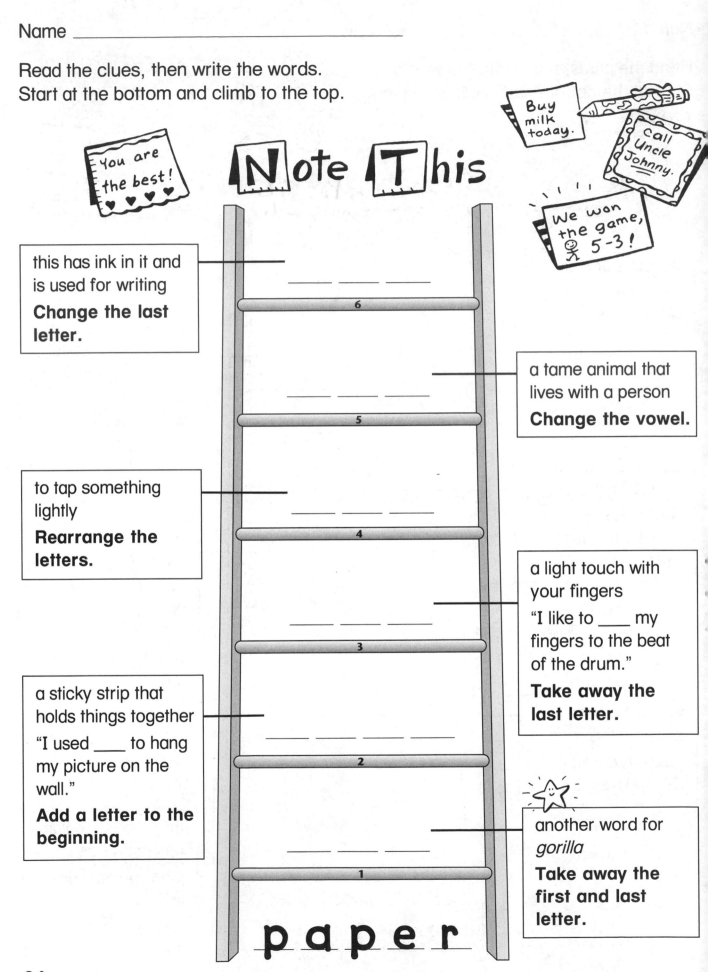

Note This

this has ink in it and is used for writing
Change the last letter.

_ _ _ _

a tame animal that lives with a person
Change the vowel.

_ _ _

to tap something lightly
Rearrange the letters.

_ _ _

a light touch with your fingers
"I like to ___ my fingers to the beat of the drum."
Take away the last letter.

a sticky strip that holds things together
"I used ___ to hang my picture on the wall."
Add a letter to the beginning.

another word for *gorilla*
Take away the first and last letter.

p a p e r

84

Name _____

Read the clues, then write the words.
Start at the bottom and climb to the top.

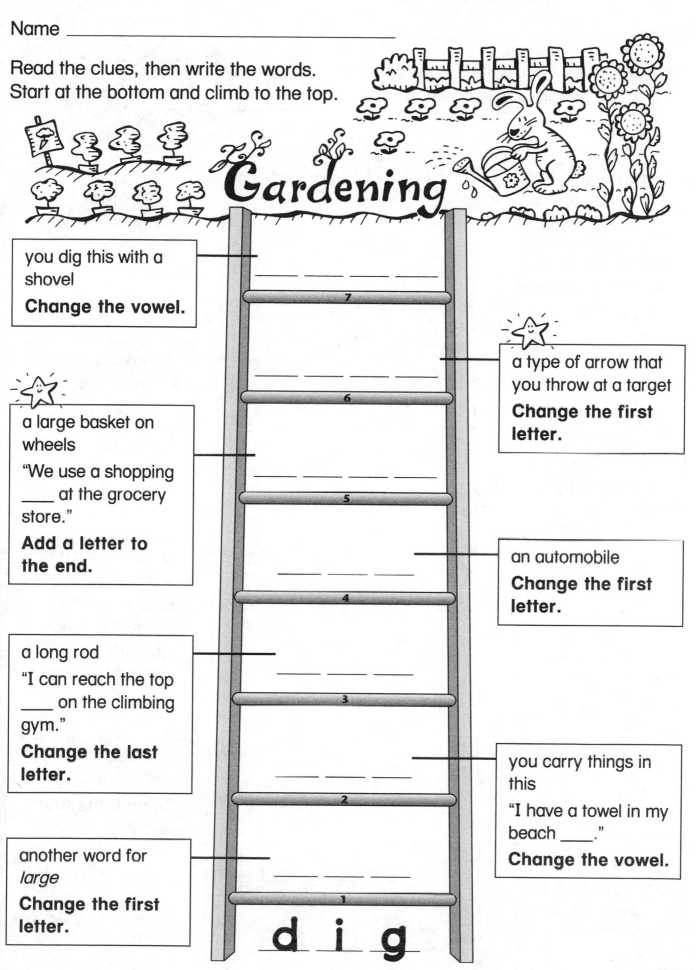

Gardening

you dig this with a shovel
Change the vowel.

a type of arrow that you throw at a target
Change the first letter.

a large basket on wheels
"We use a shopping ___ at the grocery store."
Add a letter to the end.

an automobile
Change the first letter.

a long rod
"I can reach the top ___ on the climbing gym."
Change the last letter.

you carry things in this
"I have a towel in my beach ___."
Change the vowel.

another word for *large*
Change the first letter.

7

6

5

4

3

2

1

d i g

85

Name _____

Read the clues, then write the words.
Start at the bottom and climb to the top.

Up We Go!

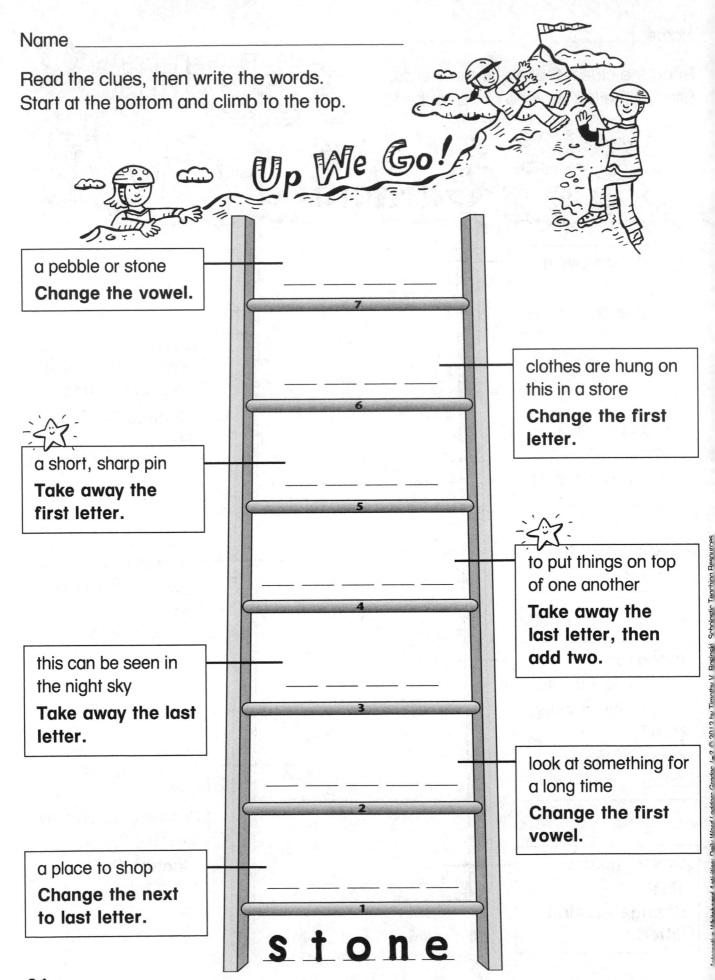

a pebble or stone
Change the vowel.

clothes are hung on this in a store
Change the first letter.

a short, sharp pin
Take away the first letter.

to put things on top of one another
Take away the last letter, then add two.

this can be seen in the night sky
Take away the last letter.

look at something for a long time
Change the first vowel.

a place to shop
Change the next to last letter.

s t o n e

The Mailbox Daily Mixed Ladders Grades 1–2 © 2012 by Timothy V. Rasinski, Scholastic Teaching Resources

Name _____

Read the clues, then write the words.
Start at the bottom and climb to the top.

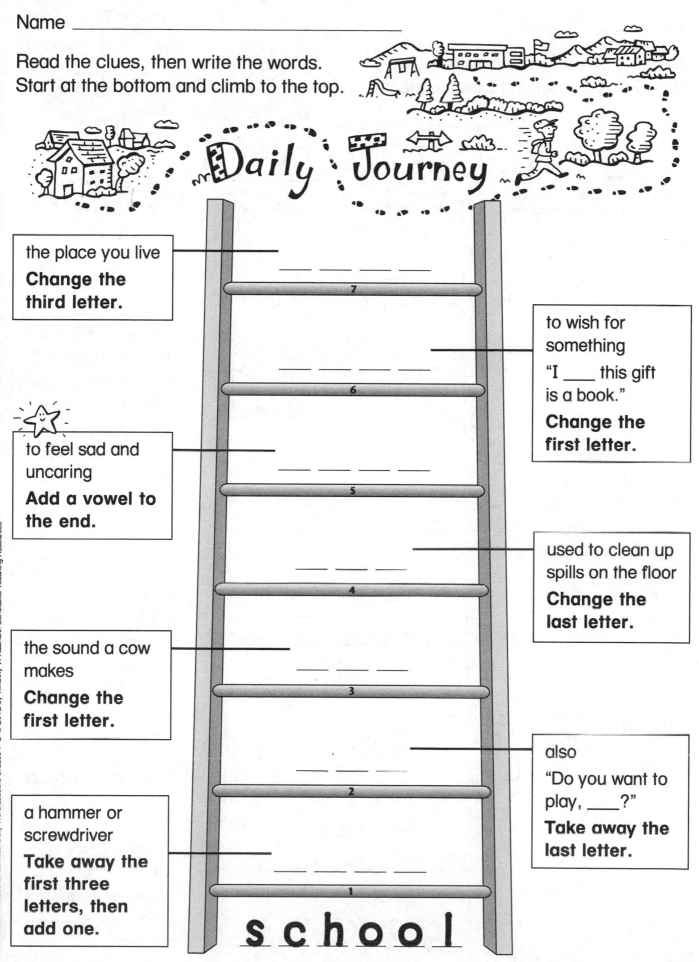

Daily Journey

the place you live
Change the third letter.

— — — — — —
7

to wish for something
"I ___ this gift is a book."
Change the first letter.

to feel sad and uncaring
Add a vowel to the end.

— — — — —
6

— — — — —
5

used to clean up spills on the floor
Change the last letter.

the sound a cow makes
Change the first letter.

— — — —
4

— — —
3

a hammer or screwdriver
Take away the first three letters, then add one.

also
"Do you want to play, ___?"
Take away the last letter.

— — — —
2

— — — — —
1

s c h o o l

Name _____

Read the clues, then write the words.
Start at the bottom and climb to the top.

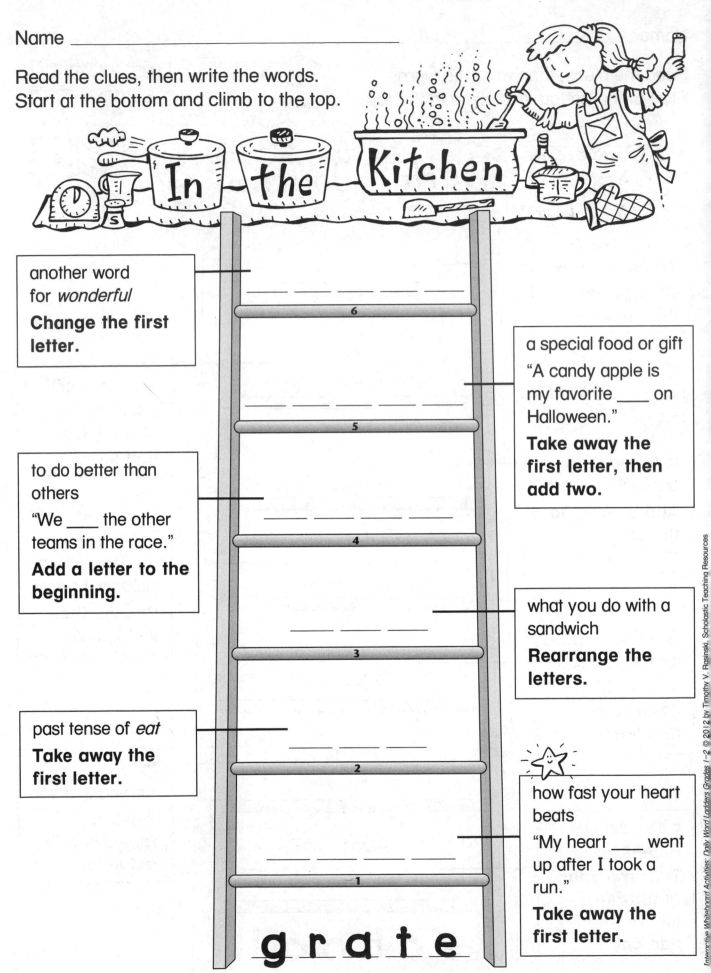

another word
for *wonderful*
**Change the first
letter.**

a special food or gift
"A candy apple is
my favorite ____ on
Halloween."
**Take away the
first letter, then
add two.**

to do better than
others
"We ____ the other
teams in the race."
**Add a letter to the
beginning.**

what you do with a
sandwich
**Rearrange the
letters.**

past tense of *eat*
**Take away the
first letter.**

how fast your heart
beats
"My heart ____ went
up after I took a
run."
**Take away the
first letter.**

6

5

4

3

2

1

g r a t e

Interactive Whiteboard Activities: *Daily Word Ladders Grades 1–2* © 2012 by Timothy V. Rasinski, Scholastic Teaching Resources

Name _____

Read the clues, then write the words.
Start at the bottom and climb to the top.

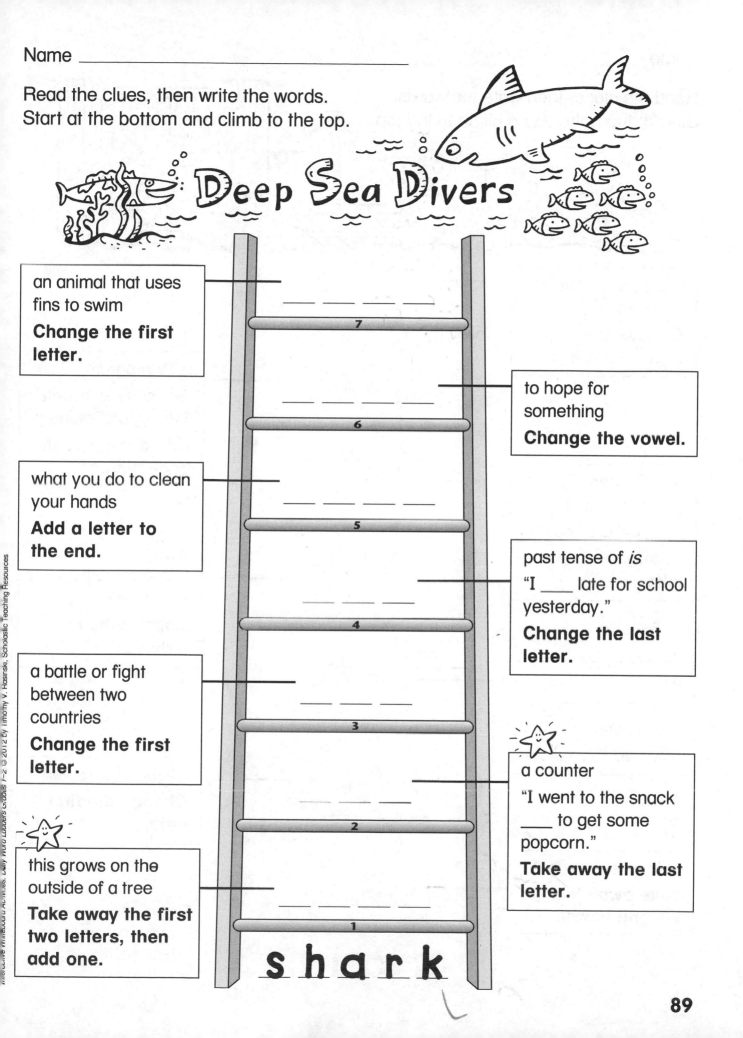

Deep Sea Divers

an animal that uses fins to swim
Change the first letter.

7 _____

to hope for something
Change the vowel.

6 _____

what you do to clean your hands
Add a letter to the end.

5 _____

past tense of *is*
"I ____ late for school yesterday."
Change the last letter.

4 _____

a battle or fight between two countries
Change the first letter.

3 _____

a counter
"I went to the snack ____ to get some popcorn."
Take away the last letter.

2 _____

this grows on the outside of a tree
Take away the first two letters, then add one.

1 _____

s h a r k

Name _____

Read the clues, then write the words.
Start at the bottom and climb to the top.

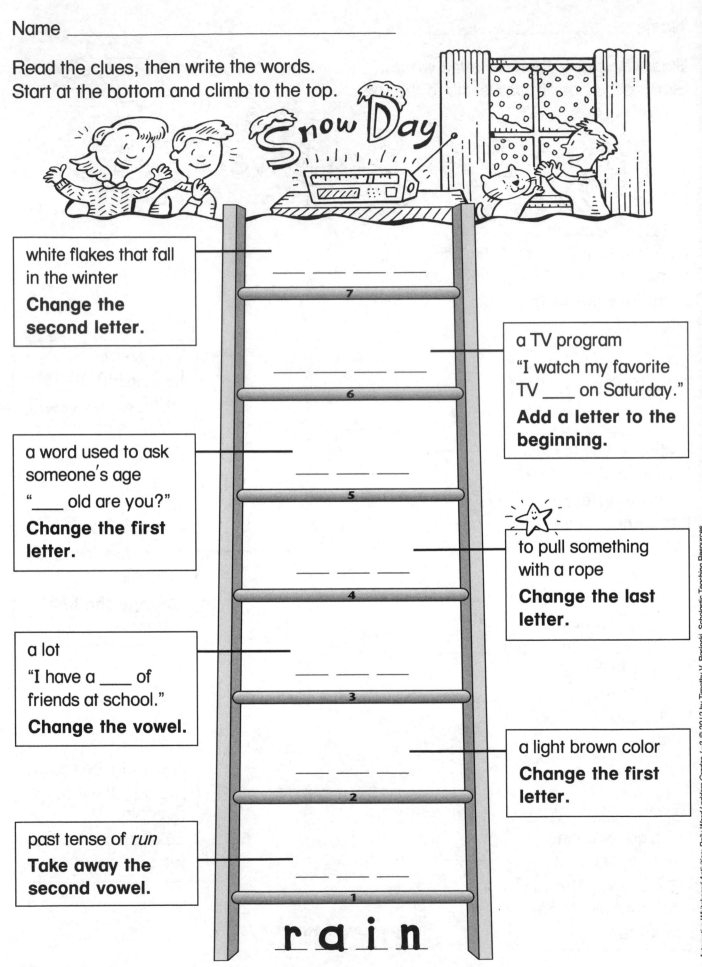

white flakes that fall
in the winter
**Change the
second letter.**

7 _ _ _ _

a TV program
"I watch my favorite
TV ___ on Saturday."
**Add a letter to the
beginning.**

6 _ _ _ _

a word used to ask
someone's age
"___ old are you?"
**Change the first
letter.**

5 _ _ _

to pull something
with a rope
**Change the last
letter.**

4 _ _ _

a lot
"I have a ___ of
friends at school."
Change the vowel.

3 _ _ _

a light brown color
**Change the first
letter.**

2 _ _ _

past tense of *run*
**Take away the
second vowel.**

1 _ _ _

r a i n

Name _____

Read the clues, then write the words.
Start at the bottom and climb to the top.

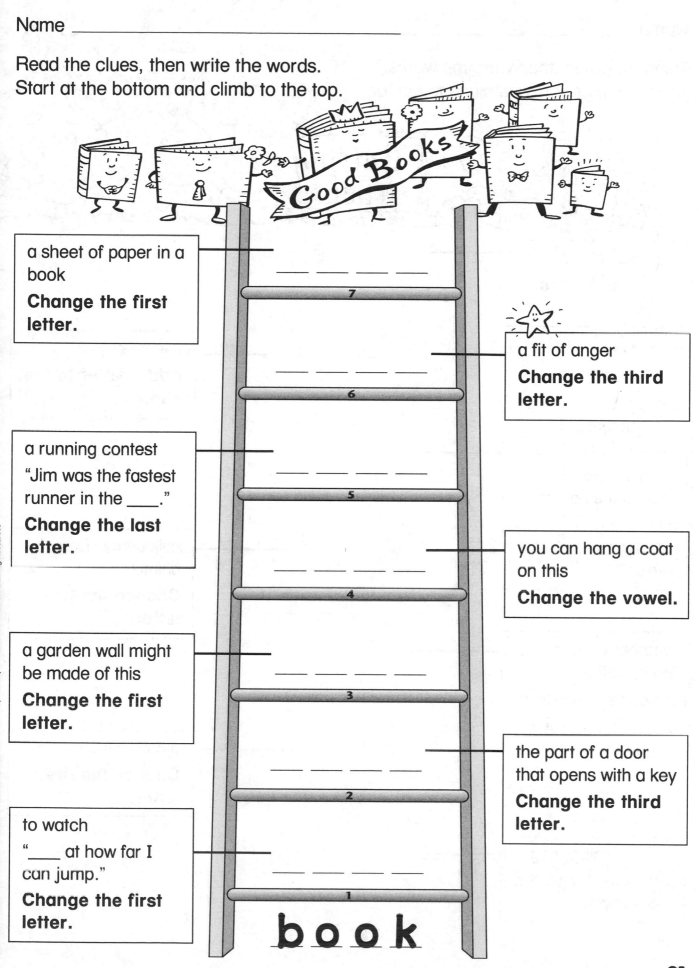

a sheet of paper in a book
Change the first letter.

a running contest
"Jim was the fastest runner in the ____."
Change the last letter.

a garden wall might be made of this
Change the first letter.

to watch
"____ at how far I can jump."
Change the first letter.

a fit of anger
Change the third letter.

you can hang a coat on this
Change the vowel.

the part of a door that opens with a key
Change the third letter.

7

6

5

4

3

2

1

b o o k

Name _____

Read the clues, then write the words.
Start at the bottom and climb to the top.

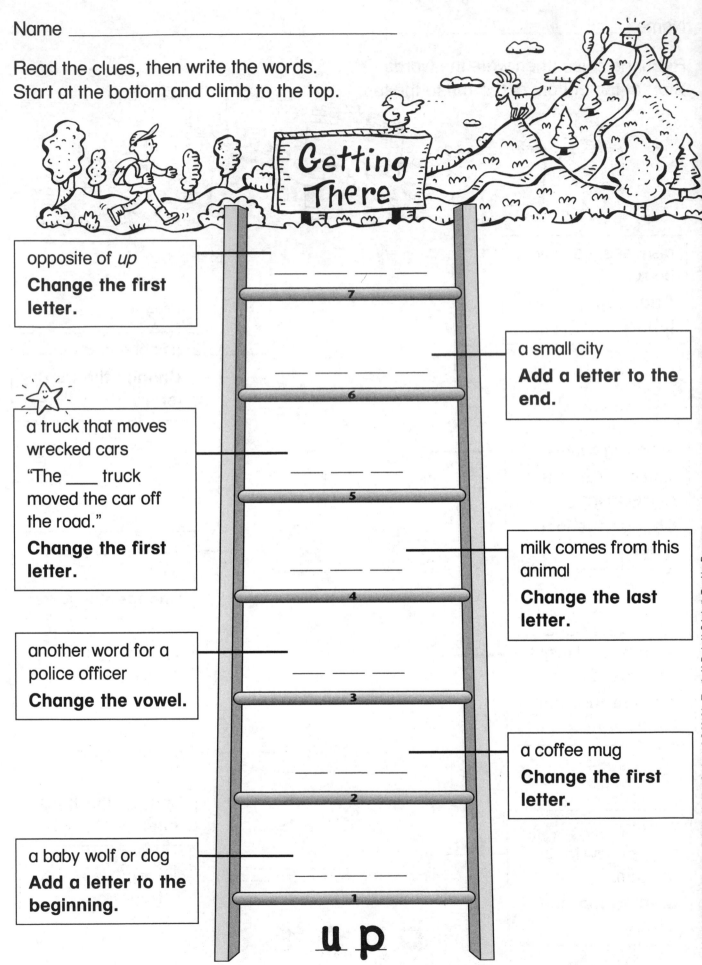

opposite of *up*
Change the first letter.

a small city
Add a letter to the end.

a truck that moves wrecked cars
"The ____ truck moved the car off the road."
Change the first letter.

milk comes from this animal
Change the last letter.

another word for a police officer
Change the vowel.

a coffee mug
Change the first letter.

a baby wolf or dog
Add a letter to the beginning.

u p

Name _____

Read the clues, then write the words.
Start at the bottom and climb to the top.

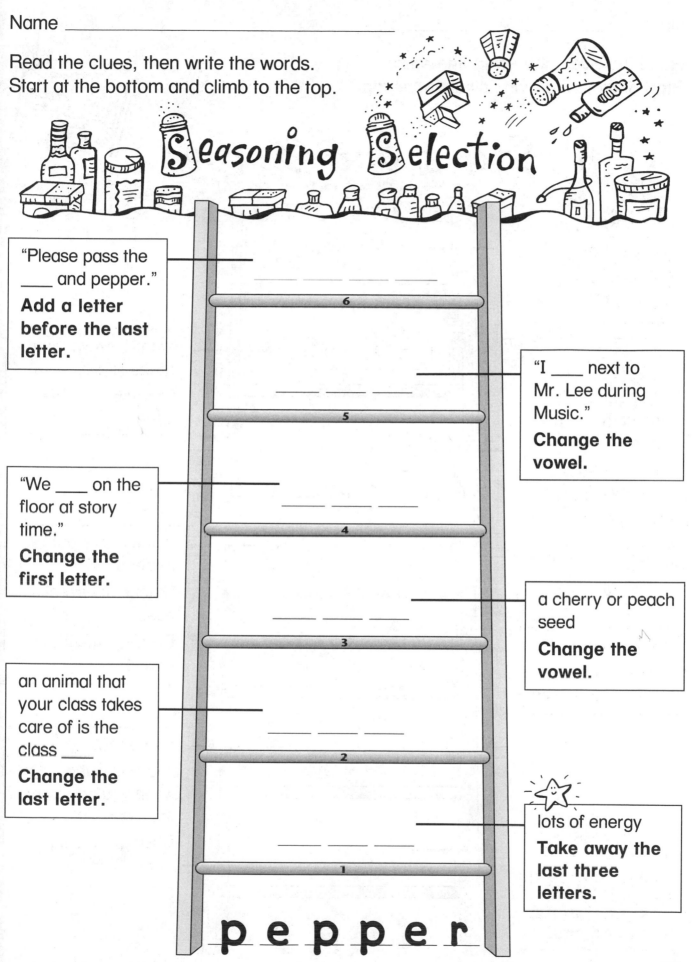

Seasoning Selection

"Please pass the ___ and pepper."
Add a letter before the last letter.

6 ___ ___ ___ ___ ___ ___

"I ___ next to Mr. Lee during Music."
Change the vowel.

5 ___ ___ ___ ___ ___

"We ___ on the floor at story time."
Change the first letter.

4 ___ ___ ___ ___

an animal that your class takes care of is the class ___
Change the last letter.

a cherry or peach seed
Change the vowel.

3 ___ ___ ___ ___

2 ___ ___ ___

lots of energy
Take away the last three letters.

1 ___ ___ ___ ___

p e p p e r

Name _____

Read the clues, then write the words.
Start at the bottom and climb to the top.

Stars and Stripes

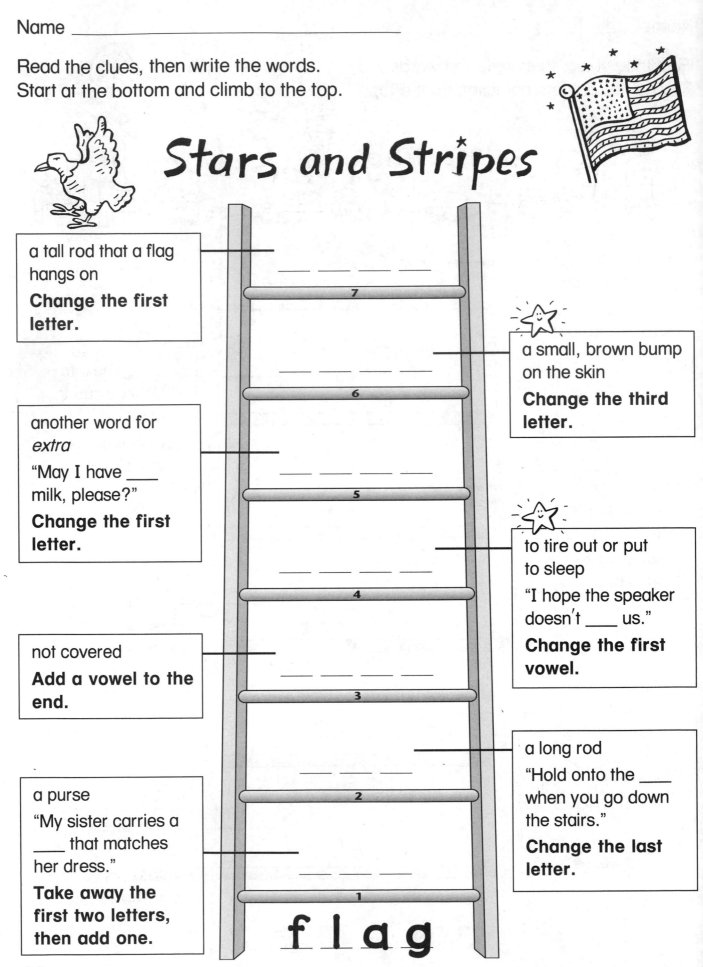

a tall rod that a flag hangs on
Change the first letter.

a small, brown bump on the skin
Change the third letter.

another word for *extra*
"May I have ___ milk, please?"
Change the first letter.

to tire out or put to sleep
"I hope the speaker doesn't ___ us."
Change the first vowel.

not covered
Add a vowel to the end.

a long rod
"Hold onto the ___ when you go down the stairs."
Change the last letter.

a purse
"My sister carries a ___ that matches her dress."
Take away the first two letters, then add one.

7
6
5
4
3
2
1

f l a g

Name _____

Read the clues, then write the words.
Start at the bottom and climb to the top.

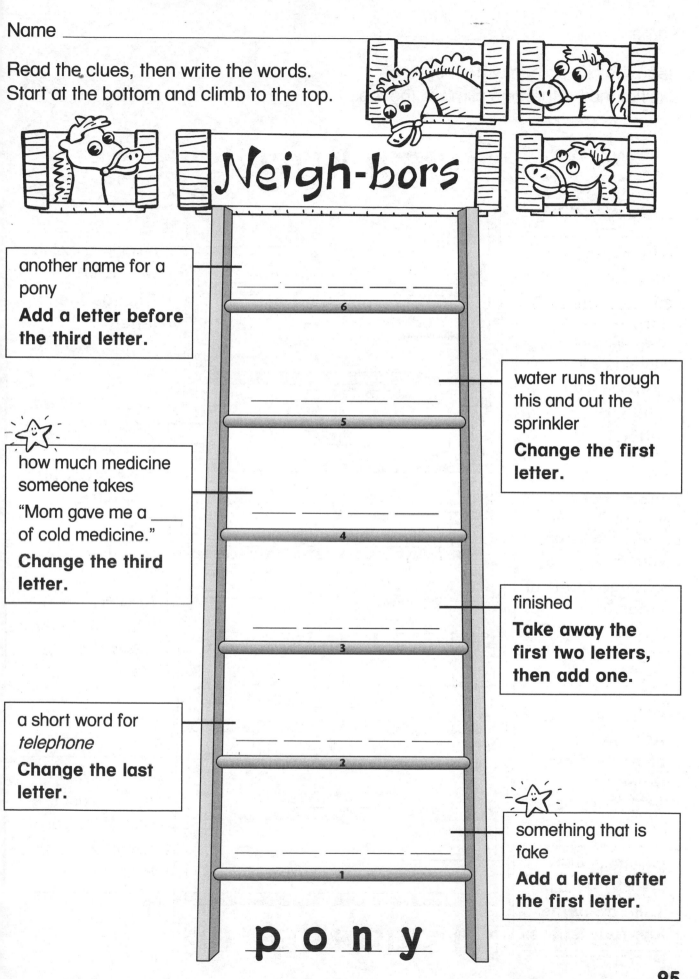

Neigh-bors

another name for a pony
Add a letter before the third letter.

water runs through this and out the sprinkler
Change the first letter.

how much medicine someone takes
"Mom gave me a ____ of cold medicine."
Change the third letter.

finished
Take away the first two letters, then add one.

a short word for *telephone*
Change the last letter.

something that is fake
Add a letter after the first letter.

6

5

4

3

2

1

p o n y

Name _____

Read the clues, then write the words.
Start at the bottom and climb to the top.

Furry Friends

an animal that lives with people
Change the last letter.

a small, green vegetable that grows in a pod
Change the first letter.

a hot drink made from leaves
Take away the last letter.

a drop of water that comes from your eye
Change the first letter.

to listen **Change the last letter.**

the top part of your body
Add a vowel after the first letter.

past tense of *has*
"I ____ a good time at the party."
Change the last letter.

pink meat that comes from a pig
Take away the last four letters.

8

7

6

5

4

3

2

1

h a m s t e r

Name _____

Read the clues, then write the words.
Start at the bottom and climb to the top.

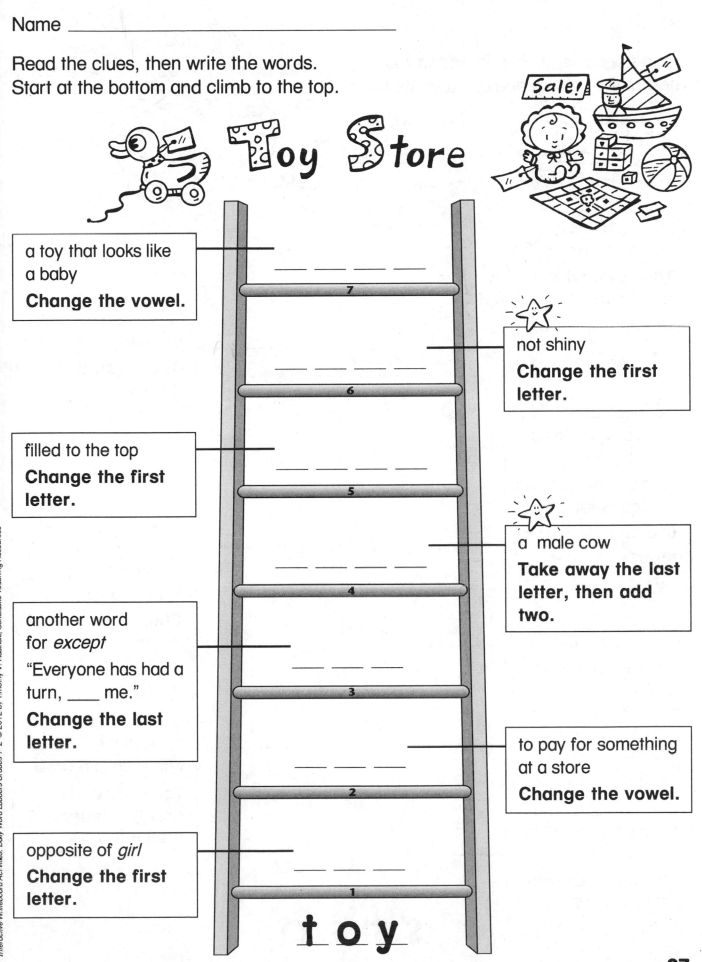

Toy Store

a toy that looks like
a baby
Change the vowel.

— — — — —
7

not shiny
**Change the first
letter.**

— — — —
6

filled to the top
**Change the first
letter.**

— — — —
5

a male cow
**Take away the last
letter, then add
two.**

— — — —
4

another word
for *except*
"Everyone has had a
turn, ___ me."
**Change the last
letter.**

— — —
3

to pay for something
at a store
Change the vowel.

— — —
2

opposite of *girl*
**Change the first
letter.**

— — —
1

t o y

Name _____

Read the clues, then write the words.
Start at the bottom and climb to the top.

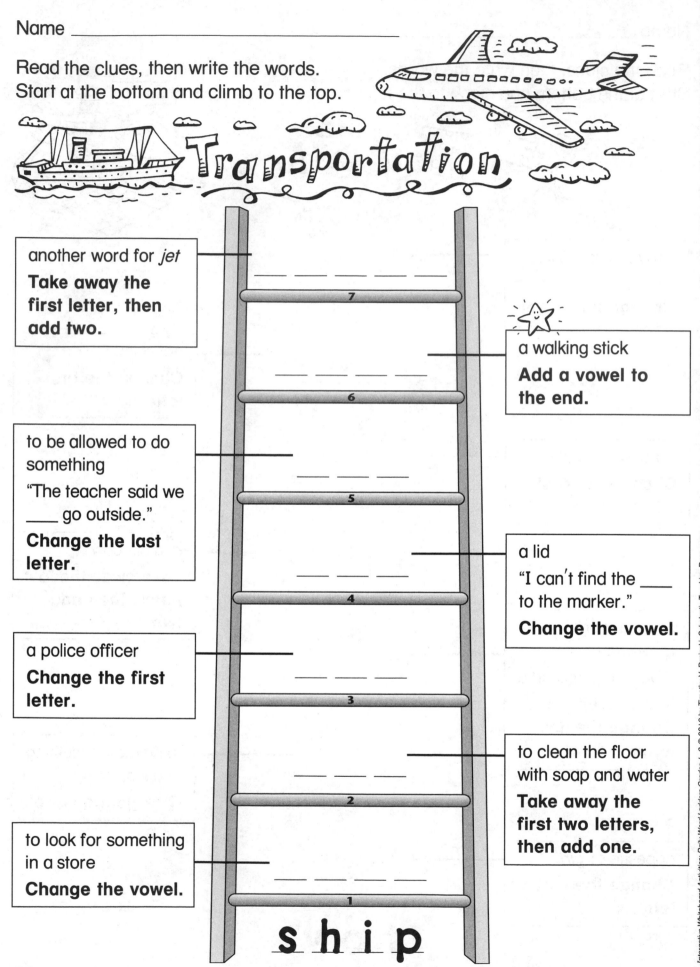

Transportation

another word for *jet*
Take away the first letter, then add two.

_ _ _ _ _ _   7

a walking stick
Add a vowel to the end.

_ _ _ _ _   6

to be allowed to do something
"The teacher said we ___ go outside."
Change the last letter.

_ _ _   5

a lid
"I can't find the ___ to the marker."
Change the vowel.

_ _ _   4

a police officer
Change the first letter.

_ _ _   3

to clean the floor with soap and water
Take away the first two letters, then add one.

_ _ _ _   2

to look for something in a store
Change the vowel.

_ _ _ _   1

s h i p

98

Interactive Whiteboard Activities: Daily Word Ladders Grades 1–2 © 2012 by Timothy V. Rasinski, Scholastic Teaching Resources

Name _____

Read the clues, then write the words.
Start at the bottom and climb to the top.

Score!

this is kicked over a goal post
Change the first letter.

a place with many stores in it
Take away the last letter, then add two.

a small rug
"Please wipe your feet on the door ___."
Change the first letter.

a pan used for making soup
Take away the last two letters, then add one.

a soft touch
"Dad gave me a ___ on the back."
Change the vowel.

a place to swim
Change the first letter.

to trick
"You tried to ___ me with that magic act."
Change the last letter.

7

6

5

4

3

2

1

f o o t

Name _____

Read the clues, then write the words.
Start at the bottom and climb to the top.

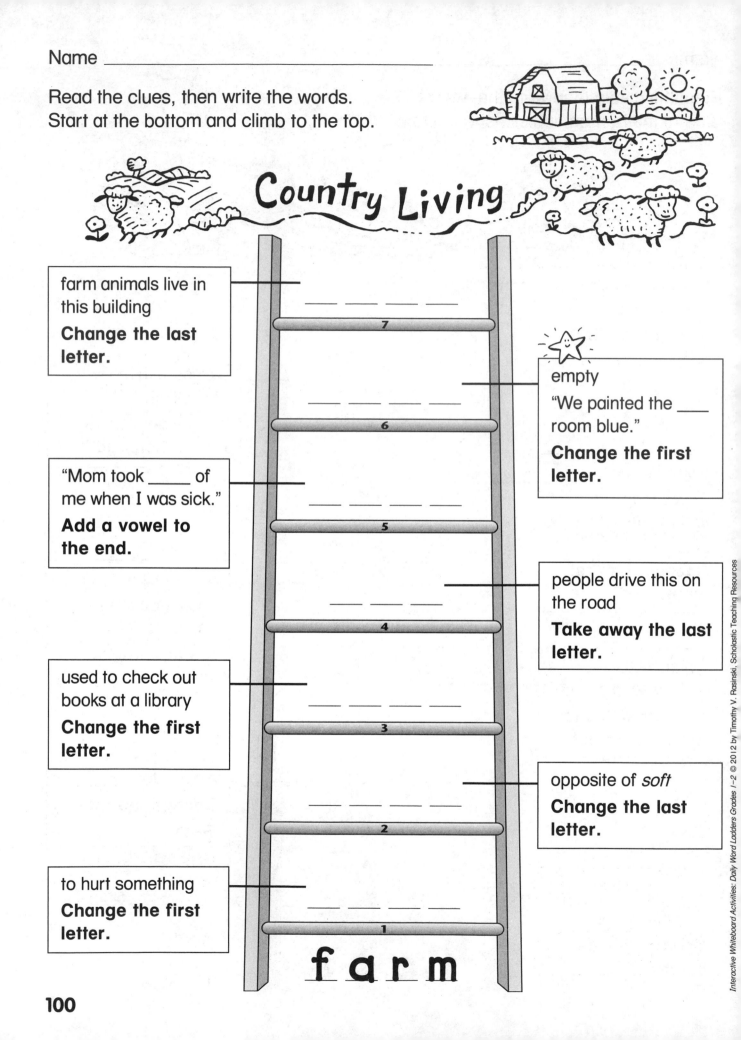

Country Living

farm animals live in this building
Change the last letter.

_ _ _ _
7

empty
"We painted the ___ room blue."
Change the first letter.

_ _ _ _
6

"Mom took _____ of me when I was sick."
Add a vowel to the end.

_ _ _ _
5

people drive this on the road
Take away the last letter.

_ _ _ _
4

used to check out books at a library
Change the first letter.

_ _ _ _
3

opposite of *soft*
Change the last letter.

_ _ _ _
2

to hurt something
Change the first letter.

_ _ _ _
1

f a r m

Interactive Whiteboard Activities: *Daily Word Ladders Grades 1–2* © 2012 by Timothy V. Rasinski, Scholastic Teaching Resources

Name _____

Read the clues, then write the words.
Start at the bottom and climb to the top.

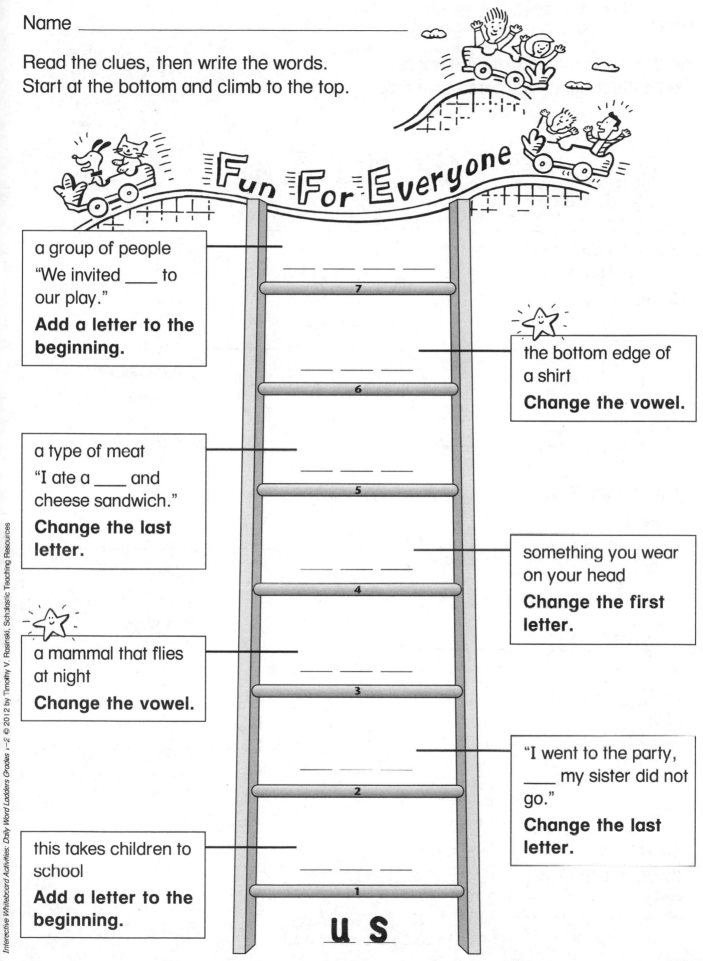

Fun For Everyone

a group of people
"We invited ___ to our play."
Add a letter to the beginning.

7

the bottom edge of a shirt
Change the vowel.

6

a type of meat
"I ate a ___ and cheese sandwich."
Change the last letter.

5

something you wear on your head
Change the first letter.

4

a mammal that flies at night
Change the vowel.

3

"I went to the party, ___ my sister did not go."
Change the last letter.

2

this takes children to school
Add a letter to the beginning.

1

U S

Name _____

Read the clues, then write the words.
Start at the bottom and climb to the top.

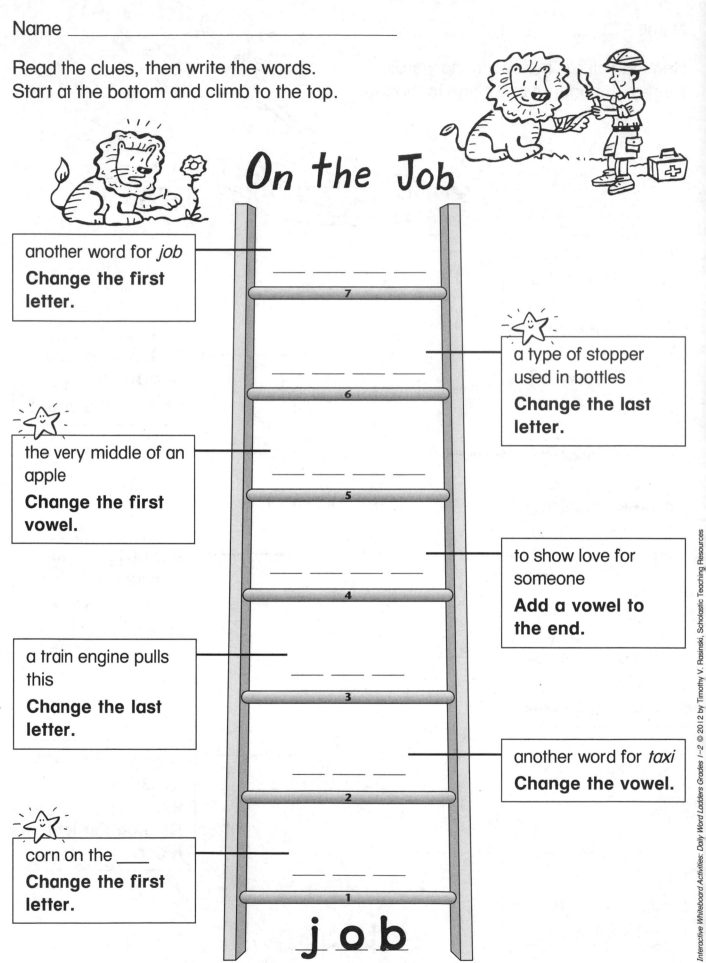

On the Job

another word for *job*
Change the first letter.

_ _ _ _
7

a type of stopper used in bottles
Change the last letter.

_ _ _ _
6

the very middle of an apple
Change the first vowel.

_ _ _ _
5

to show love for someone
Add a vowel to the end.

_ _ _ _
4

a train engine pulls this
Change the last letter.

_ _ _
3

another word for *taxi*
Change the vowel.

_ _ _
2

corn on the ____
Change the first letter.

_ _ _
1

j o b

Interactive Whiteboard Activities: Daily Word Ladders Grades 1–2 © 2012 by Timothy V. Rasinski, Scholastic Teaching Resources

Name _____

Read the clues, then write the words.
Start at the bottom and climb to the top.

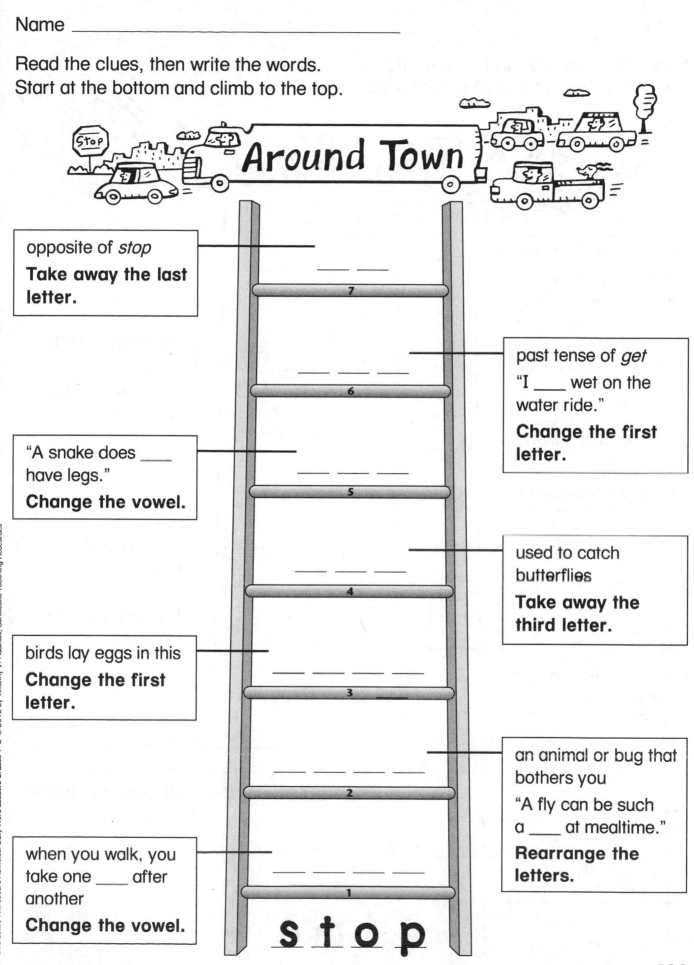

Around Town

opposite of *stop*
Take away the last letter.

past tense of *get*
"I ____ wet on the water ride."
Change the first letter.

"A snake does ____ have legs."
Change the vowel.

used to catch butterflies
Take away the third letter.

birds lay eggs in this
Change the first letter.

an animal or bug that bothers you
"A fly can be such a ____ at mealtime."
Rearrange the letters.

when you walk, you take one ____ after another
Change the vowel.

7

6

5

4

3

2

1

s t o p

Name _____

Read the clues, then write the words.
Start at the bottom and climb to the top.

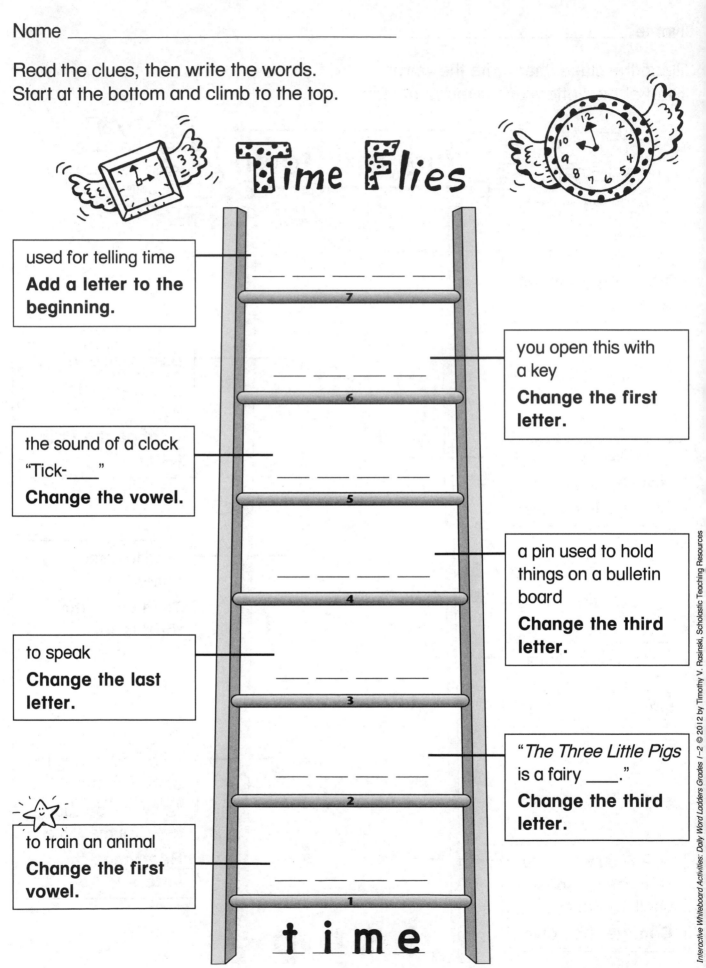

Time Flies

used for telling time
Add a letter to the beginning.

you open this with a key
Change the first letter.

the sound of a clock
"Tick-___"
Change the vowel.

a pin used to hold things on a bulletin board
Change the third letter.

to speak
Change the last letter.

"*The Three Little Pigs* is a fairy ___."
Change the third letter.

to train an animal
Change the first vowel.

t i m e

Name _____

Read the clues, then write the words.
Start at the bottom and climb to the top.

And the Winner Is...

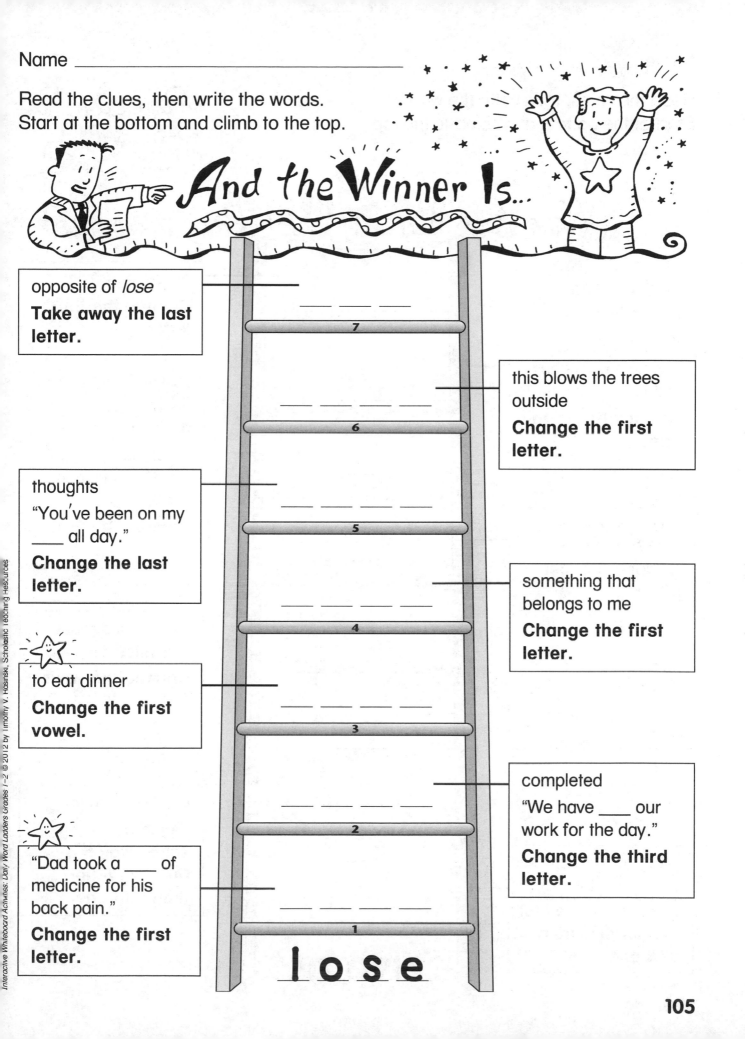

opposite of *lose*
Take away the last letter.

_ _ _ _

7

this blows the trees outside
Change the first letter.

_ _ _ _

6

thoughts
"You've been on my ___ all day."
Change the last letter.

_ _ _ _

5

something that belongs to me
Change the first letter.

_ _ _ _

4

to eat dinner
Change the first vowel.

_ _ _ _

3

completed
"We have ___ our work for the day."
Change the third letter.

_ _ _ _

2

"Dad took a ___ of medicine for his back pain."
Change the first letter.

_ _ _ _

1

l o s e

Name _____

Read the clues, then write the words.
Start at the bottom and climb to the top.

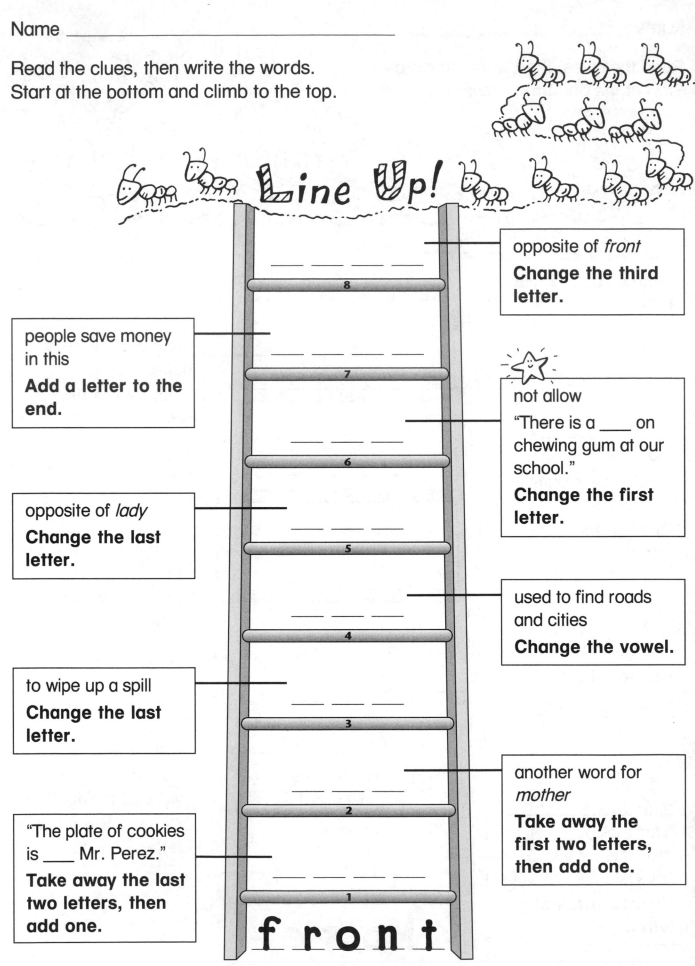

Line Up!

opposite of *front*
Change the third letter.

8 ____ ____ ____ ____ ____

people save money in this
Add a letter to the end.

7 ____ ____ ____ ____ ____

not allow
"There is a ____ on chewing gum at our school."
Change the first letter.

6 ____ ____ ____ ____

opposite of *lady*
Change the last letter.

5 ____ ____ ____ ____

used to find roads and cities
Change the vowel.

4 ____ ____ ____ ____

to wipe up a spill
Change the last letter.

3 ____ ____ ____

another word for *mother*
Take away the first two letters, then add one.

2 ____ ____ ____

"The plate of cookies is ____ Mr. Perez."
Take away the last two letters, then add one.

1 ____ ____ ____

f r o n t

Interactive Whiteboard Activities: Daily Word Ladders Grades 1–2 © 2012 by Timothy V. Rasinski, Scholastic Teaching Resources

Name _____

Read the clues, then write the words.
Start at the bottom and climb to the top.

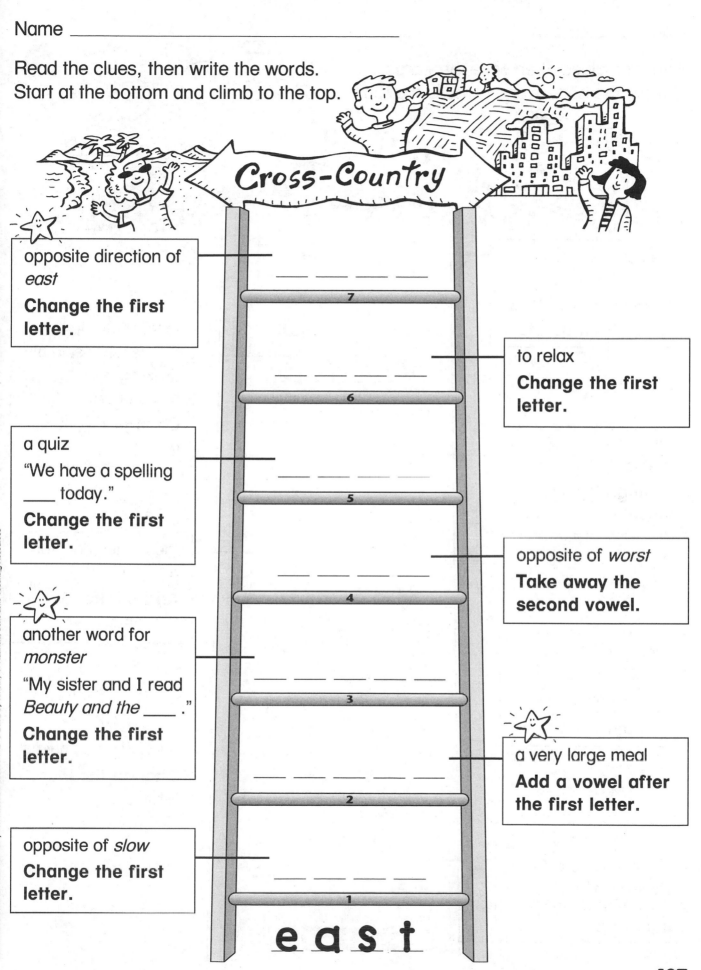

Cross-Country

opposite direction of *east*
Change the first letter.

7 _ _ _ _

to relax
Change the first letter.

6 _ _ _ _

a quiz
"We have a spelling ___ today."
Change the first letter.

5 _ _ _ _

opposite of *worst*
Take away the second vowel.

4 _ _ _ _ _

another word for *monster*
"My sister and I read *Beauty and the* ___ ."
Change the first letter.

3 _ _ _ _ _

a very large meal
Add a vowel after the first letter.

2 _ _ _ _

opposite of *slow*
Change the first letter.

1 _ _ _ _

e a s t

Name _____

Read the clues, then write the words.
Start at the bottom and climb to the top.

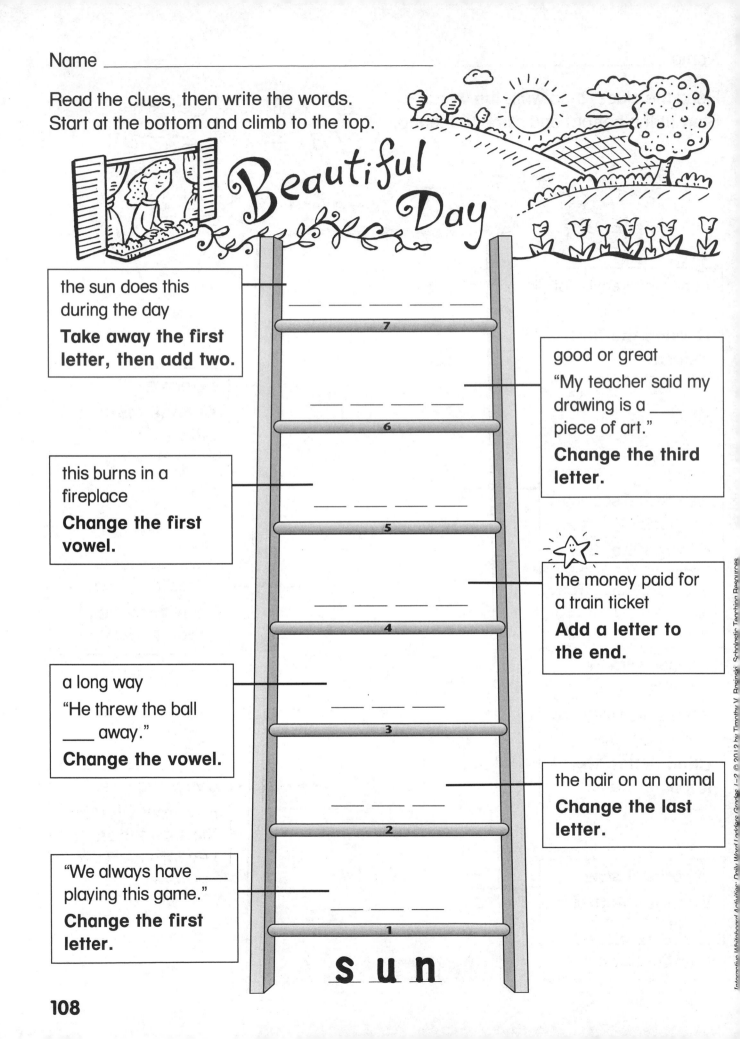

the sun does this during the day
Take away the first letter, then add two.

7 _ _ _ _ _ _

good or great
"My teacher said my drawing is a ___ piece of art."
Change the third letter.

6 _ _ _ _ _

this burns in a fireplace
Change the first vowel.

5 _ _ _ _

the money paid for a train ticket
Add a letter to the end.

4 _ _ _ _

a long way
"He threw the ball ___ away."
Change the vowel.

3 _ _ _

the hair on an animal
Change the last letter.

2 _ _ _

"We always have ___ playing this game."
Change the first letter.

1 _ _ _

s u n

108

Name _____

Read the clues, then write the words.
Start at the bottom and climb to the top.

Good Scents

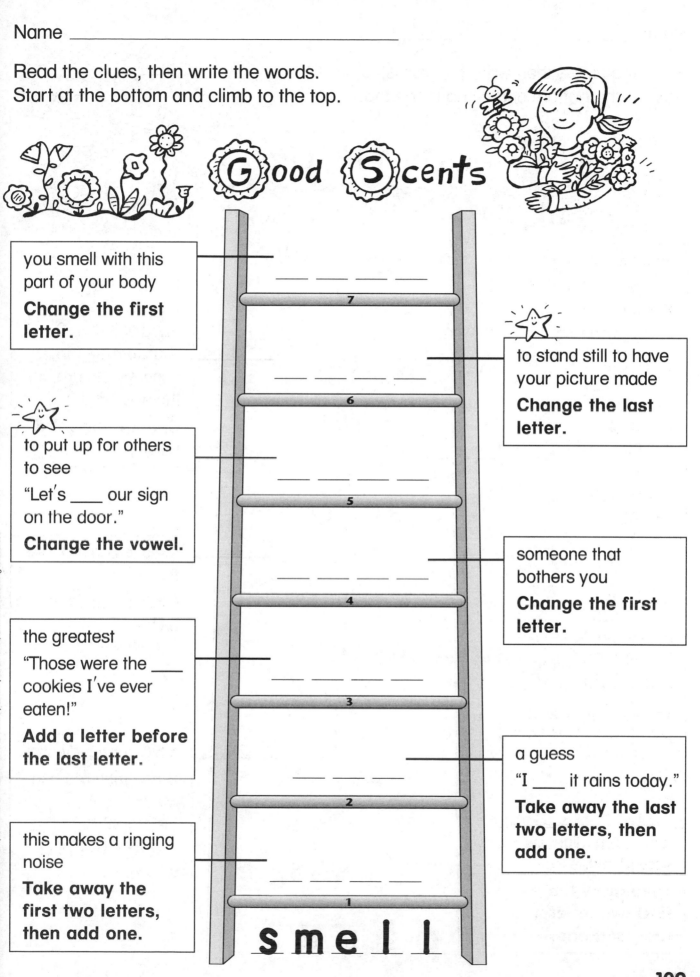

you smell with this part of your body
Change the first letter.

to stand still to have your picture made
Change the last letter.

to put up for others to see
"Let's ___ our sign on the door."
Change the vowel.

someone that bothers you
Change the first letter.

the greatest
"Those were the ___ cookies I've ever eaten!"
Add a letter before the last letter.

a guess
"I ___ it rains today."
Take away the last two letters, then add one.

this makes a ringing noise
Take away the first two letters, then add one.

7

6

5

4

3

2

1

s m e l l

Name _____

Read the clues, then write the words.
Start at the bottom and climb to the top.

On the Line

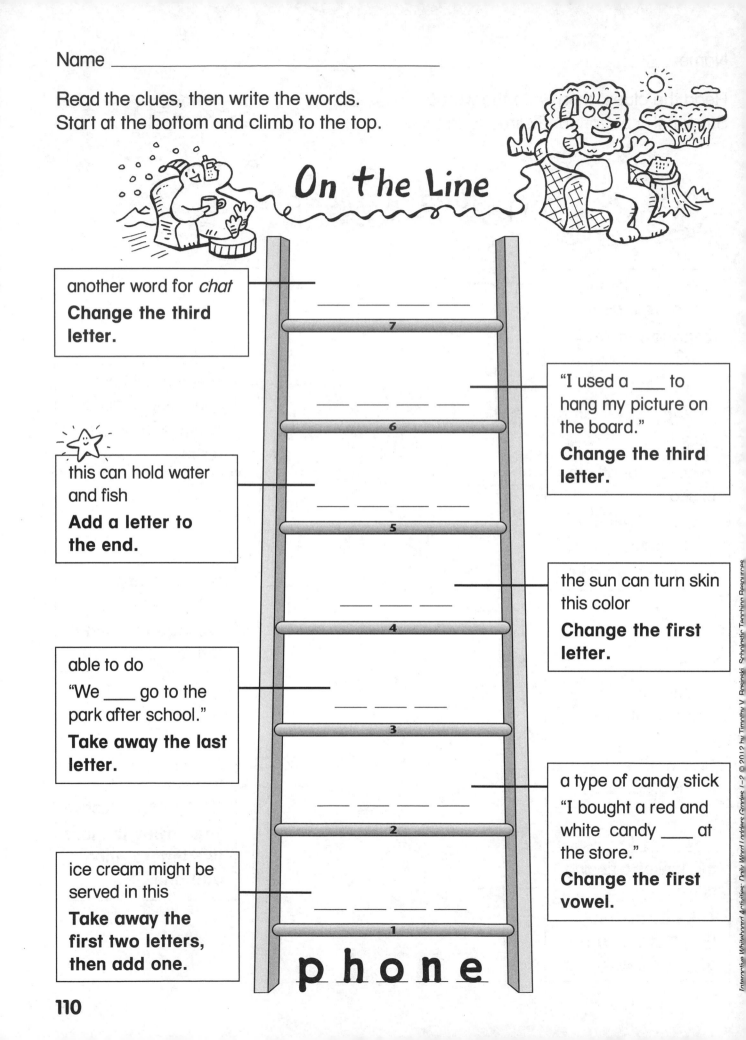

another word for *chat*
Change the third letter.

this can hold water and fish
Add a letter to the end.

able to do
"We ___ go to the park after school."
Take away the last letter.

ice cream might be served in this
Take away the first two letters, then add one.

"I used a ___ to hang my picture on the board."
Change the third letter.

the sun can turn skin this color
Change the first letter.

a type of candy stick
"I bought a red and white candy ___ at the store."
Change the first vowel.

7
6
5
4
3
2
1

p h o n e

Name _____

Read the clues, then write the words.
Start at the bottom and climb to the top.

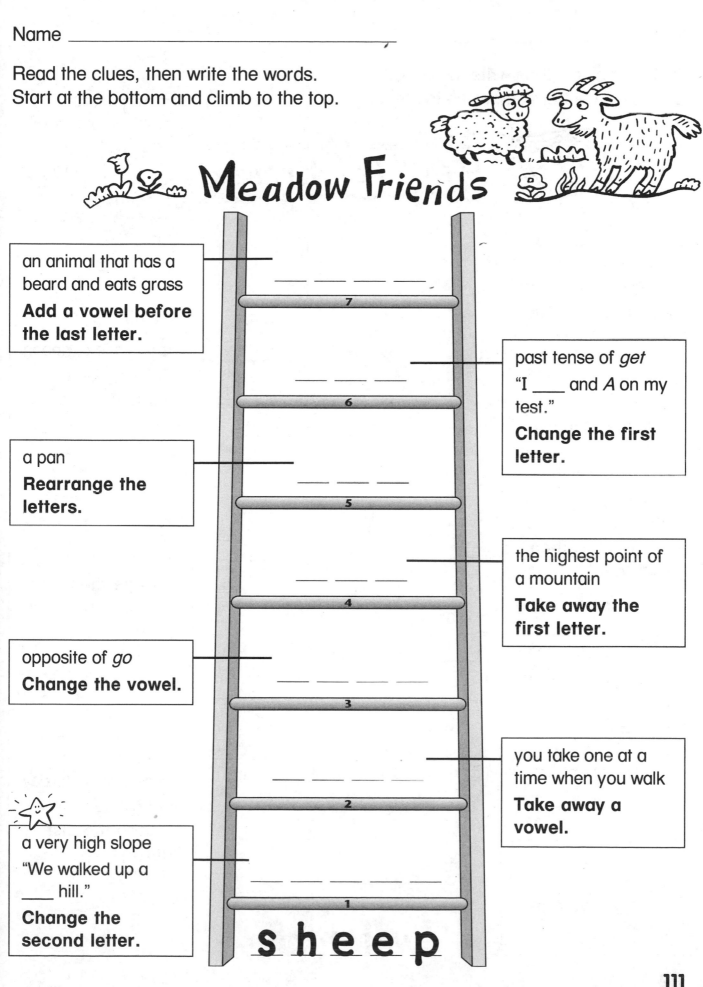

Meadow Friends

an animal that has a beard and eats grass
Add a vowel before the last letter.

7 _ _ _ _ _

past tense of *get*
"I ___ and *A* on my test."
Change the first letter.

6 _ _ _ _

a pan
Rearrange the letters.

5 _ _ _ _

the highest point of a mountain
Take away the first letter.

4 _ _ _

opposite of *go*
Change the vowel.

3 _ _ _ _

you take one at a time when you walk
Take away a vowel.

2 _ _ _ _

a very high slope
"We walked up a ___ hill."
Change the second letter.

1 s h e e p

Name _____

Read the clues, then write the words.
Start at the bottom and climb to the top.

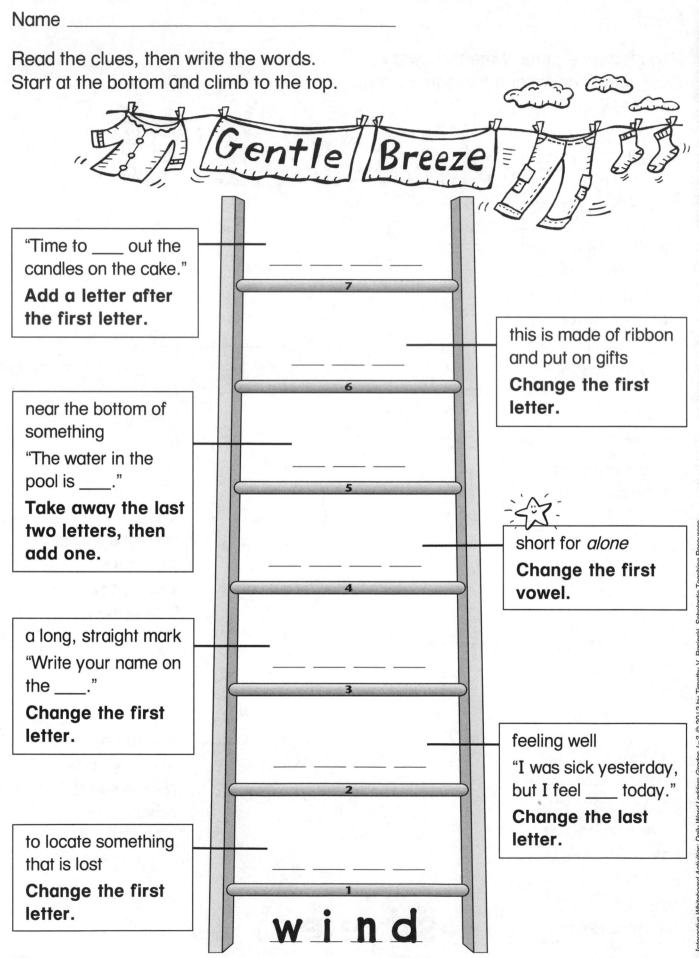

Gentle Breeze

"Time to ____ out the candles on the cake."
Add a letter after the first letter.

7 ___ ___ ___ ___ ___

6 ___ w i n ___

this is made of ribbon and put on gifts
Change the first letter.

near the bottom of something
"The water in the pool is ____."
Take away the last two letters, then add one.

5 ___ ___ ___ ___

4 ___ ___ ___ ___

short for *alone*
Change the first vowel.

a long, straight mark
"Write your name on the ____."
Change the first letter.

3 ___ ___ ___ ___

2 ___ ___ ___ ___

feeling well
"I was sick yesterday, but I feel ____ today."
Change the last letter.

to locate something that is lost
Change the first letter.

1 ___ ___ ___ ___

w i n d

Interactive Whiteboard Activities: Daily Word Ladders Grades 1–2 © 2012 by Timothy V. Rasinski, Scholastic Teaching Resources

Name _____

Read the clues, then write the words.
Start at the bottom and climb to the top.

Big and Cuddly

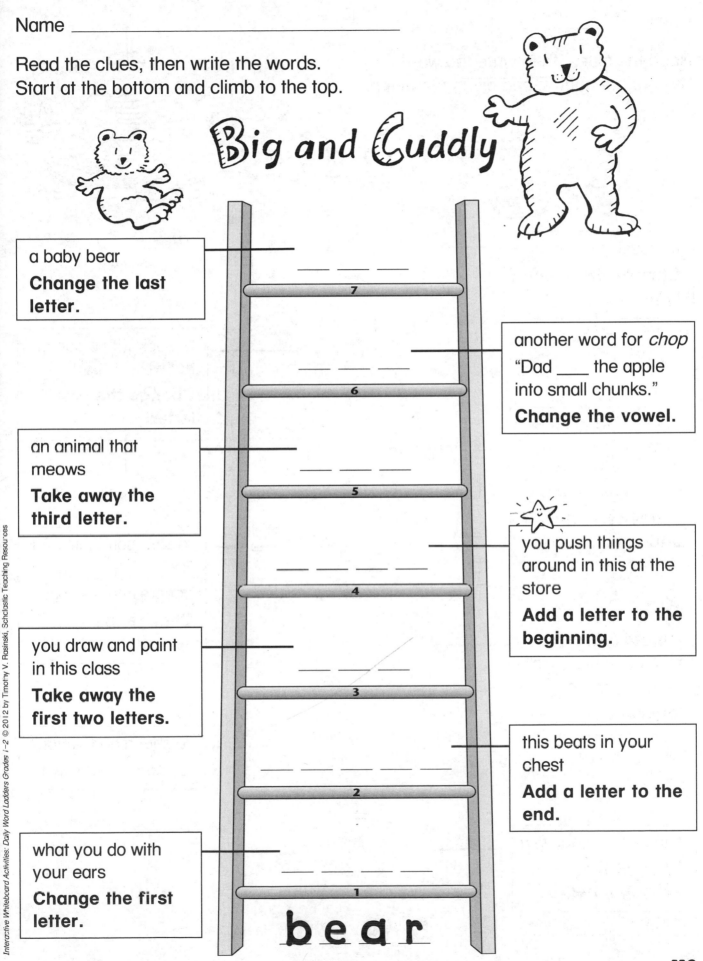

a baby bear
Change the last letter.

_ _ _ _   7

another word for *chop*
"Dad ____ the apple into small chunks."
Change the vowel.

_ _ _ _   6

an animal that meows
Take away the third letter.

_ _ _ _   5

you push things around in this at the store
Add a letter to the beginning.

_ _ _ _ _   4

you draw and paint in this class
Take away the first two letters.

_ _ _ _   3

this beats in your chest
Add a letter to the end.

_ _ _ _ _   2

what you do with your ears
Change the first letter.

_ _ _ _   1

b e a r

Name _____

Read the clues, then write the words.
Start at the bottom and climb to the top.

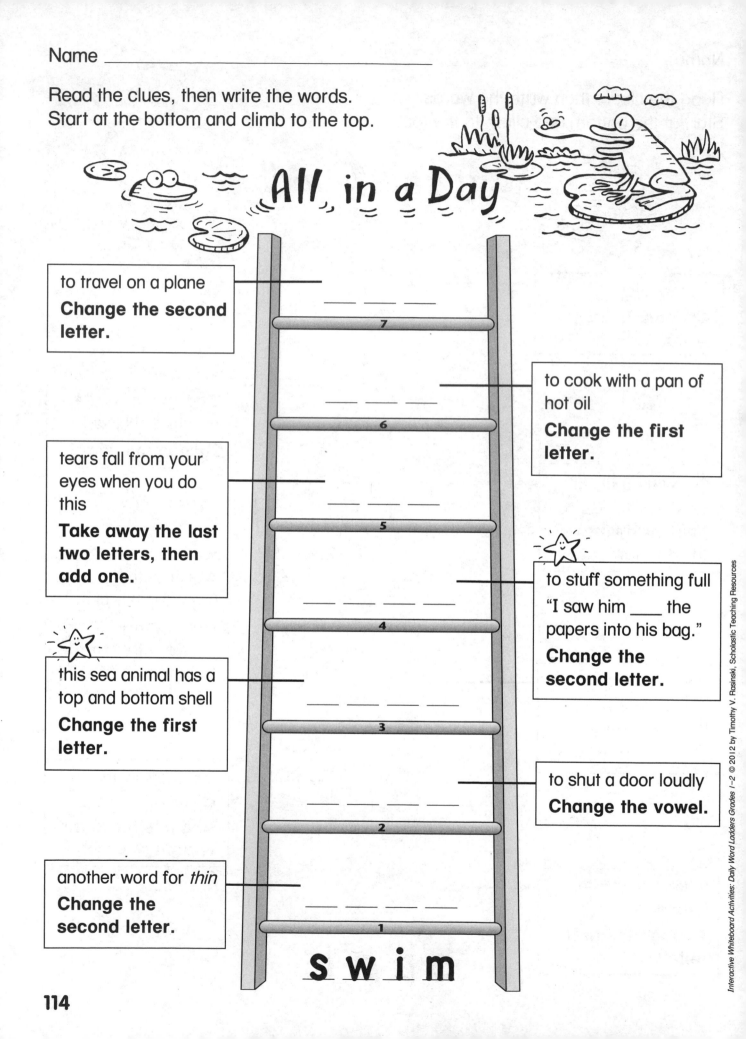

All in a Day

to travel on a plane
Change the second letter.

_ _ _ _   7

to cook with a pan of hot oil
Change the first letter.

_ _ _   6

tears fall from your eyes when you do this
Take away the last two letters, then add one.

_ _ _ _   5

to stuff something full
"I saw him ___ the papers into his bag."
Change the second letter.

_ _ _ _   4

this sea animal has a top and bottom shell
Change the first letter.

_ _ _ _   3

to shut a door loudly
Change the vowel.

_ _ _ _   2

another word for *thin*
Change the second letter.

_ _ _ _   1

s w i m

114

Name _____

Read the clues, then write the words.
Start at the bottom and climb to the top.

Open Wide!

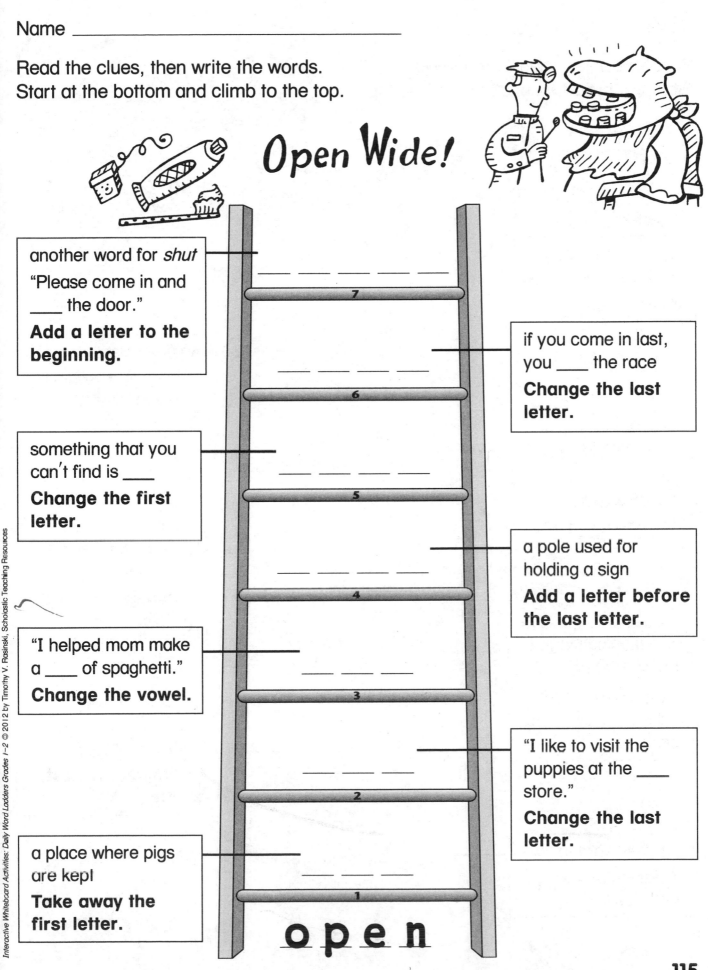

another word for *shut*
"Please come in and
___ the door."
Add a letter to the beginning.

if you come in last,
you ___ the race
Change the last letter.

something that you
can't find is ___
Change the first letter.

a pole used for
holding a sign
Add a letter before the last letter.

"I helped mom make
a ___ of spaghetti."
Change the vowel.

"I like to visit the
puppies at the ___ store."
Change the last letter.

a place where pigs
are kept
Take away the first letter.

7

6

5

4

3

2

1

o p e n

Interactive Whiteboard Activities: Daily Word Ladders Grades 1–2 © 2012 by Timothy V. Rasinski, Scholastic Teaching Resources

Name _____

Read the clues, then write the words.
Start at the bottom and climb to the top.

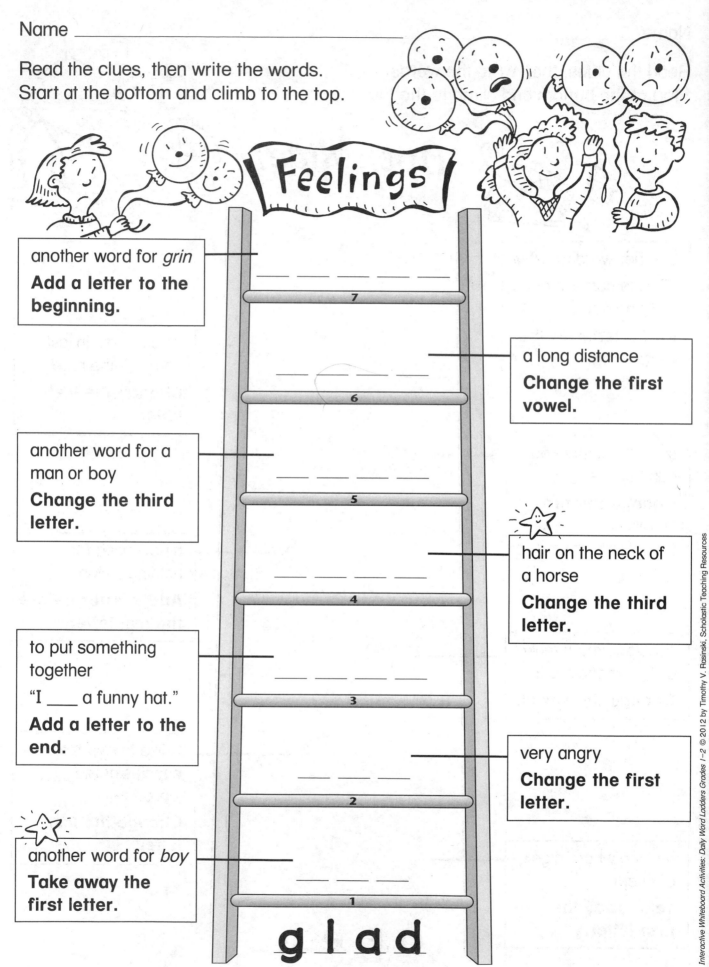

Feelings

another word for *grin*
Add a letter to the beginning.

a long distance
Change the first vowel.

another word for a man or boy
Change the third letter.

hair on the neck of a horse
Change the third letter.

to put something together
"I ___ a funny hat."
Add a letter to the end.

very angry
Change the first letter.

another word for *boy*
Take away the first letter.

7

6

5

4

3

2

1

g l a d

Interactive Whiteboard Activities: Daily Word Ladders Grades 1–2 © 2012 by Timothy V. Rasinski, Scholastic Teaching Resources

Name _____

Read the clues, then write the words.
Start at the bottom and climb to the top.

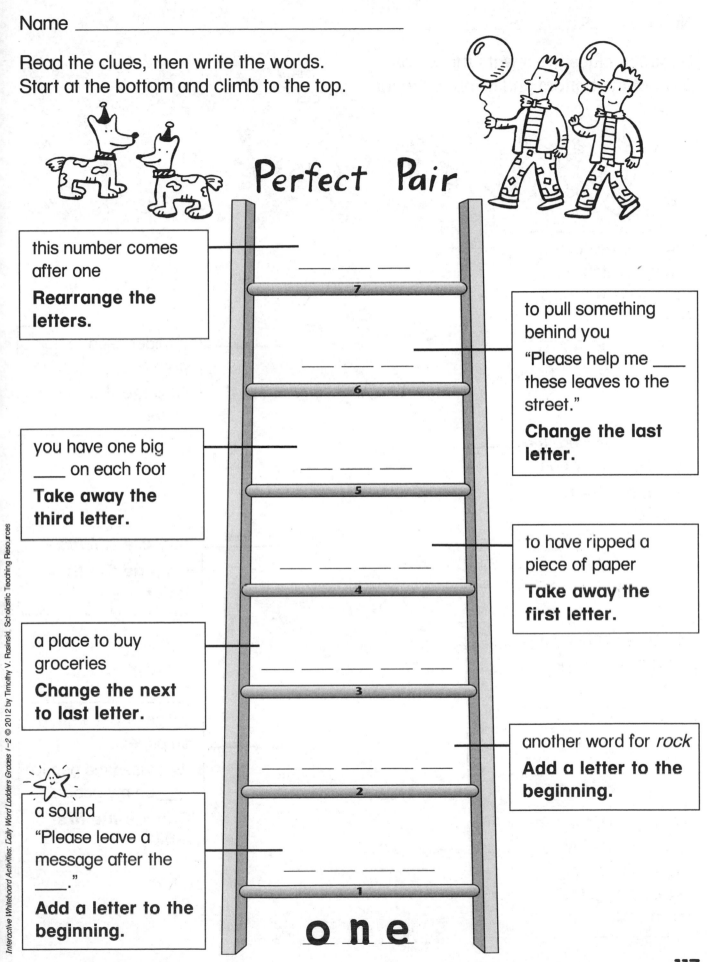

Perfect Pair

this number comes after one
Rearrange the letters.

_ _ _   7

to pull something behind you
"Please help me ___ these leaves to the street."
Change the last letter.

_ _ _ _   6

you have one big ___ on each foot
Take away the third letter.

_ _ _   5

to have ripped a piece of paper
Take away the first letter.

_ _ _ _   4

a place to buy groceries
Change the next to last letter.

_ _ _ _   3

another word for *rock*
Add a letter to the beginning.

_ _ _ _   2

a sound
"Please leave a message after the ___."
Add a letter to the beginning.

_ _ _   1

o n e

Name _____

Read the clues, then write the words.
Start at the bottom and climb to the top.

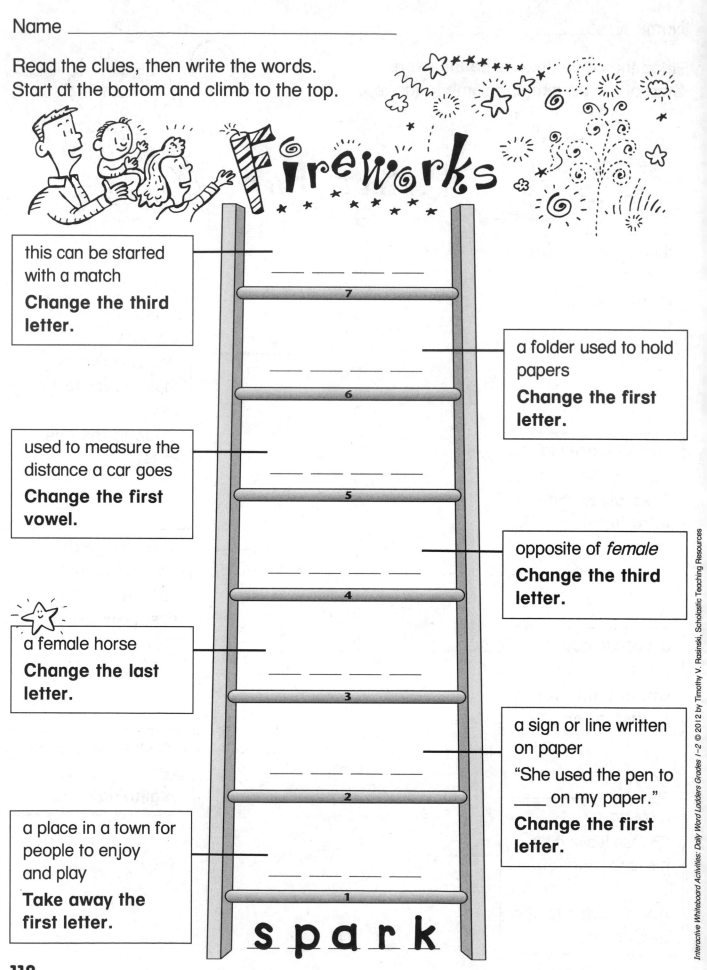

Fireworks

this can be started
with a match
**Change the third
letter.**

a folder used to hold
papers
**Change the first
letter.**

used to measure the
distance a car goes
**Change the first
vowel.**

opposite of *female*
**Change the third
letter.**

a female horse
**Change the last
letter.**

a sign or line written
on paper
"She used the pen to
___ on my paper."
**Change the first
letter.**

a place in a town for
people to enjoy
and play
**Take away the
first letter.**

7

6

5

4

3

2

1

s p a r k

Interactive Whiteboard Activities: Daily Word Ladders Grades 1–2 © 2012 by Timothy V. Rasinski, Scholastic Teaching Resources

Name _____

Read the clues, then write the words.
Start at the bottom and climb to the top.

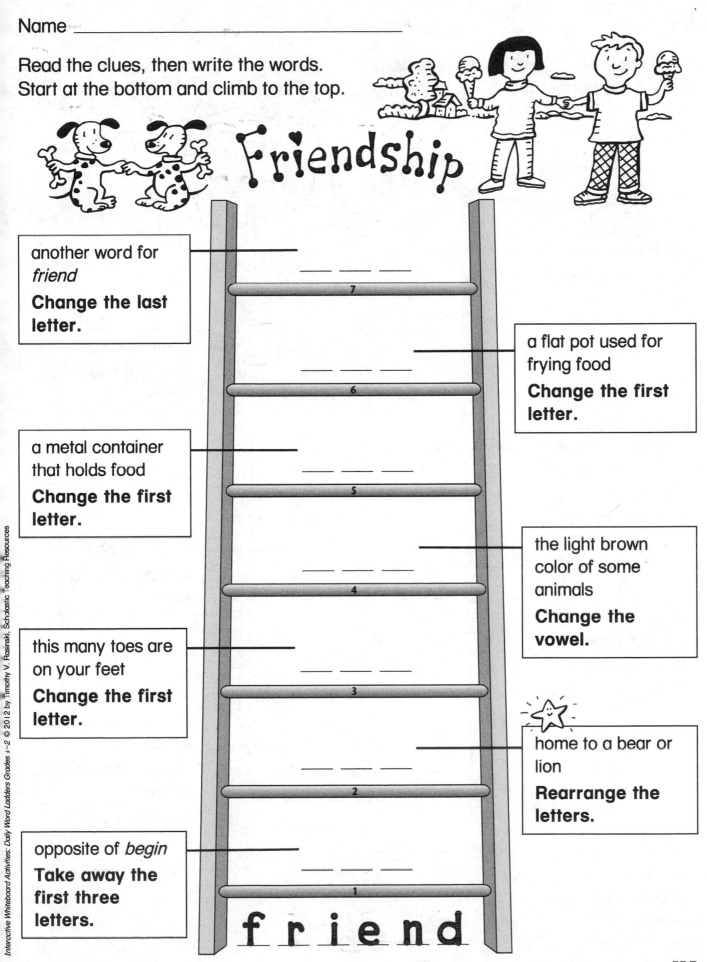

Friendship

another word for *friend*
Change the last letter.

7 _ _ _ _ _

a flat pot used for frying food
Change the first letter.

6 _ _ _ _

a metal container that holds food
Change the first letter.

5 _ _ _

the light brown color of some animals
Change the vowel.

4 _ _ _ _

this many toes are on your feet
Change the first letter.

3 _ _ _ _ _

home to a bear or lion
Rearrange the letters.

2 _ _ _

opposite of *begin*
Take away the first three letters.

1 _ _ _ _ _

f r i e n d

Name _____

Read the clues, then write the words.
Start at the bottom and climb to the top.

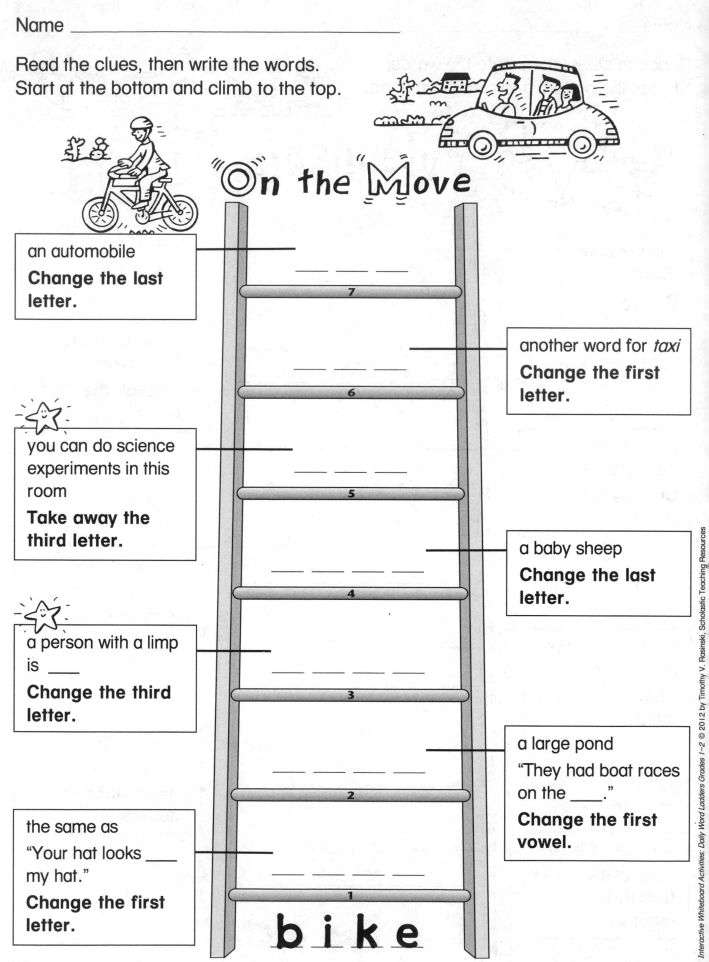

On the Move

an automobile
Change the last letter.

another word for *taxi*
Change the first letter.

you can do science experiments in this room
Take away the third letter.

a baby sheep
Change the last letter.

a person with a limp is ___
Change the third letter.

a large pond
"They had boat races on the ___."
Change the first vowel.

the same as
"Your hat looks ___ my hat."
Change the first letter.

b i k e

Interactive Whiteboard Activities: Daily Word Ladders Grades 1–2 © 2012 by Timothy V. Rasinski, Scholastic Teaching Resources

Name _____

Read the clues, then write the words.
Start at the bottom and climb to the top.

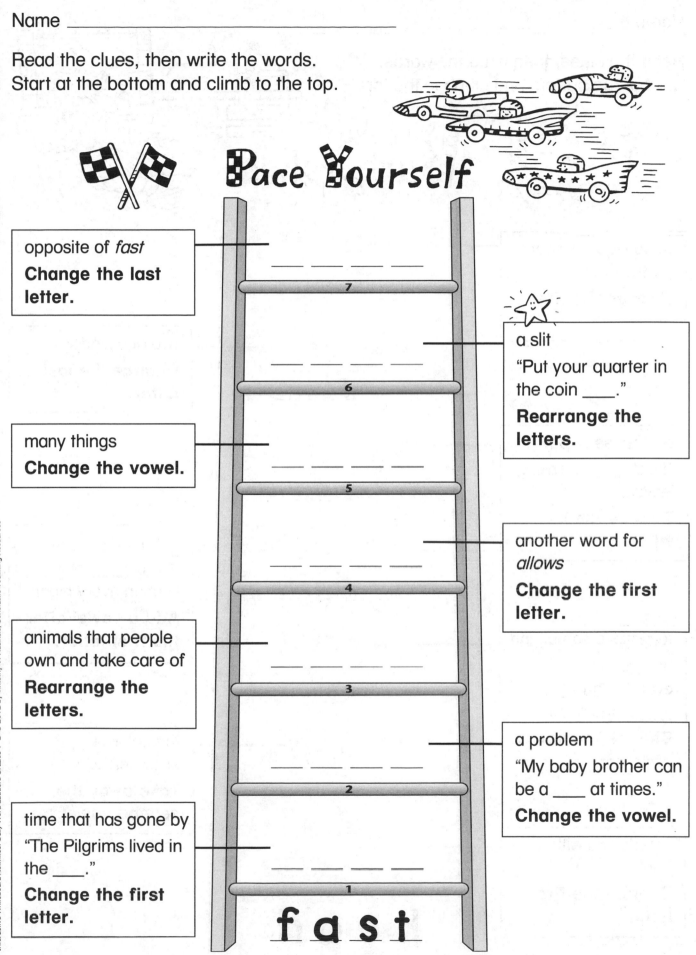

Pace Yourself

opposite of *fast*
Change the last letter.

7 _ _ _ _

a slit
"Put your quarter in the coin ____."
Rearrange the letters.

6 _ _ _ _

many things
Change the vowel.

5 _ _ _ _

another word for *allows*
Change the first letter.

4 _ _ _ _

animals that people own and take care of
Rearrange the letters.

3 _ _ _ _

a problem
"My baby brother can be a ____ at times."
Change the vowel.

2 _ _ _ _

time that has gone by
"The Pilgrims lived in the ____."
Change the first letter.

1 _ _ _ _

f a s t

Name _____

Read the clues, then write the words.
Start at the bottom and climb to the top.

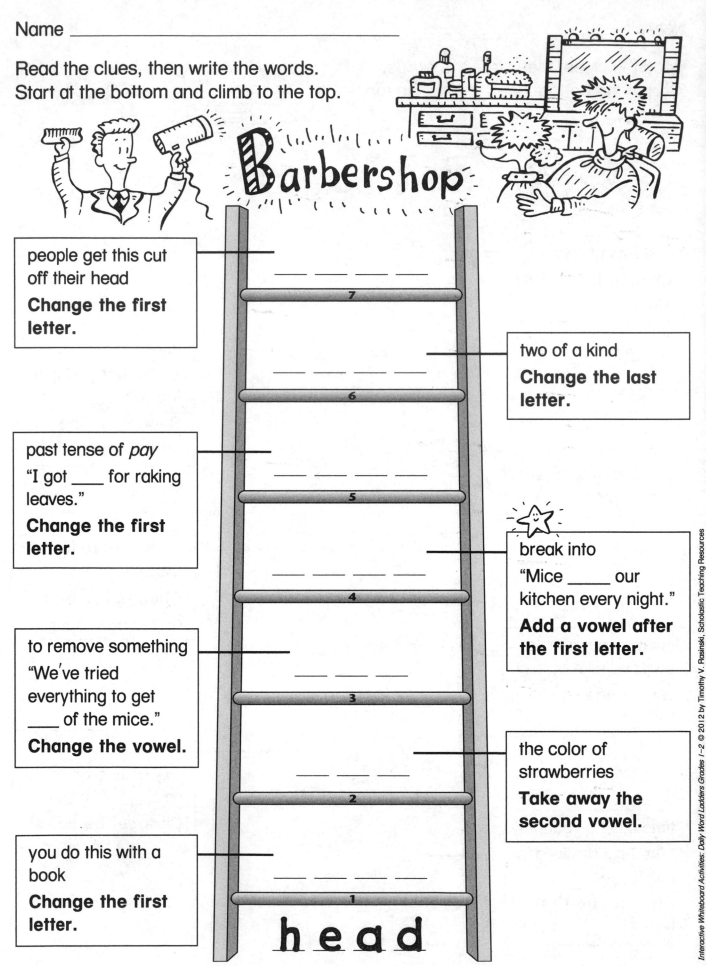

Barbershop

people get this cut off their head
Change the first letter.

two of a kind
Change the last letter.

past tense of *pay*
"I got ___ for raking leaves."
Change the first letter.

break into
"Mice ____ our kitchen every night."
Add a vowel after the first letter.

to remove something
"We've tried everything to get ___ of the mice."
Change the vowel.

the color of strawberries
Take away the second vowel.

you do this with a book
Change the first letter.

7
6
5
4
3
2
1

h e a d

Interactive Whiteboard Activities: Daily Word Ladders Grades 1–2 © 2012 by Timothy V. Rasinski, Scholastic Teaching Resources

Name _____

Read the clues, then write the words.
Start at the bottom and climb to the top.

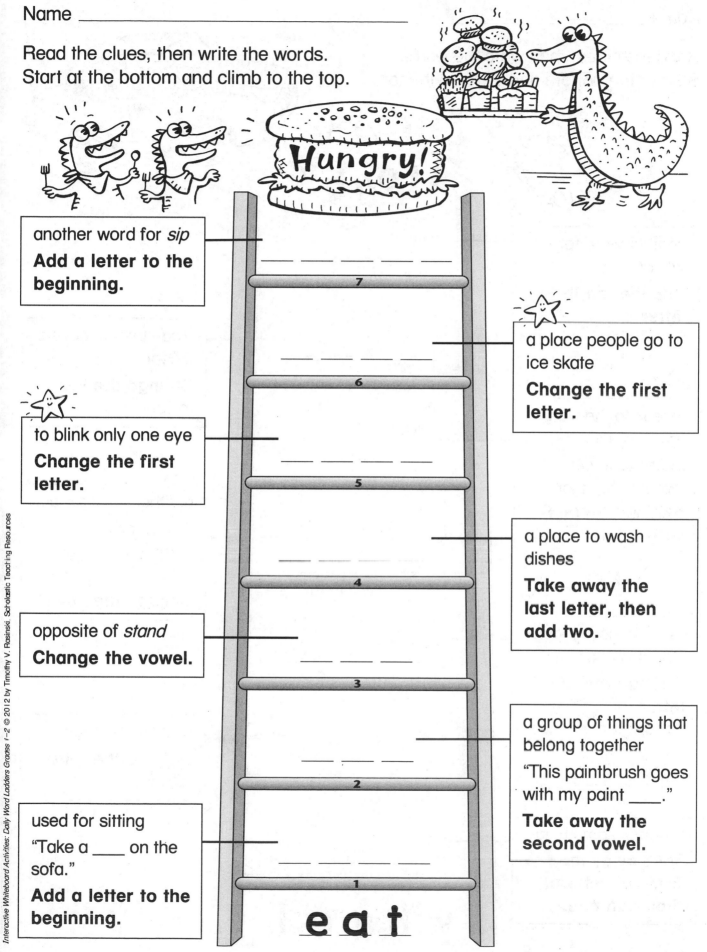

another word for *sip*
Add a letter to the beginning.

— — — —   7

a place people go to ice skate
Change the first letter.

— — — —   6

to blink only one eye
Change the first letter.

— — — —   5

a place to wash dishes
Take away the last letter, then add two.

— — — —   4

opposite of *stand*
Change the vowel.

— — — —   3

a group of things that belong together
"This paintbrush goes with my paint ____."
Take away the second vowel.

— — — —   2

used for sitting
"Take a ____ on the sofa."
Add a letter to the beginning.

— — — —   1

e a t

Name _____

Read the clues, then write the words.
Start at the bottom and climb to the top.

Car Trouble

another word for *wheel*
Change the third letter.

a square that covers a floor
Change the last letter.

to lean to the side
"They had to ___ the chair to get it through the door."
Change the last letter.

another word for *until*
"We won't start the game ___ you get here."
Change the vowel.

to let someone know something
Change the first letter.

past tense of *fall*
Change the third letter.

to touch something
Take away the first two letters, then add one.

w h e e l

7

6

5

4

3

2

1

Interactive Whiteboard Activities: Daily Word Ladders Grades 1–2 © 2012 by Timothy V. Rasinski, Scholastic Teaching Resources

Name _____

Read the clues, then write the words.
Start at the bottom and climb to the top.

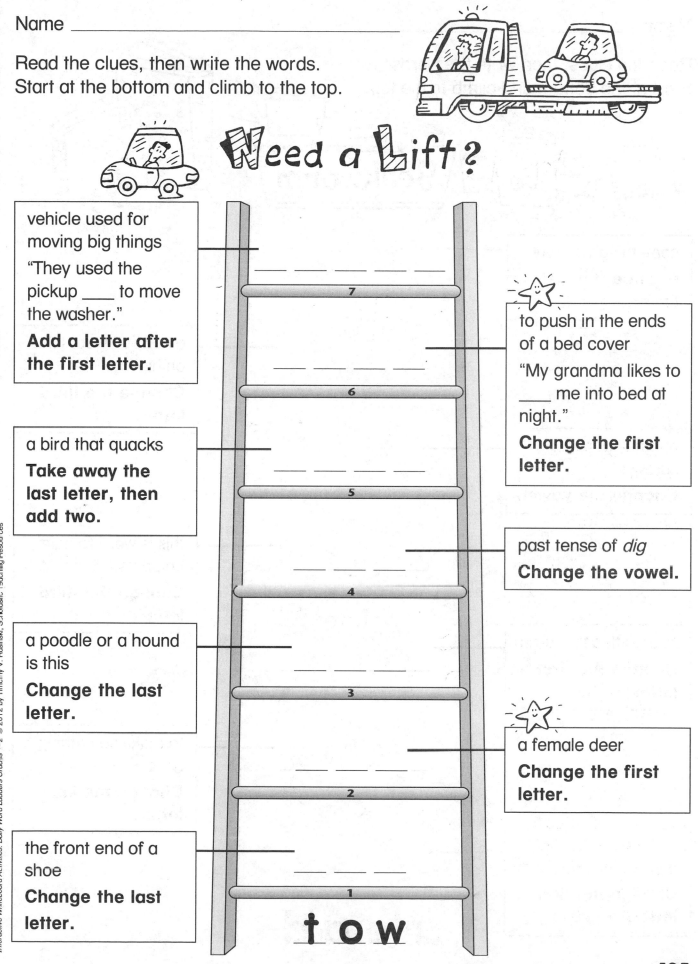

Need a Lift?

vehicle used for moving big things
"They used the pickup ___ to move the washer."
Add a letter after the first letter.

to push in the ends of a bed cover
"My grandma likes to ___ me into bed at night."
Change the first letter.

a bird that quacks
Take away the last letter, then add two.

past tense of *dig*
Change the vowel.

a poodle or a hound is this
Change the last letter.

a female deer
Change the first letter.

the front end of a shoe
Change the last letter.

t o w

Interactive Whiteboard Activities: Daily Word Ladders Grades 1–2 © 2012 by Timothy V. Rasinski, Scholastic Teaching Resources

Name _____

Read the clues, then write the words.
Start at the bottom and climb to the top.

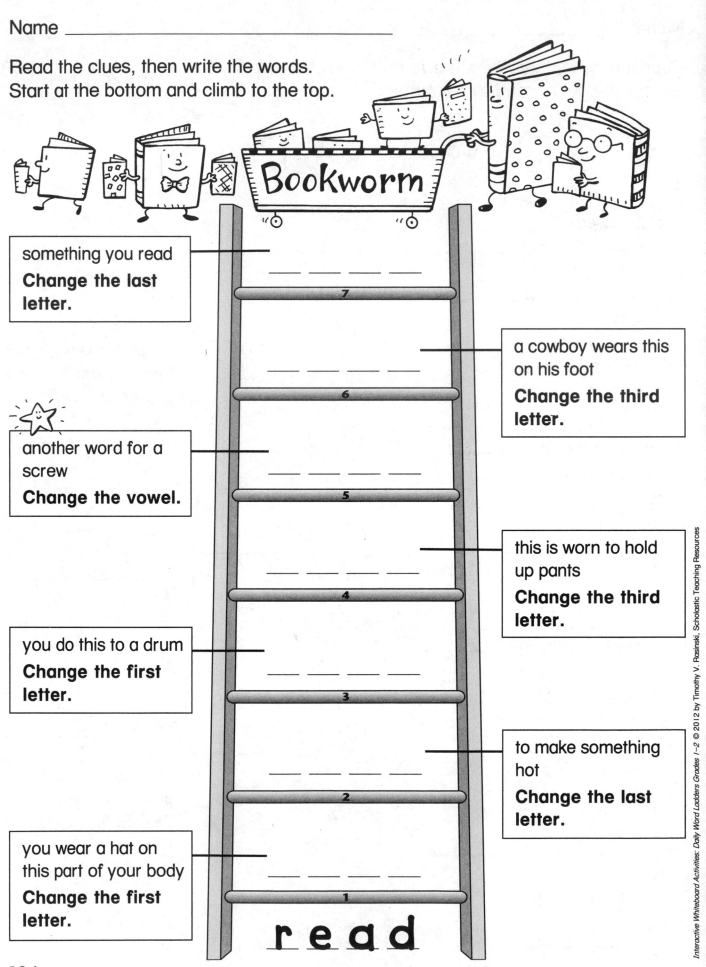

something you read
Change the last letter.

7 ___ ___ ___ ___

a cowboy wears this on his foot
Change the third letter.

6 ___ ___ ___ ___

another word for a screw
Change the vowel.

5 ___ ___ ___ ___

this is worn to hold up pants
Change the third letter.

4 ___ ___ ___ ___

you do this to a drum
Change the first letter.

3 ___ ___ ___ ___

to make something hot
Change the last letter.

2 ___ ___ ___ ___

you wear a hat on this part of your body
Change the first letter.

1 ___ ___ ___ ___

r e a d

Name _____

Read the clues, then write the words.
Start at the bottom and climb to the top.

A Little Light

this makes the light that comes from a candle
Add a vowel to the end.

7 _ _ _ _ _ _

a type of evergreen tree
Change the last letter.

6 _ _ _ _

to be the right size
"This shirt is a perfect ____."
Change the first letter.

5 _ _ _ _

a small amount
Change the vowel.

4 _ _ _ _

a flying mammal that lives in caves
Take away the last letter.

3 _ _ _

you take a ____ to get clean
Take away the next to last letter.

2 _ _ _ _

a group of things
"Let's bake a ____ of cookies."
Change the first letter.

1 _ _ _ _ _

m a t c h

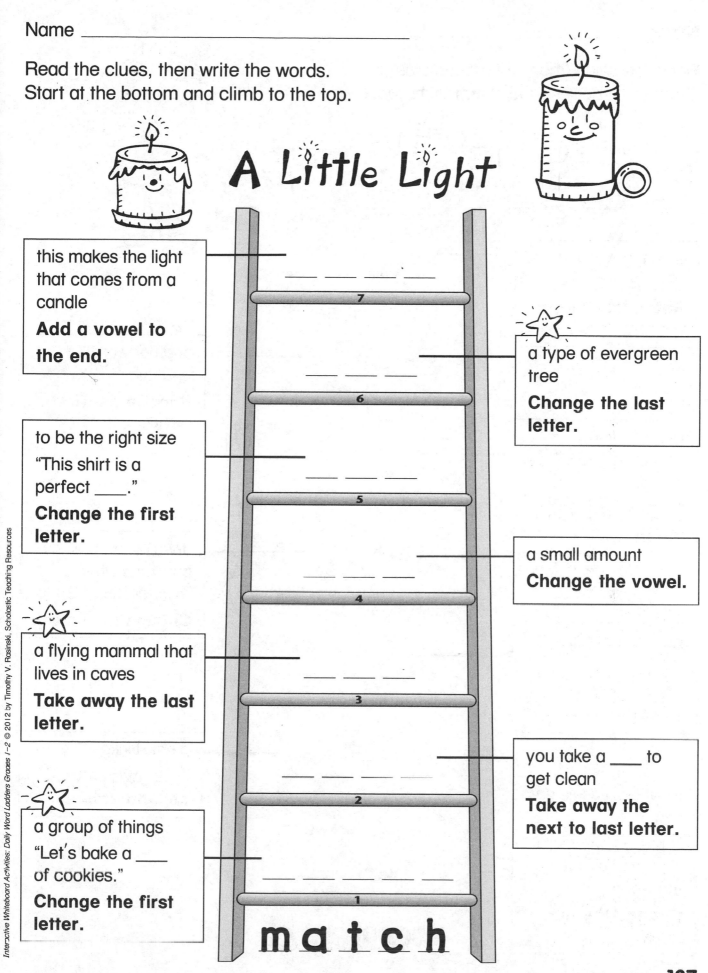

Name _____

Read the clues, then write the words.
Start at the bottom and climb to the top.

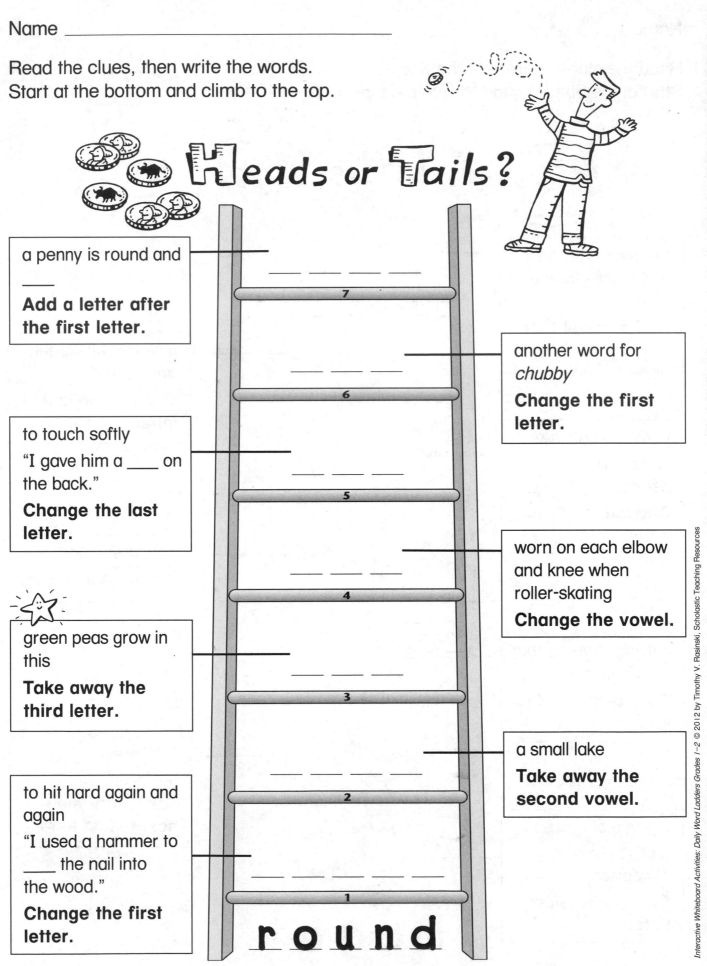

Heads or Tails?

a penny is round and ____

Add a letter after the first letter.

another word for *chubby*

Change the first letter.

to touch softly

"I gave him a ____ on the back."

Change the last letter.

worn on each elbow and knee when roller-skating

Change the vowel.

green peas grow in this

Take away the third letter.

a small lake

Take away the second vowel.

to hit hard again and again

"I used a hammer to ____ the nail into the wood."

Change the first letter.

7

6

5

4

3

2

1

r o u n d

Interactive Whiteboard Activities: Daily Word Ladders Grades 1–2 © 2012 by Timothy V. Rasinski, Scholastic Teaching Resources

Name _____

Read the clues, then write the words.
Start at the bottom and climb to the top.

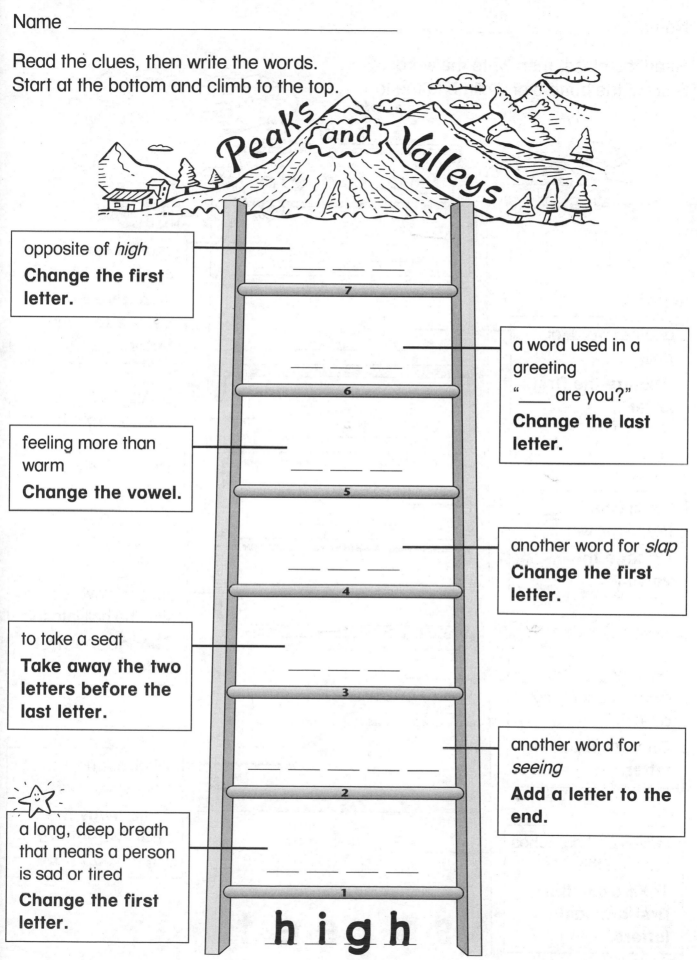

opposite of *high*
Change the first letter.

7 _ _ _

a word used in a greeting
"___ are you?"
Change the last letter.

6 _ _ _

feeling more than warm
Change the vowel.

5 _ _ _

another word for *slap*
Change the first letter.

4 _ _ _

to take a seat
Take away the two letters before the last letter.

3 _ _ _

another word for *seeing*
Add a letter to the end.

2 _ _ _ _ _

a long, deep breath that means a person is sad or tired
Change the first letter.

1 _ _ _ _

h i g h

Name _____

Read the clues, then write the words.
Start at the bottom and climb to the top.

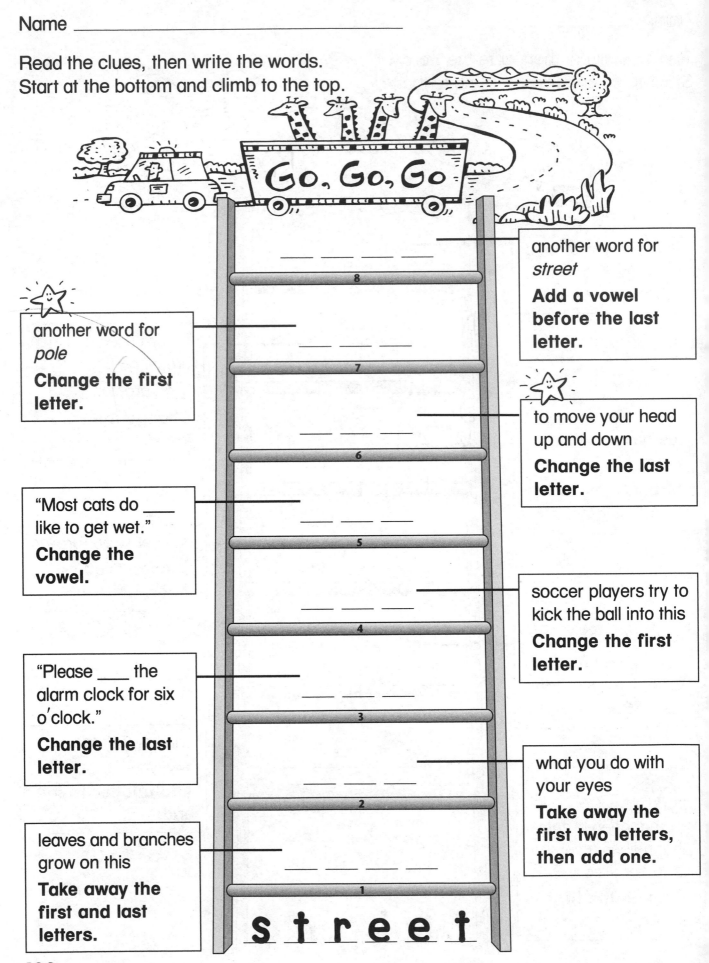

Go, Go, Go

8 — — — — —

another word for *street*
Add a vowel before the last letter.

7 — — — —

another word for *pole*
Change the first letter.

6 — — — —

to move your head up and down
Change the last letter.

5 — — — —

"Most cats do ____ like to get wet."
Change the vowel.

4 — — — —

soccer players try to kick the ball into this
Change the first letter.

3 — — — —

"Please ____ the alarm clock for six o'clock."
Change the last letter.

2 — — — —

what you do with your eyes
Take away the first two letters, then add one.

1 — — — — —

leaves and branches grow on this
Take away the first and last letters.

s t r e e t

Name _____

Read the clues, then write the words.
Start at the bottom and climb to the top.

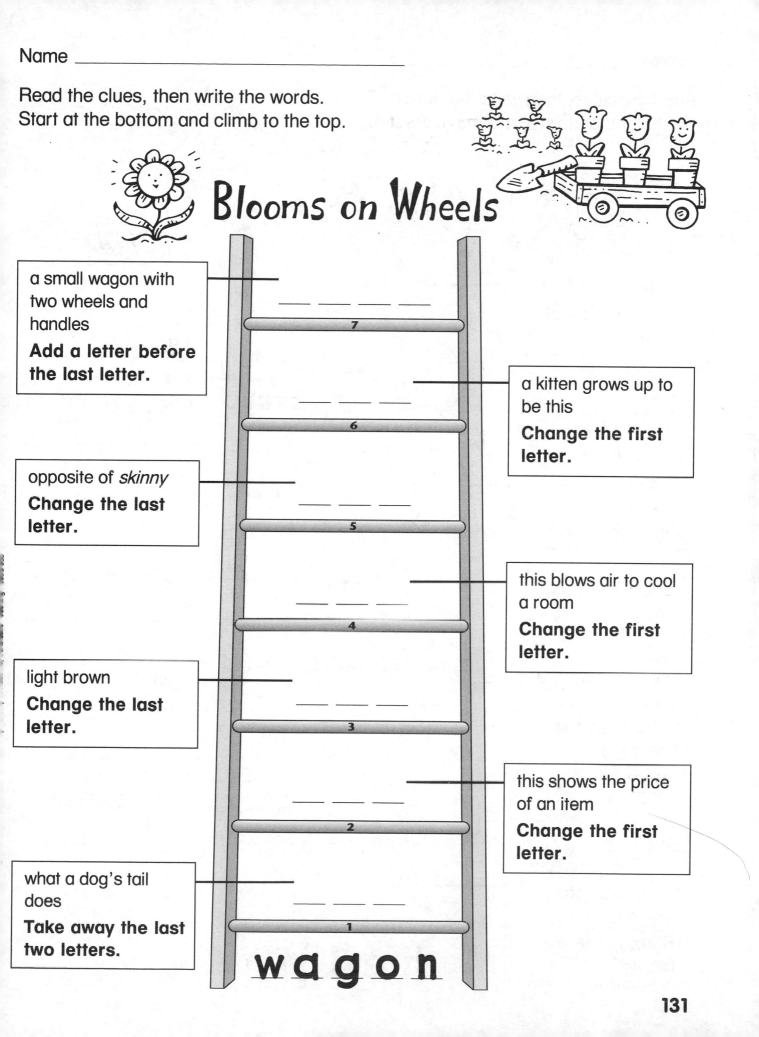

Blooms on Wheels

a small wagon with two wheels and handles
Add a letter before the last letter.

7 ___ ___ ___ ___

a kitten grows up to be this
Change the first letter.

6 ___ ___ ___

opposite of *skinny*
Change the last letter.

5 ___ ___ ___ ___

this blows air to cool a room
Change the first letter.

4 ___ ___ ___

light brown
Change the last letter.

3 ___ ___ ___

this shows the price of an item
Change the first letter.

2 ___ ___ ___ ___

what a dog's tail does
Take away the last two letters.

1 ___ ___ ___

w a g o n

Name _____

Read the clues, then write the words.
Start at the bottom and climb to the top.

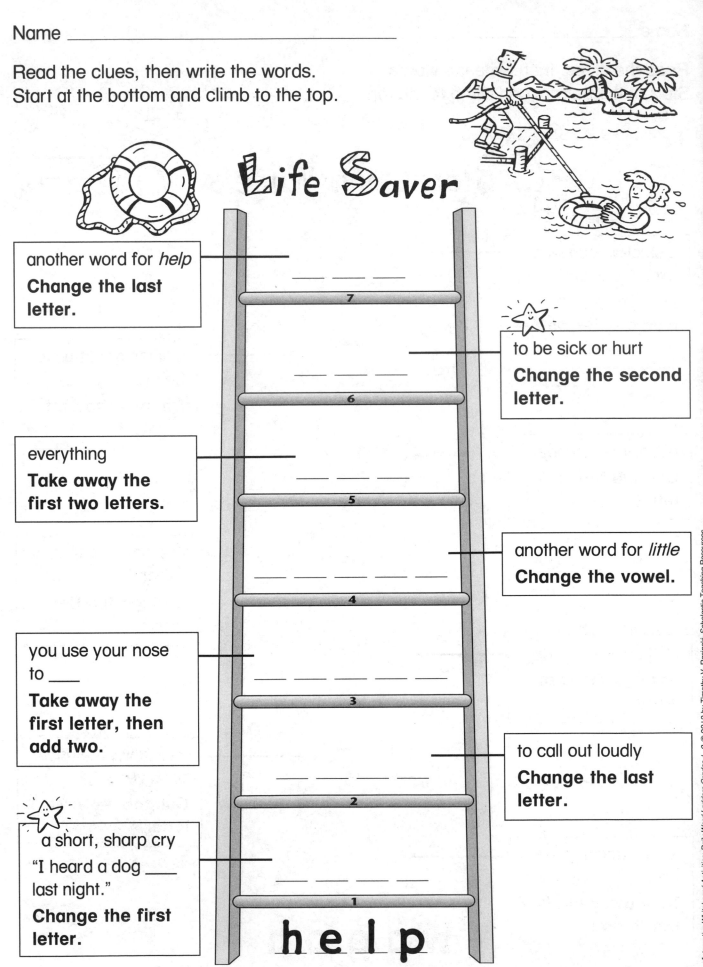

Life Saver

another word for *help*
Change the last letter.

7 ___ ___ ___ ___

to be sick or hurt
Change the second letter.

6 ___ ___ ___

everything
Take away the first two letters.

5 ___ ___ ___

another word for *little*
Change the vowel.

4 ___ ___ ___ ___ ___

you use your nose to ___
Take away the first letter, then add two.

3 ___ ___ ___ ___

to call out loudly
Change the last letter.

2 ___ ___ ___ ___ ___

a short, sharp cry
"I heard a dog ___ last night."
Change the first letter.

1 ___ ___ ___ ___

h e l p

Name _____

Read the clues, then write the words.
Start at the bottom and climb to the top.

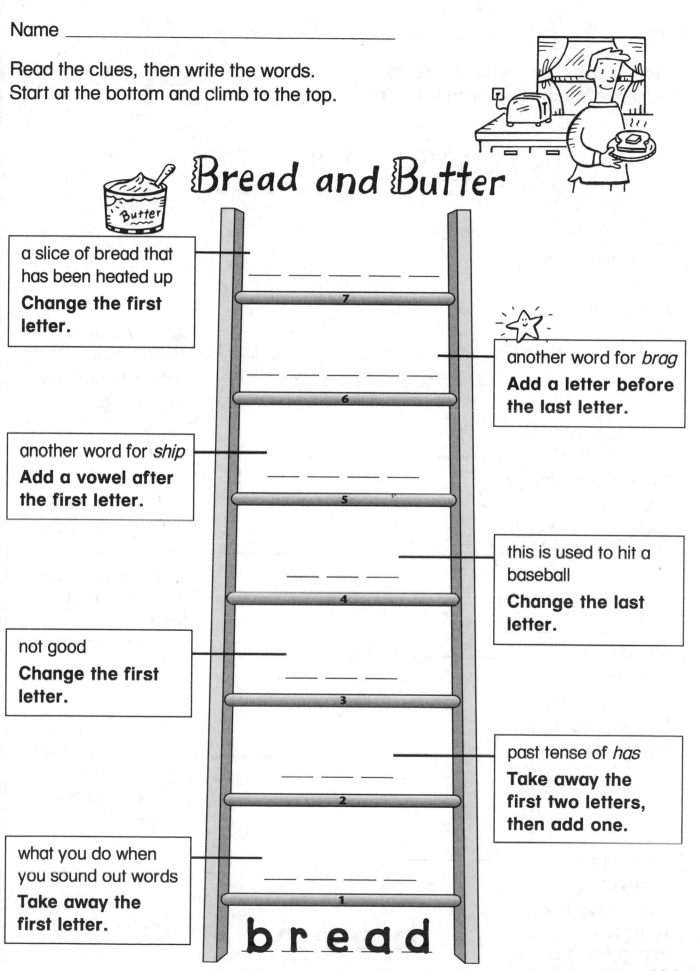

Bread and Butter

a slice of bread that
has been heated up
**Change the first
letter.**

another word for *ship*
**Add a vowel after
the first letter.**

not good
**Change the first
letter.**

what you do when
you sound out words
**Take away the
first letter.**

another word for *brag*
**Add a letter before
the last letter.**

this is used to hit a
baseball
**Change the last
letter.**

past tense of *has*
**Take away the
first two letters,
then add one.**

7

6

5

4

3

2

1

b r e a d

Name _____

Read the clues, then write the words.
Start at the bottom and climb to the top.

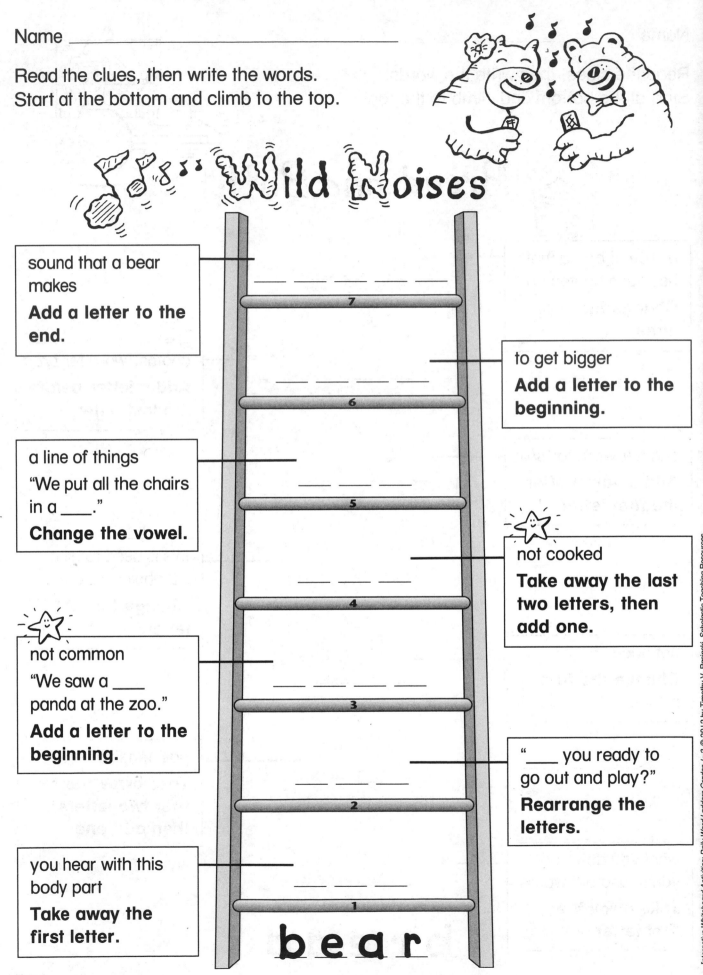

Wild Noises

sound that a bear makes
Add a letter to the end.

_ _ _ _ _ 7

to get bigger
Add a letter to the beginning.

_ _ _ _ 6

a line of things
"We put all the chairs in a ___."
Change the vowel.

_ _ _ _ 5

not cooked
Take away the last two letters, then add one.

_ _ _ _ 4

not common
"We saw a ___ panda at the zoo."
Add a letter to the beginning.

_ _ _ _ _ 3

"___ you ready to go out and play?"
Rearrange the letters.

_ _ _ _ 2

you hear with this body part
Take away the first letter.

_ _ _ 1

bear

Name _____

Read the clues, then write the words.
Start at the bottom and climb to the top.

Open-Air Ride

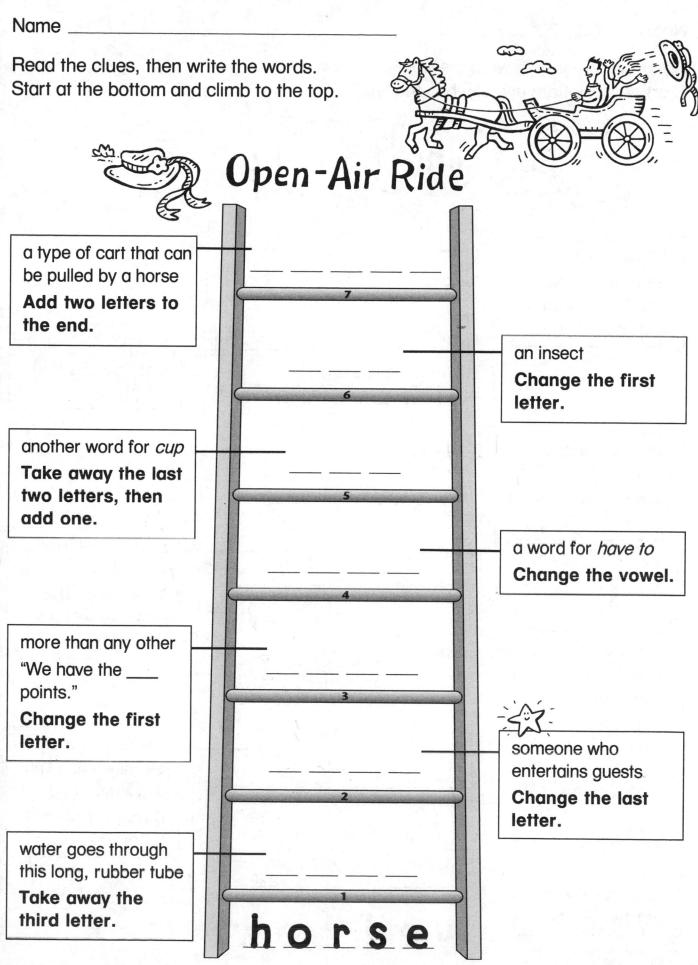

a type of cart that can be pulled by a horse
Add two letters to the end.

— — — — — — 7

an insect
Change the first letter.

— — — — 6

another word for *cup*
Take away the last two letters, then add one.

— — — — 5

a word for *have to*
Change the vowel.

— — — — — 4

more than any other
"We have the ___ points."
Change the first letter.

— — — — — 3

someone who entertains guests
Change the last letter.

— — — — — 2

water goes through this long, rubber tube
Take away the third letter.

— — — — — 1

h o r s e

Name _____

Read the clues, then write the words.
Start at the bottom and climb to the top.

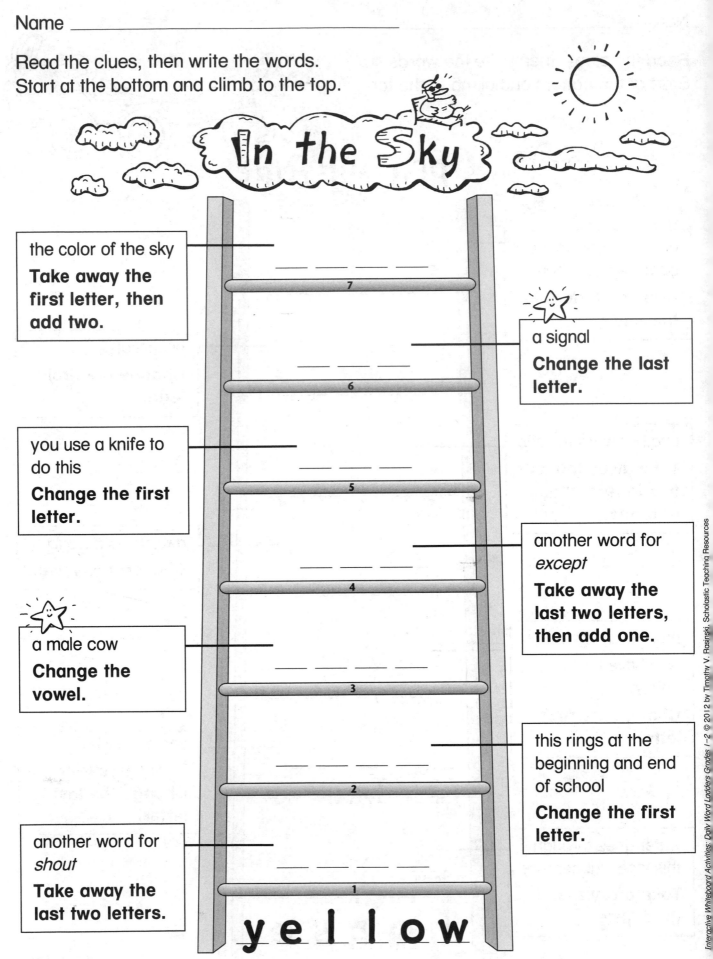

In the Sky

the color of the sky
Take away the first letter, then add two.

a signal
Change the last letter.

you use a knife to do this
Change the first letter.

another word for *except*
Take away the last two letters, then add one.

a male cow
Change the vowel.

this rings at the beginning and end of school
Change the first letter.

another word for *shout*
Take away the last two letters.

7
6
5
4
3
2
1

y e l l o w

Interactive Whiteboard Activities: Daily Word Ladders Grades 1–2 © 2012 by Timothy V. Rasinski, Scholastic Teaching Resources

Name _____

Read the clues, then write the words.
Start at the bottom and climb to the top.

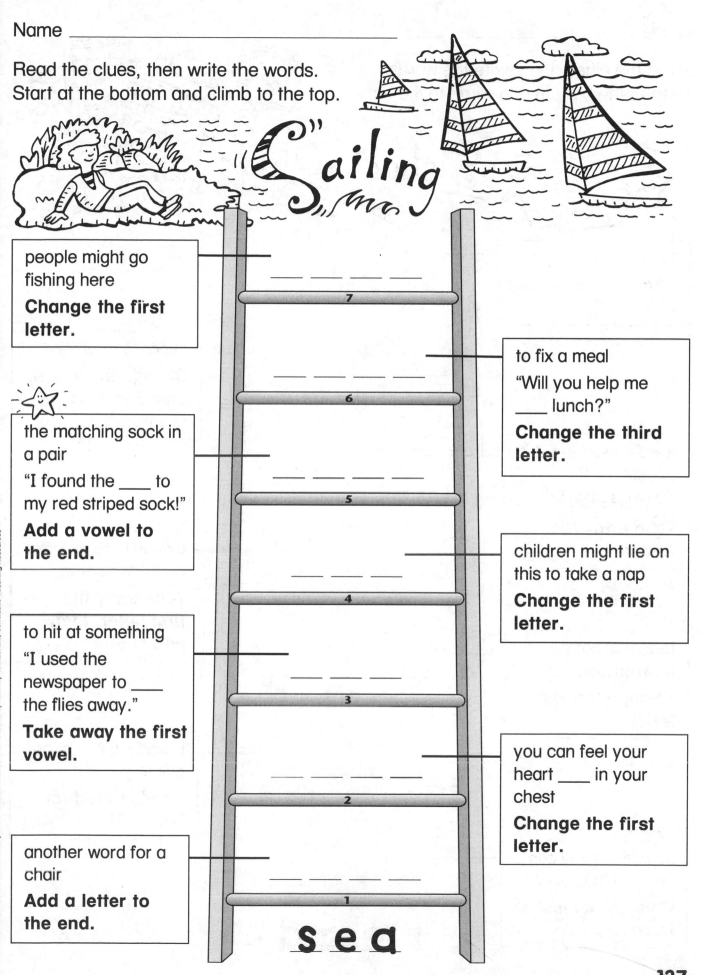

Sailing

people might go fishing here
Change the first letter.

— — — —   7

the matching sock in a pair
"I found the ___ to my red striped sock!"
Add a vowel to the end.

— — — —   6

to hit at something
"I used the newspaper to ___ the flies away."
Take away the first vowel.

— — — —   5

another word for a chair
Add a letter to the end.

— — —   4

— — —   3

— — —   2

— — —   1

to fix a meal
"Will you help me ___ lunch?"
Change the third letter.

children might lie on this to take a nap
Change the first letter.

you can feel your heart ___ in your chest
Change the first letter.

s e a

Name _____

Read the clues, then write the words.
Start at the bottom and climb to the top.

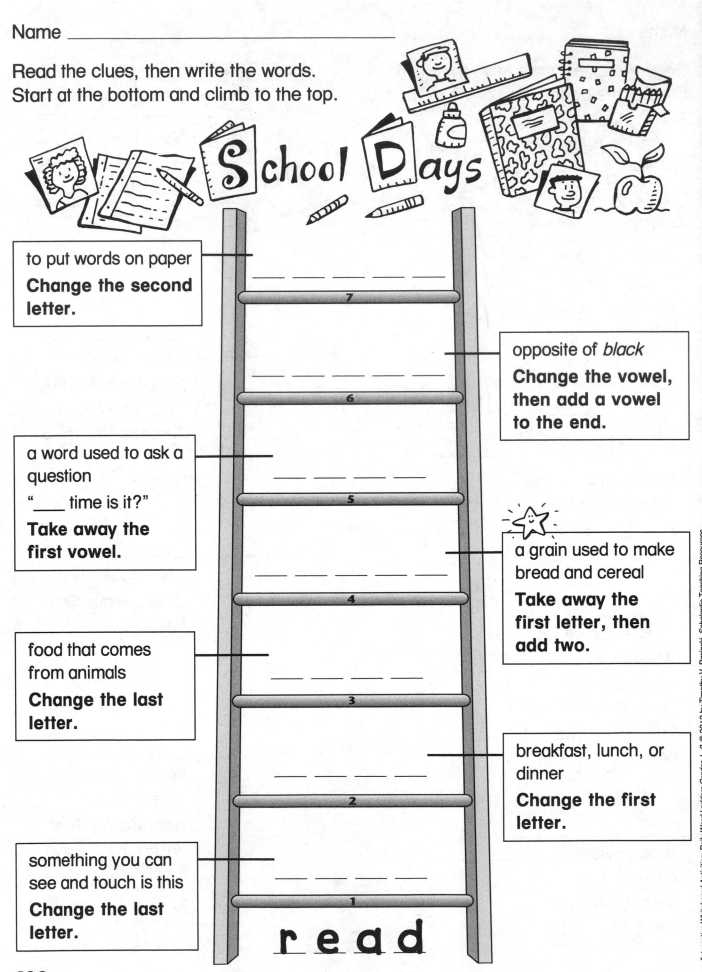

School Days

to put words on paper
Change the second letter.

opposite of *black*
Change the vowel, then add a vowel to the end.

a word used to ask a question
"___ time is it?"
Take away the first vowel.

a grain used to make bread and cereal
Take away the first letter, then add two.

food that comes from animals
Change the last letter.

breakfast, lunch, or dinner
Change the first letter.

something you can see and touch is this
Change the last letter.

7
6
5
4
3
2
1

r e a d

Interactive Whiteboard Activities: Daily Word Ladders Grades 1–2 © 2012 by Timothy V. Rasinski; Scholastic Teaching Resources

Name _____

Read the clues, then write the words.
Start at the bottom and climb to the top.

Toe-Tapping Tunes

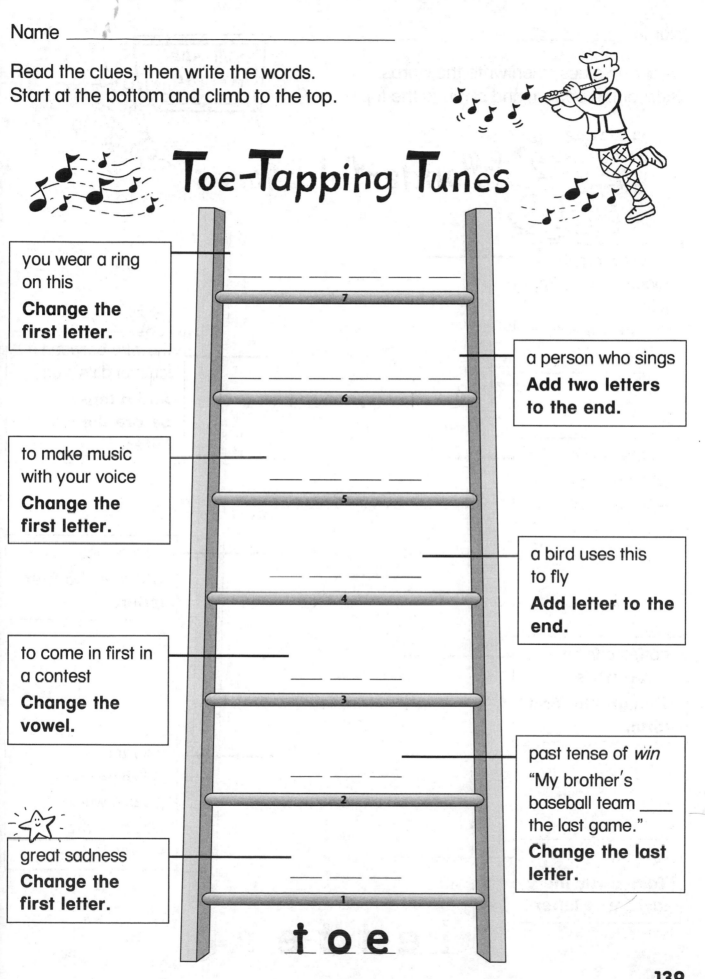

you wear a ring on this
Change the first letter.

to make music with your voice
Change the first letter.

to come in first in a contest
Change the vowel.

great sadness
Change the first letter.

a person who sings
Add two letters to the end.

a bird uses this to fly
Add letter to the end.

past tense of *win*
"My brother's baseball team ____ the last game."
Change the last letter.

t o e

Name _____

Read the clues, then write the words.
Start at the bottom and climb to the top.

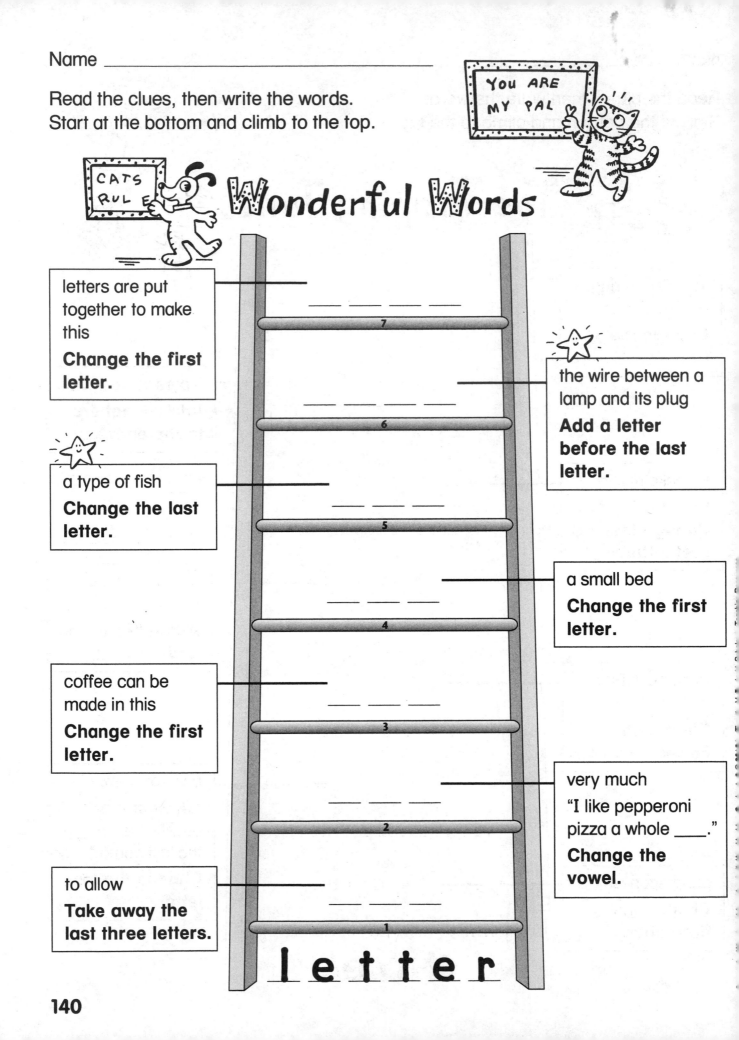

You ARE MY PAL

CATS RULE

Wonderful Words

letters are put together to make this
Change the first letter.

the wire between a lamp and its plug
Add a letter before the last letter.

a type of fish
Change the last letter.

a small bed
Change the first letter.

coffee can be made in this
Change the first letter.

very much
"I like pepperoni pizza a whole ____."
Change the vowel.

to allow
Take away the last three letters.

7

6

5

4

3

2

1

letter

Name _____

Read the clues, then write the words.
Start at the bottom and climb to the top.

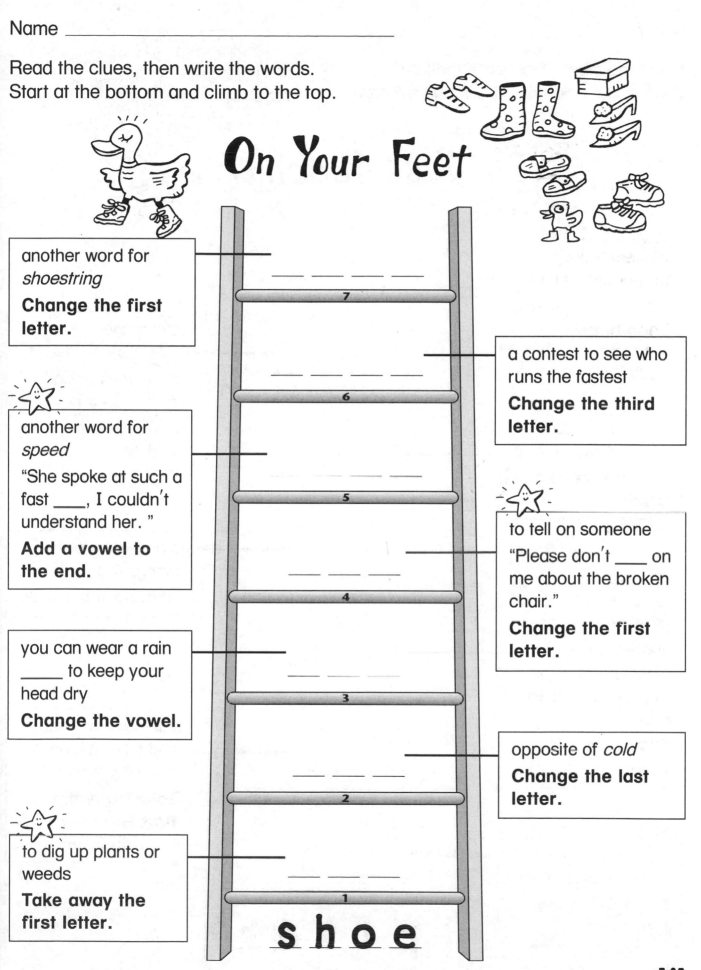

On Your Feet

another word for
shoestring
Change the first letter.

a contest to see who runs the fastest
Change the third letter.

another word for
speed
"She spoke at such a fast ____, I couldn't understand her. "
Add a vowel to the end.

to tell on someone
"Please don't ____ on me about the broken chair."
Change the first letter.

you can wear a rain ____ to keep your head dry
Change the vowel.

opposite of *cold*
Change the last letter.

to dig up plants or weeds
Take away the first letter.

s h o e

Name _____

Read the clues, then write the words.
Start at the bottom and climb to the top.

Just Peachy!

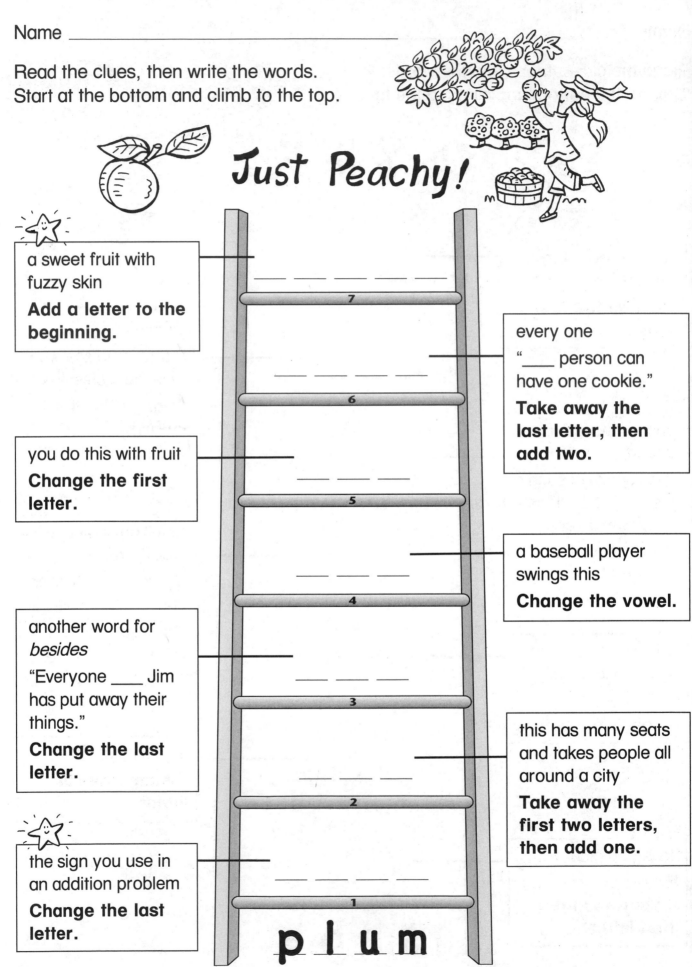

a sweet fruit with fuzzy skin
Add a letter to the beginning.

every one
"____ person can have one cookie."
Take away the last letter, then add two.

you do this with fruit
Change the first letter.

a baseball player swings this
Change the vowel.

another word for *besides*
"Everyone ____ Jim has put away their things."
Change the last letter.

this has many seats and takes people all around a city
Take away the first two letters, then add one.

the sign you use in an addition problem
Change the last letter.

7
6
5
4
3
2
1

p l u m

Name _____

Read the clues, then write the words.
Start at the bottom and climb to the top.

More Is Better

the number after
three
**Add a letter to the
beginning.**

_____ _____ _____ _____
7

_____ _____ _____
6

something that
belongs to us
"That is ____ poster
on the wall."
**Change the last
letter.**

not in
**Change the first
letter.**

_____ _____ _____
5

_____ _____ _____
4

another word for
stomach
Change the vowel.

go for
"I'll ____ your coat
for you."
**Change the first
letter.**

_____ _____ _____
3

_____ _____ _____ _____
2

opposite of *dry*
**Change the last
letter.**

another word for *tiny*
**Take away the
first three letters,
then add one.**

_____ _____ _____
1

three

Read the clues, then write the words.
Start at the bottom and climb to the top.

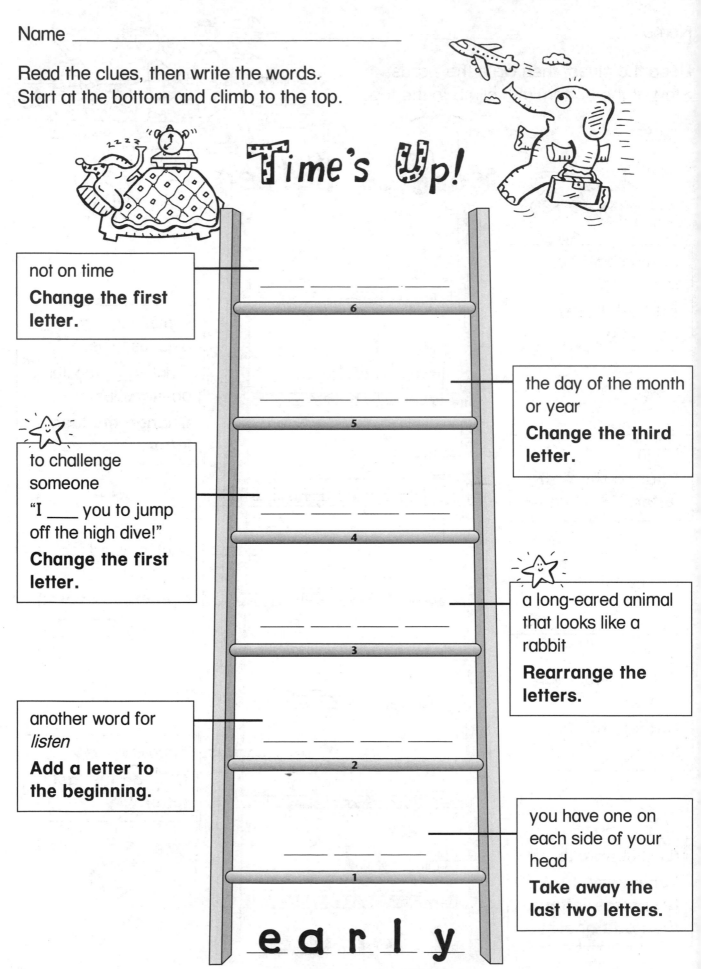

Time's Up!

not on time
Change the first letter.

6 ___ ___ ___ ___

the day of the month or year
Change the third letter.

5 ___ ___ ___ ___

to challenge someone
"I ___ you to jump off the high dive!"
Change the first letter.

4 ___ ___ ___ ___

a long-eared animal that looks like a rabbit
Rearrange the letters.

3 ___ ___ ___ ___

another word for *listen*
Add a letter to the beginning.

2 ___ ___ ___ ___

you have one on each side of your head
Take away the last two letters.

1 ___ ___ ___

e a r l y

Name _____

Read the clues, then write the words.
Start at the bottom and climb to the top.

Yard Sale

opposite of *buy*
Take away the second letter.

7 _ _ _ _ _

an odor or scent
"I love the _____ of roses."
Change the vowel.

6 _ _ _ _ _

a baby is this size
Add a letter at the beginning.

5 _ _ _ _

a shopping center
Change the first letter.

4 _ _ _ _

you can throw and catch this
Take away the last letter, then add two.

3 _ _ _ _

"My lunch is in a paper ____."
Change the vowel.

2 _ _ _

to bother someone
"I like to ____ my sister."
Change the last letter.

1 _ _ _

b u y

Name _____

Read the clues, then write the words.
Start at the bottom and climb to the top.

In the Tree

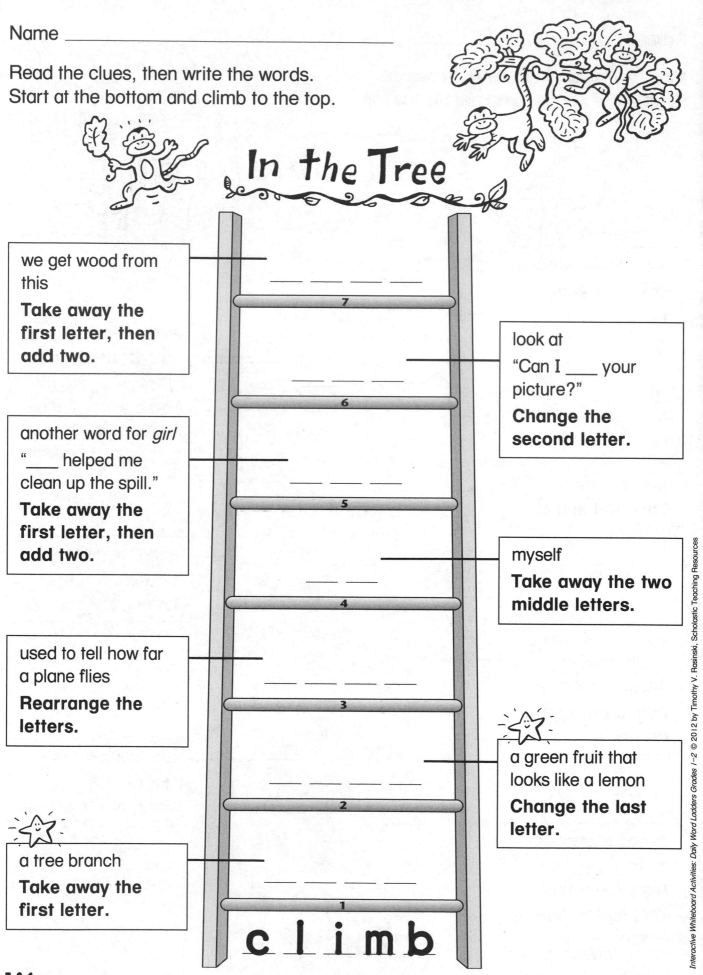

we get wood from this
Take away the first letter, then add two.

7 _ _ _ _ _

look at
"Can I ___ your picture?"
Change the second letter.

6 _ _ _ _

another word for *girl*
"___ helped me clean up the spill."
Take away the first letter, then add two.

5 _ _ _ _

myself
Take away the two middle letters.

4 _ _ _

used to tell how far a plane flies
Rearrange the letters.

3 _ _ _ _ _

a green fruit that looks like a lemon
Change the last letter.

2 _ _ _ _ _

a tree branch
Take away the first letter.

1 c l i m b

c l i m b

Interactive Whiteboard Activities: Daily Word Ladders Grades 1–2 © 2012 by Timothy V. Rasinski, Scholastic Teaching Resources

Name _____

Read the clues, then write the words.
Start at the bottom and climb to the top.

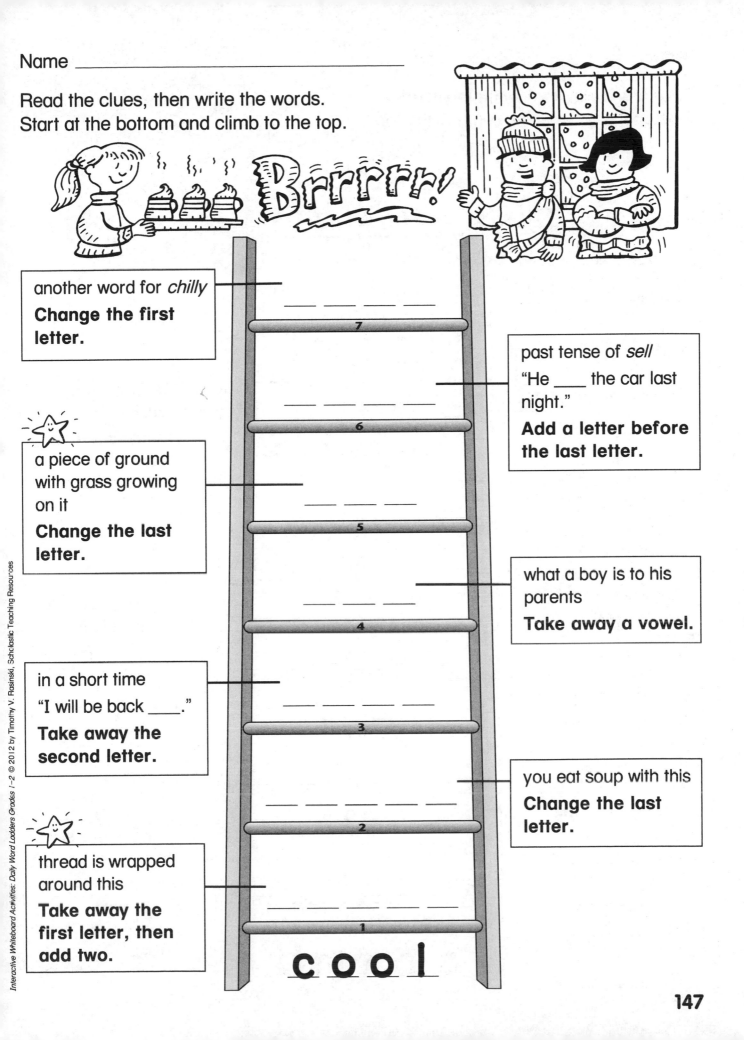

another word for *chilly*
Change the first letter.

a piece of ground with grass growing on it
Change the last letter.

in a short time
"I will be back ____."
Take away the second letter.

thread is wrapped around this
Take away the first letter, then add two.

past tense of *sell*
"He ____ the car last night."
Add a letter before the last letter.

what a boy is to his parents
Take away a vowel.

you eat soup with this
Change the last letter.

7
6
5
4
3
2
1

c o o l

Interactive Whiteboard Activities: Daily Word Ladders Grades 1–2 © 2012 by Timothy V. Rasinski, Scholastic Teaching Resources

Name _____

Read the clues, then write the words.
Start at the bottom and climb to the top.

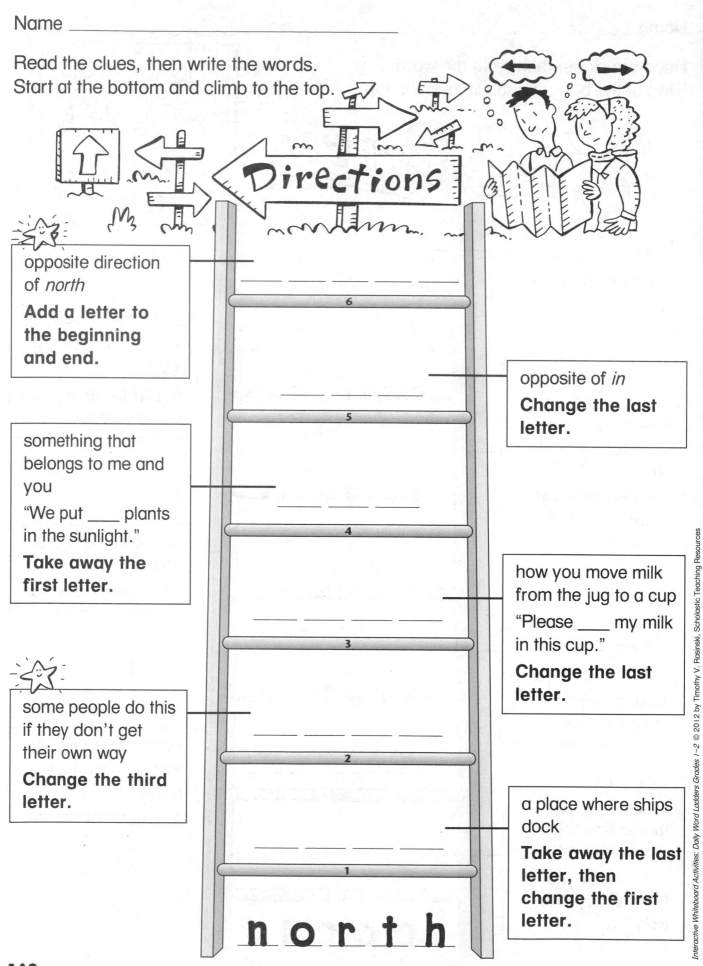

opposite direction of *north*

Add a letter to the beginning and end.

_ _ _ _ _ _   6

opposite of *in*

Change the last letter.

_ _ _ _ _   5

something that belongs to me and you

"We put ___ plants in the sunlight."

Take away the first letter.

_ _ _ _ _   4

how you move milk from the jug to a cup

"Please ___ my milk in this cup."

Change the last letter.

_ _ _ _ _   3

some people do this if they don't get their own way

Change the third letter.

_ _ _ _   2

a place where ships dock

Take away the last letter, then change the first letter.

_ _ _ _   1

n o r t h

Interactive Whiteboard Activities: Daily Word Ladders Grades 1–2 © 2012 by Timothy V. Rasinski, Scholastic Teaching Resources

Name _____

Read the clues, then write the words.
Start at the bottom and climb to the top.

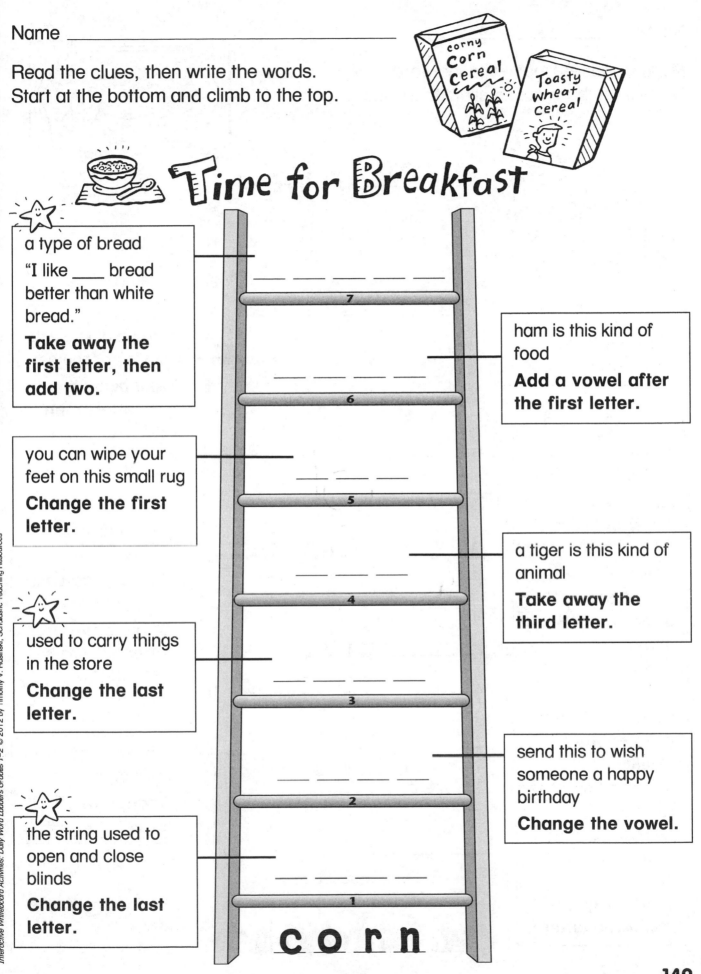

Time for Breakfast

a type of bread

"I like ___ bread better than white bread."

Take away the first letter, then add two.

you can wipe your feet on this small rug

Change the first letter.

used to carry things in the store

Change the last letter.

the string used to open and close blinds

Change the last letter.

ham is this kind of food

Add a vowel after the first letter.

a tiger is this kind of animal

Take away the third letter.

send this to wish someone a happy birthday

Change the vowel.

7

6

5

4

3

2

1

c o r n

corny Corn Cereal

Toasty wheat Cereal

149

Name _____

Read the clues, then write the words.
Start at the bottom and climb to the top.

A Clear View

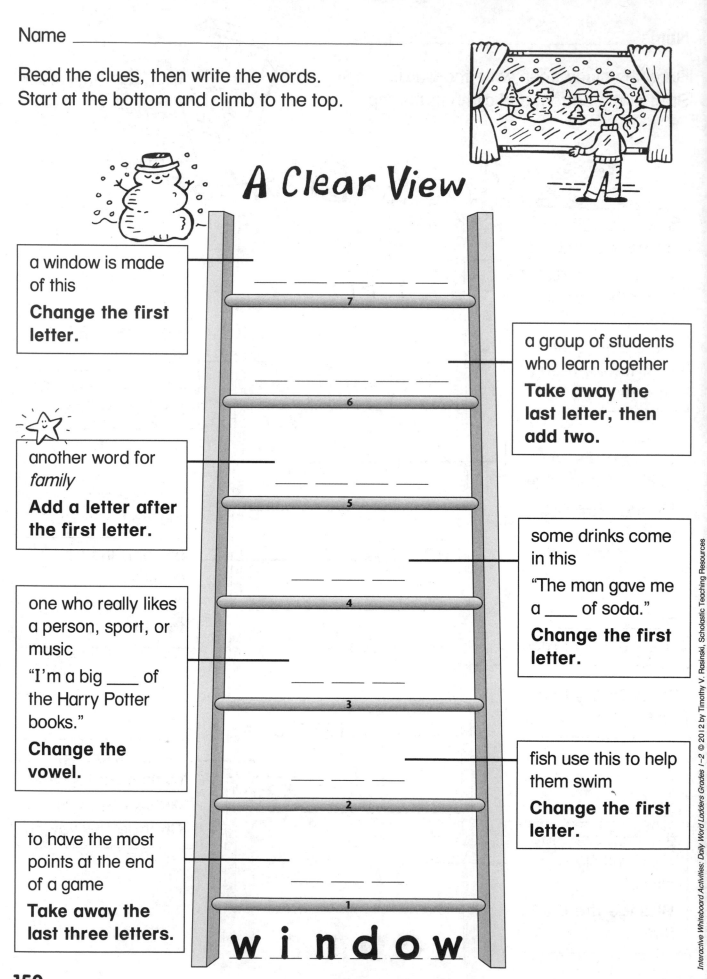

a window is made of this
Change the first letter.

_ _ _ _ _
7

a group of students who learn together
Take away the last letter, then add two.

_ _ _ _ _
6

another word for *family*
Add a letter after the first letter.

_ _ _ _ _
5

some drinks come in this
"The man gave me a ___ of soda."
Change the first letter.

_ _ _ _
4

one who really likes a person, sport, or music
"I'm a big ___ of the Harry Potter books."
Change the vowel.

_ _ _
3

fish use this to help them swim
Change the first letter.

_ _ _
2

to have the most points at the end of a game
Take away the last three letters.

_ _ _
1

w i n d o w

Name _____

Read the clues, then write the words.
Start at the bottom and climb to the top.

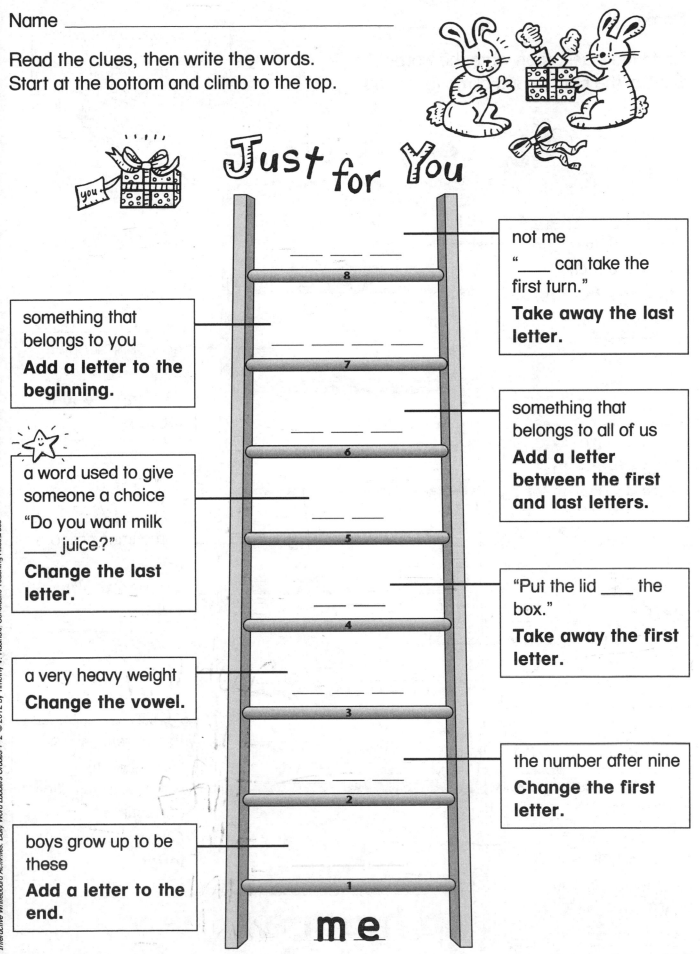

Just for You

not me
"___ can take the
first turn."
**Take away the last
letter.**

something that
belongs to you
**Add a letter to the
beginning.**

something that
belongs to all of us
**Add a letter
between the first
and last letters.**

a word used to give
someone a choice
"Do you want milk
___ juice?"
**Change the last
letter.**

"Put the lid ___ the
box."
**Take away the first
letter.**

a very heavy weight
Change the vowel.

the number after nine
**Change the first
letter.**

boys grow up to be
these
**Add a letter to the
end.**

me

Name _____

Read the clues, then write the words.
Start at the bottom and climb to the top.

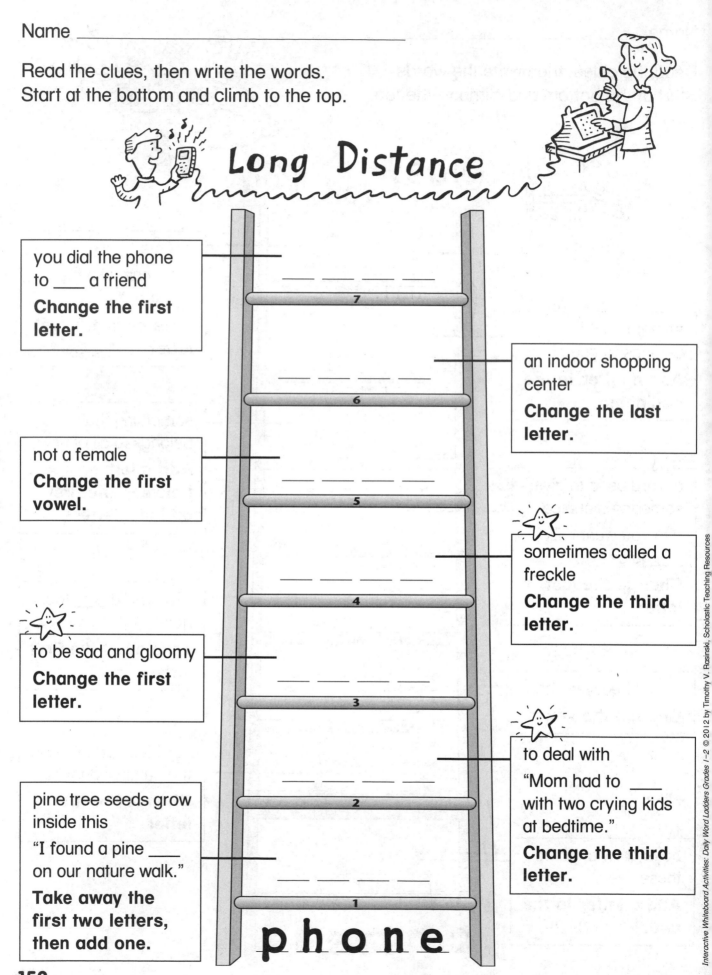

Long Distance

you dial the phone
to ___ a friend
**Change the first
letter.**

an indoor shopping
center
**Change the last
letter.**

not a female
**Change the first
vowel.**

sometimes called a
freckle
**Change the third
letter.**

to be sad and gloomy
**Change the first
letter.**

to deal with
"Mom had to ___
with two crying kids
at bedtime."
**Change the third
letter.**

pine tree seeds grow
inside this
"I found a pine ___
on our nature walk."
**Take away the
first two letters,
then add one.**

7

6

5

4

3

2

1

p h o n e

Interactive Whiteboard Activities: Daily Word Ladders Grades 1–2 © 2012 by Timothy V. Rasinski, Scholastic Teaching Resources

Name _____

Read the clues, then write the words.
Start at the bottom and climb to the top.

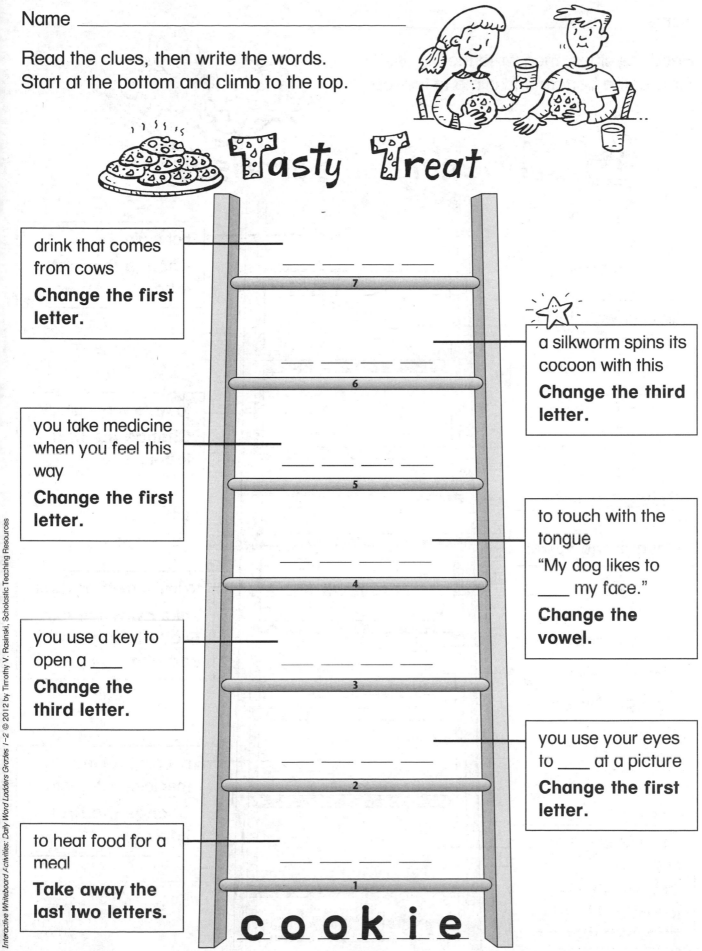

Tasty Treat

drink that comes from cows
Change the first letter.

_ _ _ _   7

a silkworm spins its cocoon with this
Change the third letter.

_ _ _ _   6

you take medicine when you feel this way
Change the first letter.

_ _ _ _   5

to touch with the tongue
"My dog likes to ___ my face."
Change the vowel.

_ _ _ _   4

you use a key to open a ___
Change the third letter.

_ _ _ _   3

you use your eyes to ___ at a picture
Change the first letter.

_ _ _ _   2

to heat food for a meal
Take away the last two letters.

_ _ _ _   1

c o o k i e

Name _____

Read the clues, then write the words.
Start at the bottom and climb to the top.

A Bundle of Surprises

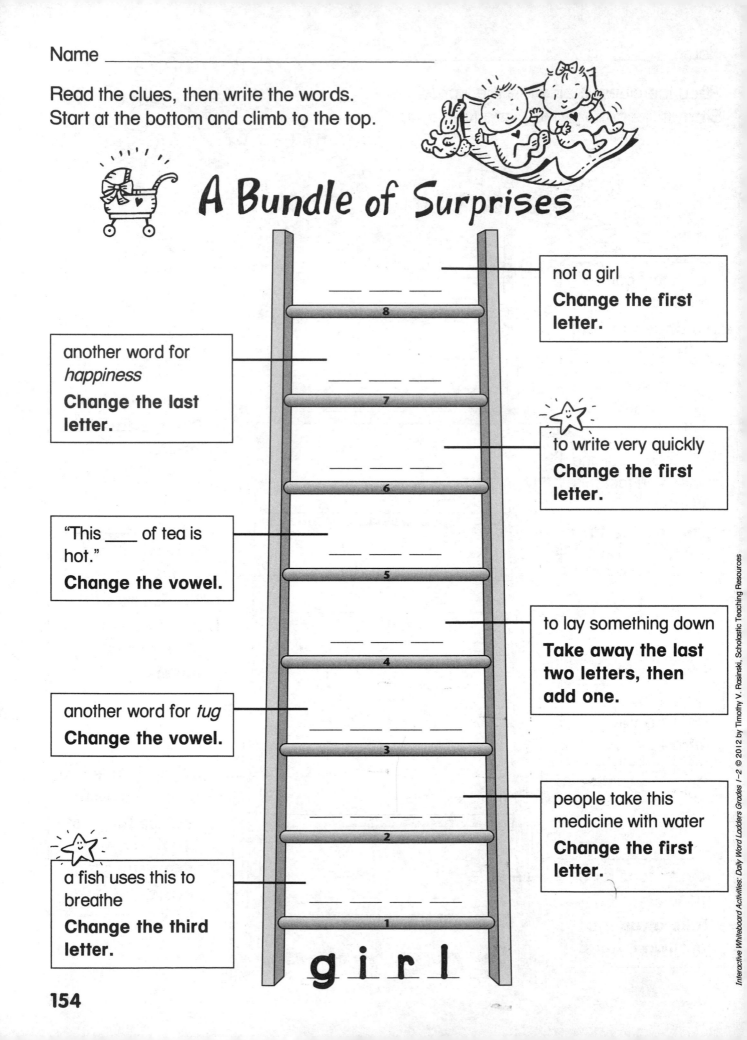

not a girl
Change the first letter.

8 _ _ _ _

another word for *happiness*
Change the last letter.

7

to write very quickly
Change the first letter.

6 _ _ _ _

"This ____ of tea is hot."
Change the vowel.

5 _ _ _ _

to lay something down
Take away the last two letters, then add one.

4 _ _ _ _

another word for *tug*
Change the vowel.

3

people take this medicine with water
Change the first letter.

2

a fish uses this to breathe
Change the third letter.

1

g i r l

Interactive Whiteboard Activities: Daily Word Ladders Grades 1–2 © 2012 by Timothy V. Rasinski, Scholastic Teaching Resources

Name _____

Read the clues, then write the words.
Start at the bottom and climb to the top.

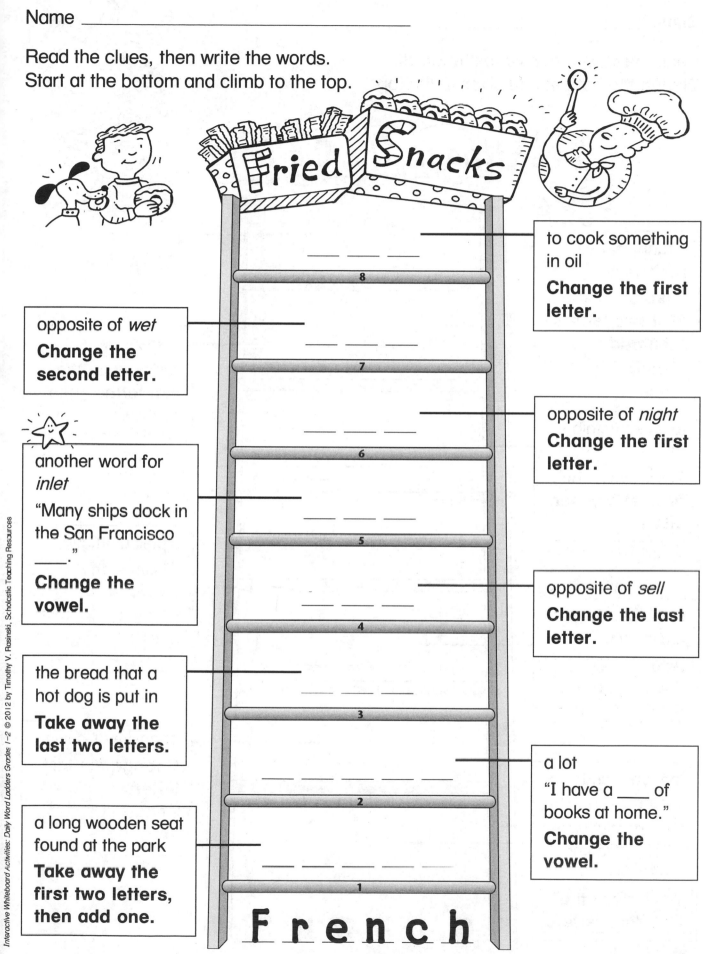

to cook something
in oil
**Change the first
letter.**

opposite of *wet*
**Change the
second letter.**

opposite of *night*
**Change the first
letter.**

another word for
inlet
"Many ships dock in
the San Francisco
____."
**Change the
vowel.**

opposite of *sell*
**Change the last
letter.**

the bread that a
hot dog is put in
**Take away the
last two letters.**

a lot
"I have a ____ of
books at home."
**Change the
vowel.**

a long wooden seat
found at the park
**Take away the
first two letters,
then add one.**

F r e n c h

Name _____

Read the clues, then write the words.
Start at the bottom and climb to the top.

Under the Big Top

a funny circus performer
Take away the first two letters, then add two.

_ _ _ _ _ _   7

6

to let something fall
Take away the first letter, then add two.

_ _ _ _ _   5

4

some people drink tea in this
Add a letter to the beginning.

_ _ _ _   3

_ _ _   2

me, you, and others
"The dentist gave all of ___ some toothpaste."
Take away the first four letters.

_ _   1

to die in water
Take away the last letter, then add two.

a police officer
Change the vowel.

opposite of *down*
Change the last letter.

c i r c u s

156

Name _____

Read the clues, then write the words.
Start at the bottom and climb to the top.

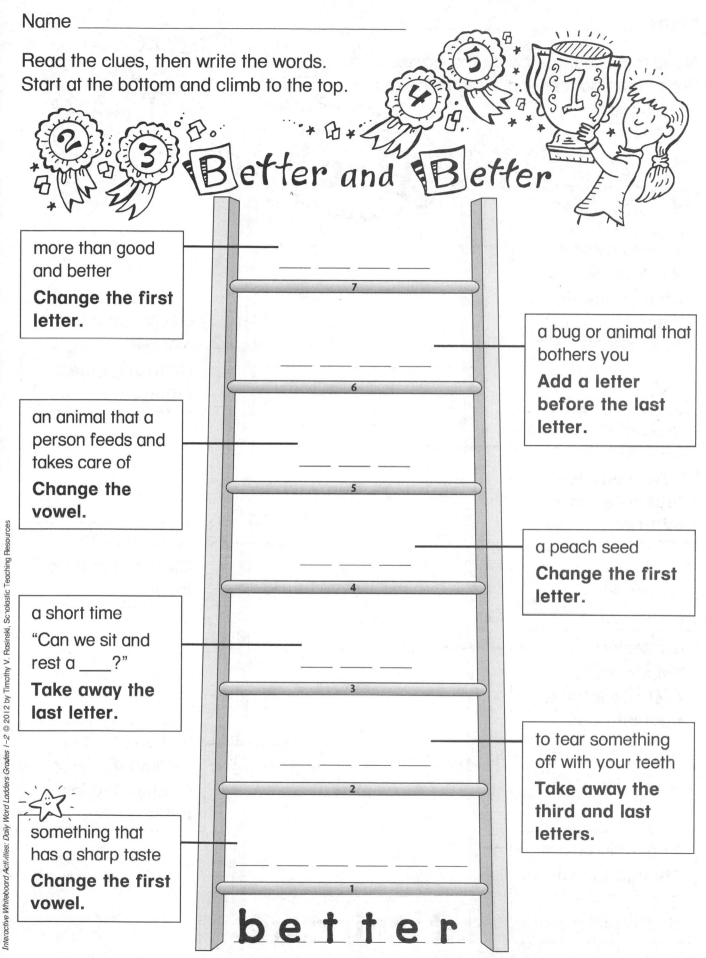

Better and Better

more than good
and better
**Change the first
letter.**
— — — — — —
7

a bug or animal that
bothers you
**Add a letter
before the last
letter.**
— — — — — —
6

an animal that a
person feeds and
takes care of
**Change the
vowel.**
— — — —
5

a peach seed
**Change the first
letter.**
— — — —
4

a short time
"Can we sit and
rest a ___?"
**Take away the
last letter.**
— — — —
3

to tear something
off with your teeth
**Take away the
third and last
letters.**
— — — — —
2

something that
has a sharp taste
**Change the first
vowel.**
— — — — — —
1

b e t t e r

Name _____

Read the clues, then write the words.
Start at the bottom and climb to the top.

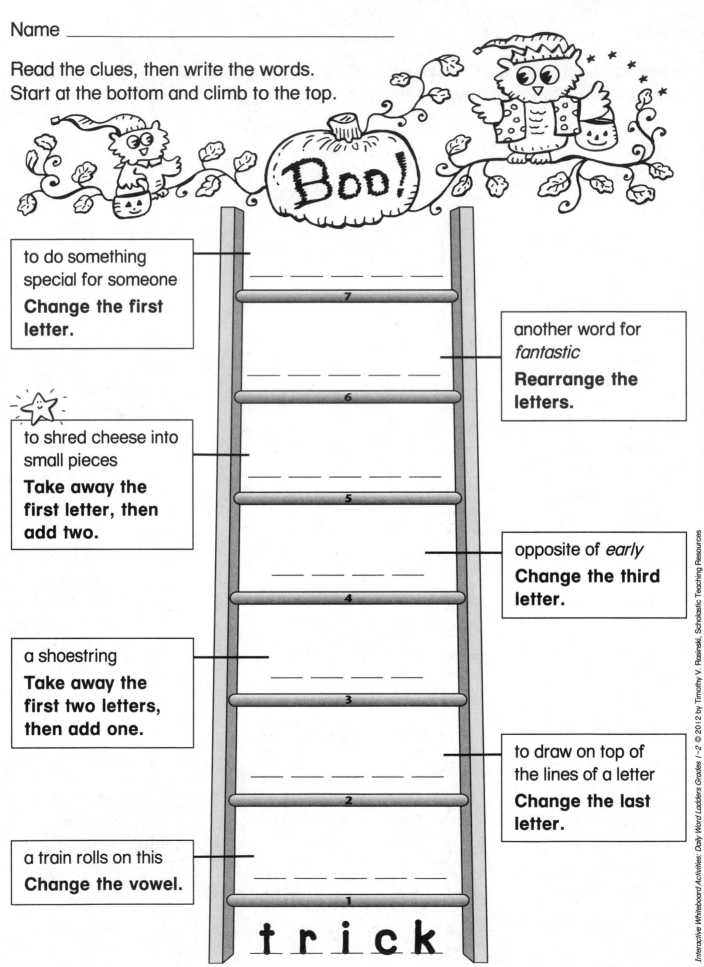

Boo!

to do something
special for someone
**Change the first
letter.**

another word for
fantastic
**Rearrange the
letters.**

to shred cheese into
small pieces
**Take away the
first letter, then
add two.**

opposite of *early*
**Change the third
letter.**

a shoestring
**Take away the
first two letters,
then add one.**

to draw on top of
the lines of a letter
**Change the last
letter.**

a train rolls on this
Change the vowel.

t r i c k

7

6

5

4

3

2

1

158

Interactive Whiteboard Activities: Daily Word Ladders Grades 1–2 © 2012 by Timothy V. Rasinski, Scholastic Teaching Resources

Name _____

Read the clues, then write the words.
Start at the bottom and climb to the top.

Up, Up and Away

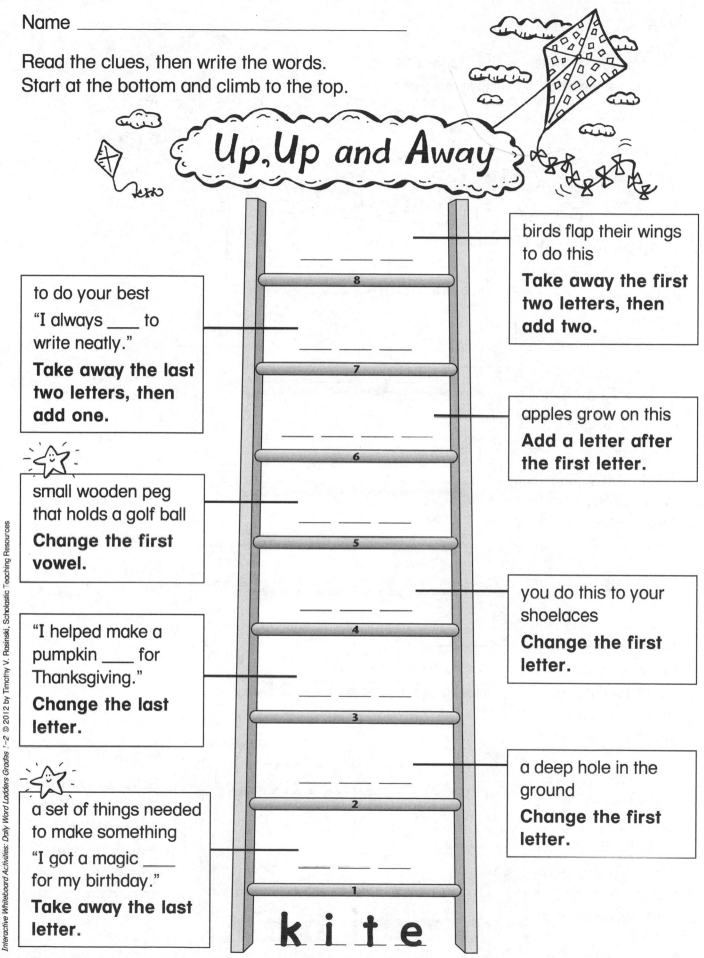

birds flap their wings to do this
Take away the first two letters, then add two.

to do your best
"I always ___ to write neatly."
Take away the last two letters, then add one.

apples grow on this
Add a letter after the first letter.

small wooden peg that holds a golf ball
Change the first vowel.

you do this to your shoelaces
Change the first letter.

"I helped make a pumpkin ___ for Thanksgiving."
Change the last letter.

a deep hole in the ground
Change the first letter.

a set of things needed to make something
"I got a magic ___ for my birthday."
Take away the last letter.

k i t e

Name _____

Read the clues, then write the words.
Start at the bottom and climb to the top.

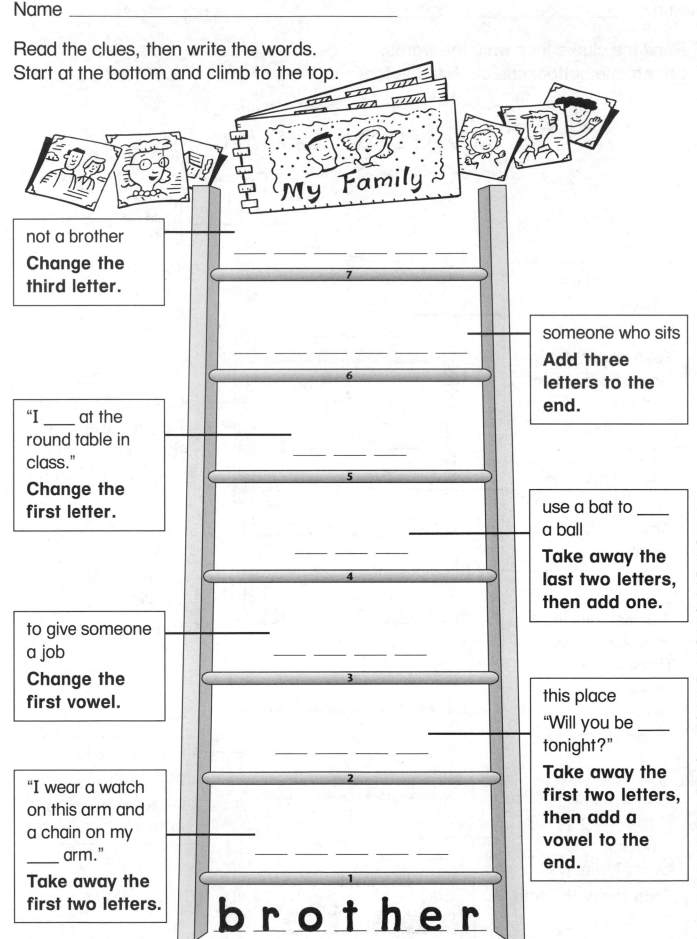

My Family

not a brother
Change the third letter.

7 _____

someone who sits
Add three letters to the end.

6 _____

"I ___ at the round table in class."
Change the first letter.

5 _ _ _ _

use a bat to ___ a ball
Take away the last two letters, then add one.

4 _ _ _ _

to give someone a job
Change the first vowel.

3 _ _ _ _ _

this place
"Will you be ___ tonight?"
Take away the first two letters, then add a vowel to the end.

2 _ _ _ _ _

"I wear a watch on this arm and a chain on my ___ arm."
Take away the first two letters.

1

b r o t h e r

Interactive Whiteboard Activities: Daily Word Ladders Grades 1–2 © 2012 by Timothy V. Rasinski, Scholastic Teaching Resources

Name _____

Read the clues, then write the words.
Start at the bottom and climb to the top.

On the Set

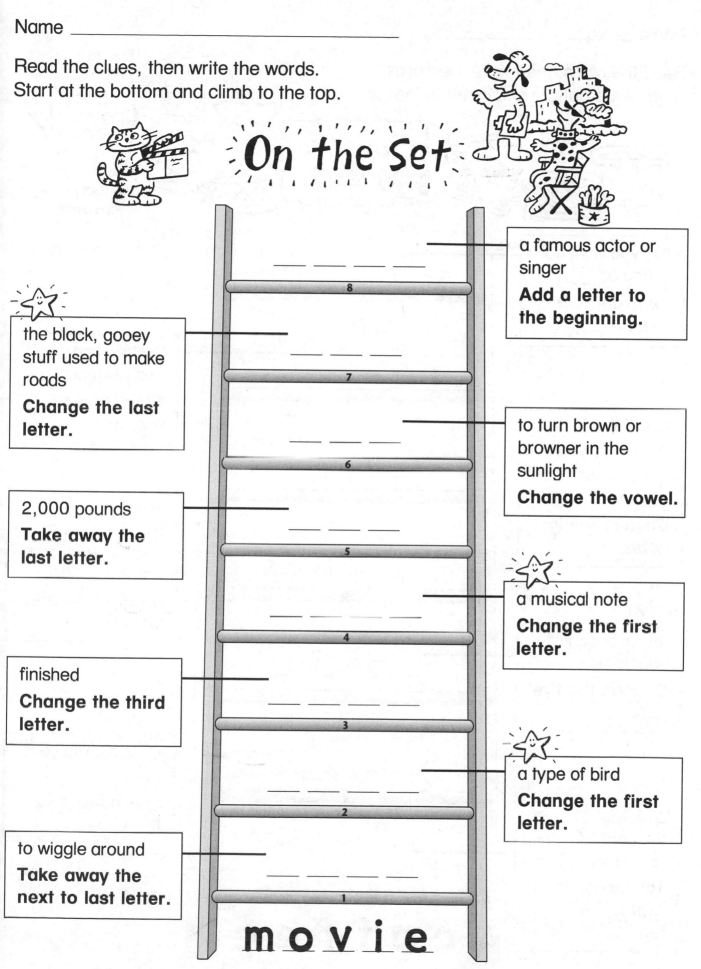

a famous actor or singer
Add a letter to the beginning.

the black, gooey stuff used to make roads
Change the last letter.

to turn brown or browner in the sunlight
Change the vowel.

2,000 pounds
Take away the last letter.

a musical note
Change the first letter.

finished
Change the third letter.

a type of bird
Change the first letter.

to wiggle around
Take away the next to last letter.

8
7
6
5
4
3
2
1

m o v i e

Name _____

Read the clues, then write the words.
Start at the bottom and climb to the top.

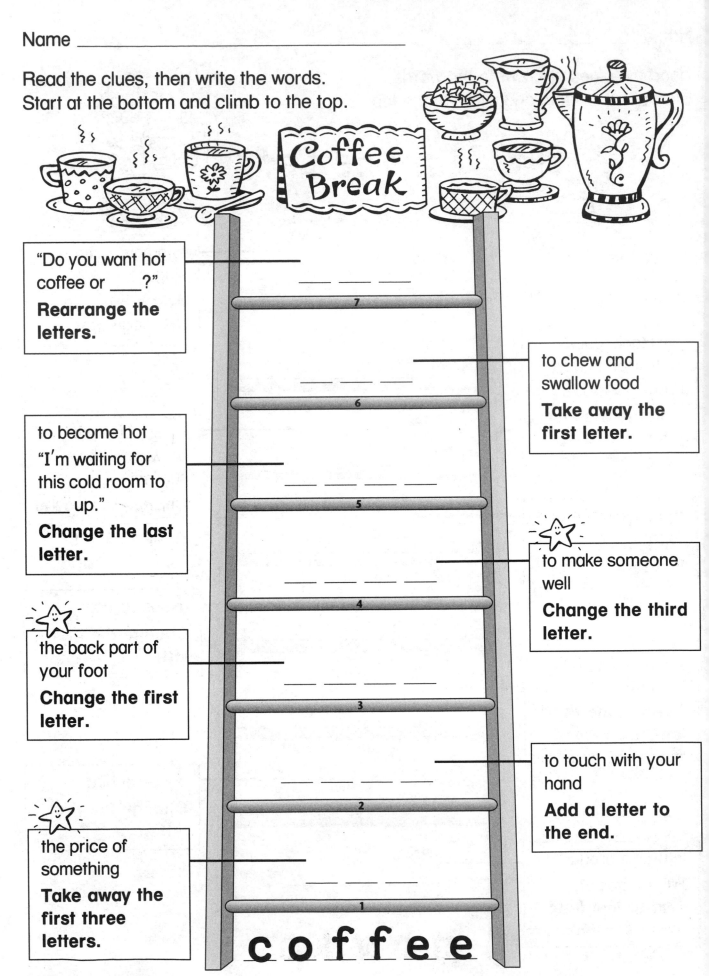

Coffee Break

"Do you want hot coffee or ___?"
Rearrange the letters.

to chew and swallow food
Take away the first letter.

to become hot
"I'm waiting for this cold room to ___ up."
Change the last letter.

to make someone well
Change the third letter.

the back part of your foot
Change the first letter.

to touch with your hand
Add a letter to the end.

the price of something
Take away the first three letters.

7
6
5
4
3
2
1

c o f f e e

Name _____

Read the clues, then write the words.
Start at the bottom and climb to the top.

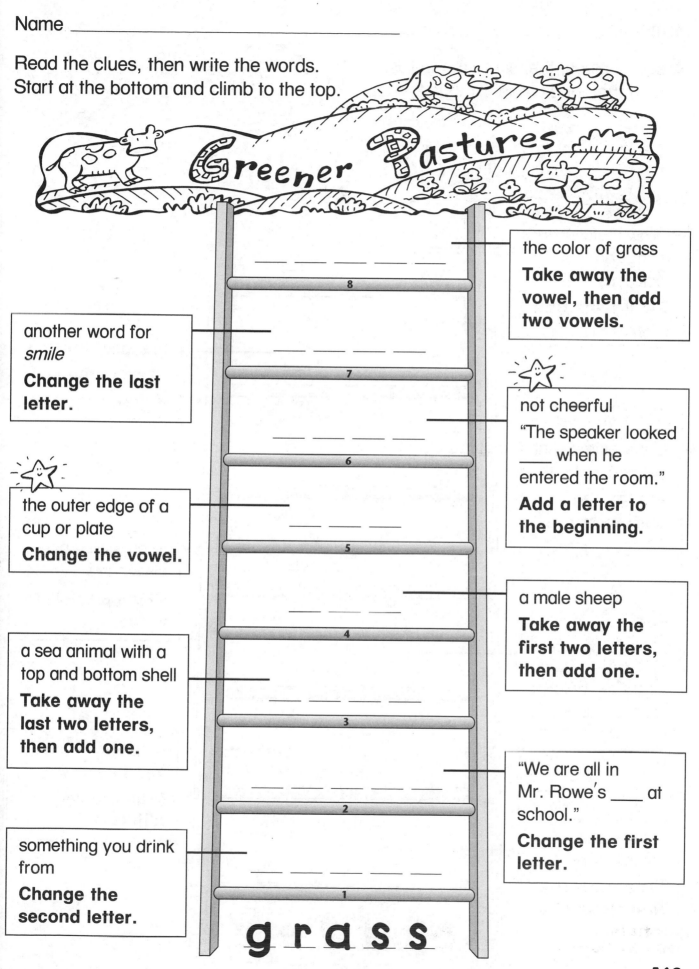

Greener Pastures

the color of grass
Take away the vowel, then add two vowels.

another word for *smile*
Change the last letter.

not cheerful
"The speaker looked ___ when he entered the room."
Add a letter to the beginning.

the outer edge of a cup or plate
Change the vowel.

a male sheep
Take away the first two letters, then add one.

a sea animal with a top and bottom shell
Take away the last two letters, then add one.

"We are all in Mr. Rowe's ___ at school."
Change the first letter.

something you drink from
Change the second letter.

g r a s s

Name _____

Read the clues, then write the words.
Start at the bottom and climb to the top.

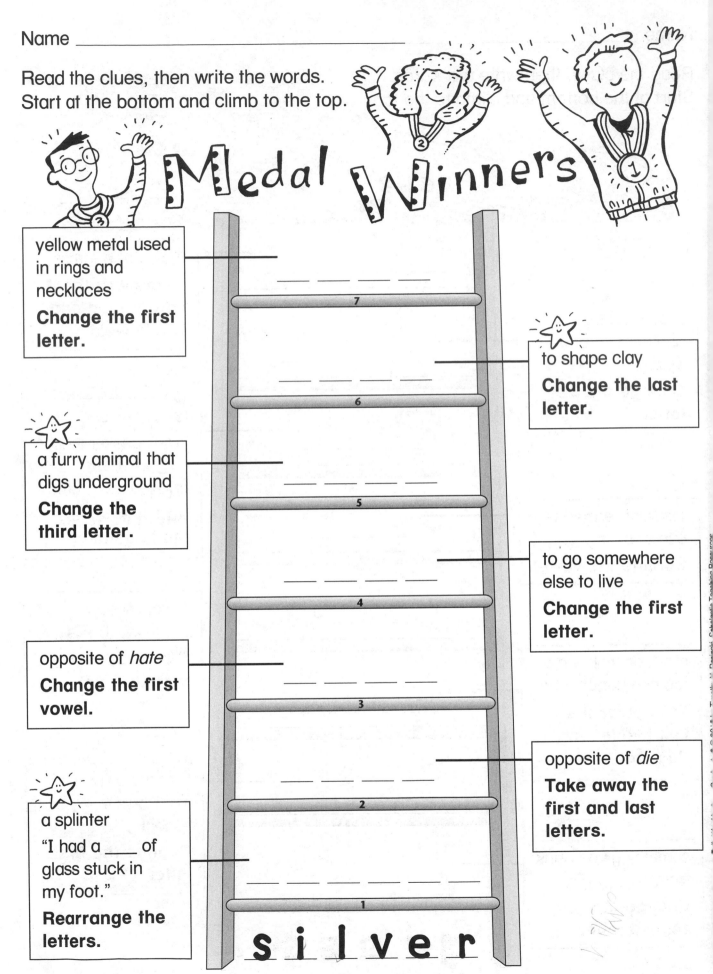

Medal Winners

yellow metal used in rings and necklaces
Change the first letter.

7

to shape clay
Change the last letter.

6

a furry animal that digs underground
Change the third letter.

5

to go somewhere else to live
Change the first letter.

4

opposite of *hate*
Change the first vowel.

3

opposite of *die*
Take away the first and last letters.

2

a splinter
"I had a ____ of glass stuck in my foot."
Rearrange the letters.

1

s i l v e r

Name _____

Read the clues, then write the words.
Start at the bottom and climb to the top.

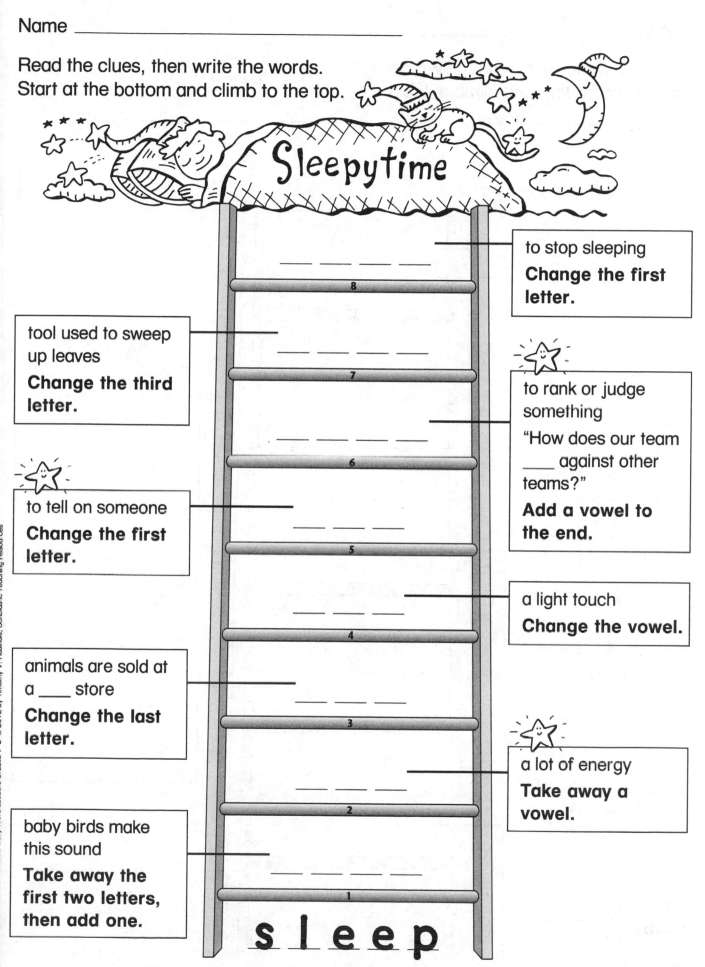

Sleepytime

to stop sleeping
Change the first letter.

tool used to sweep up leaves
Change the third letter.

to rank or judge something

"How does our team ___ against other teams?"
Add a vowel to the end.

to tell on someone
Change the first letter.

a light touch
Change the vowel.

animals are sold at a ___ store
Change the last letter.

a lot of energy
Take away a vowel.

baby birds make this sound
Take away the first two letters, then add one.

s l e e p

Name _____

Read the clues, then write the words.
Start at the bottom and climb to the top.

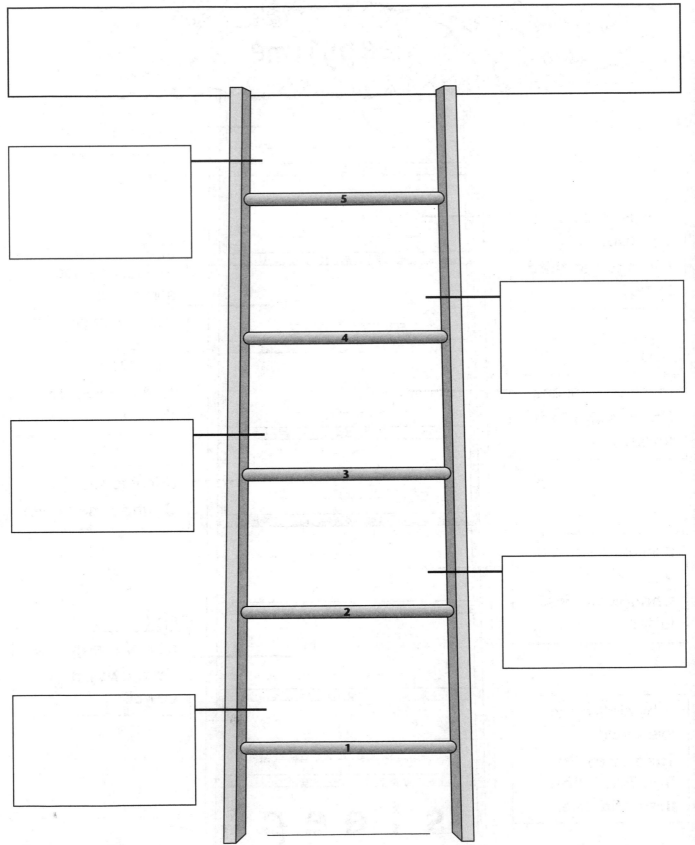

Name _____

Read the clues, then write the words.
Start at the bottom and climb to the top.

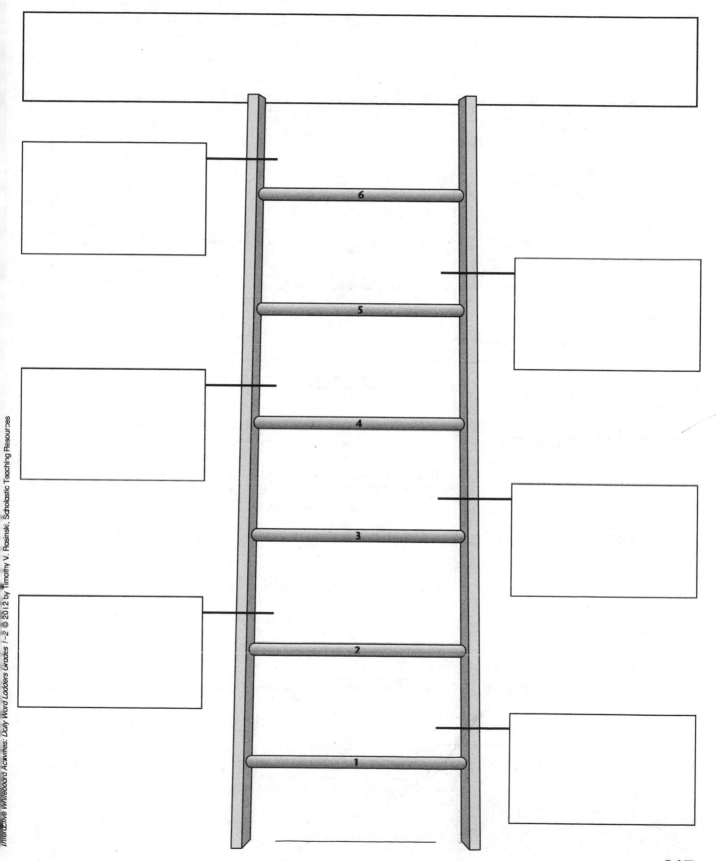

Name _____

Read the clues, then write the words.
Start at the bottom and climb to the top.

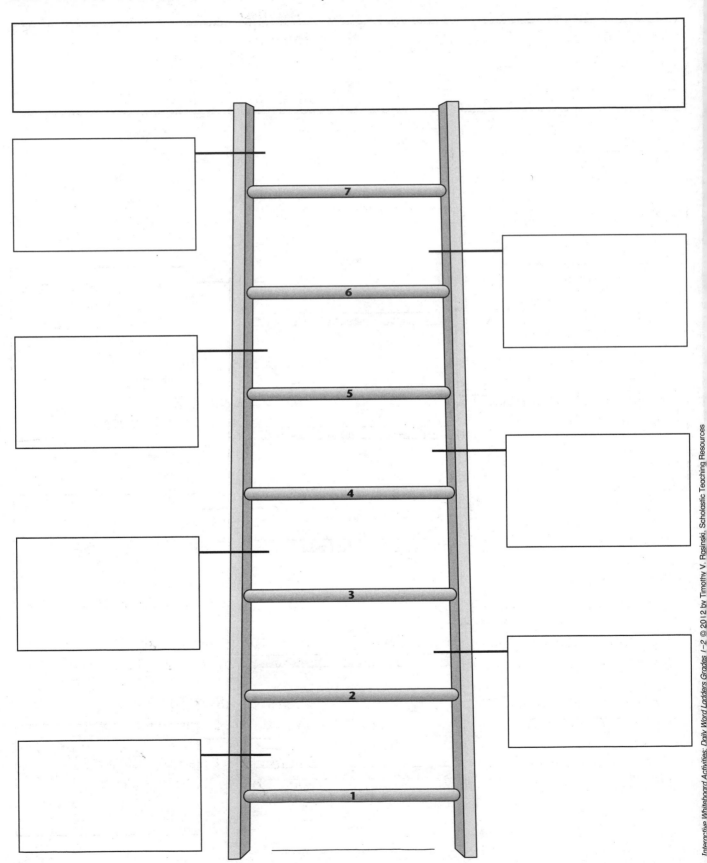

Interactive Whiteboard Activities: Daily Word Ladders Grades 1–2 © 2012 by Timothy V. Rasinski. Scholastic Teaching Resources

Answer Key

Farm Fun, page 8
cow, cot, pot, pet, pit, pig

Dinner's Ready, page 9
bite, bit, hit, hat, fat, eat

Inside Out, page 10
in, fin, fan, fat, cat, cut, out

Color Change, page 11
red, bed, bet, pet, pit, pin, pink

Animal Enemies, page 12
dog, dot, pot, pop, top, tap, cap, cat

Air Travel, page 13
plane, plan, pan, pen, men, met, jet

A Matter of Size, page 14
big, bit, bill, ball, mall, small

Around the Clock, page 15
tick, sick, sack, rack, rock, tock

Family Ties, page 16
mom, mop, top, tap, tan, man, mad, dad

Fun on a Bun, page 17
hot, lot, let, pet, pit, pig, dig, dog

Opposites Attract, page 18
fat, fit, hit, his, this, thin

Sweet Sounds, page 19
ear, eat, rat, ran, rang, ring

Give a Dog a Bone, page 20
tail, sail, said, sad, bad, bag, wag

Here to There, page 21
walk, wall, fall, full, fun, run

Get Well Soon, page 22
ill, pill, hill, sill, silk, sick

In the Can, page 23
trash, crash, cash, cast, cat, can

America's Pastime, page 24
base, case, care, bare, bale, ball

Hop to It!, page 25
frog, jog, jug, tug, tag, tad, toad

On the Playground, page 26
sit, hit, hat, had, hand, sand, stand

Fur Facts, page 27
hair, hail, fail, fall, ball, bald

Ship Shape, page 28
ship, slip, slap, sap, sat, set, sea

Pail Problem, page 29
pail, tail, tall, tale, sale, pale

Fancy Footwear, page 30
sock, rock, row, how, show, shoe

In the Doghouse, page 31
dog, hog, hag, bag, bar, barn, bark

Counting Up, page 32
few, dew, den, men, man, many

Personality Change, page 33
good, gold, cold, bold, bald, bad

Notes